Feminism on the Border

Feminism on the Border

Chicana Gender Politics and Literature

Sonia Saldívar-Hull

UNIVERSITY OF CALIFORNIA PRESS

Berkeley / Los Angeles / London

University of California Press

Berkeley and Los Angeles, California

University of California Press, Ltd.
London, England

Grateful acknowledgment is made for the quotations from Angela de Hoyos's *Arise Chicano and Other Poems* and *Chicano Poems for the Barrio* (both published by M&A Editions, San Antonio; by permission of Arte Público Press); *The House on Mango Street,* copyright © 1984 by Sandra Cisneros (published by Vintage Books, a division of Random House, Inc., New York, and in hardcover by Alfred A. Knopf in 1994; reprinted by permission of Susan Bergholz Literary Services, New York; all rights reserved); *Loose Woman,* copyright © 1994 by Sandra Cisneros (published by Vintage Books, a division of Random House, Inc., New York, and originally in hardcover by Alfred A. Knopf, Inc.; reprinted by permission of Susan Bergholz Literary Services, New York; all rights reserved); *Woman Hollering Creek,* copyright © 1991 by Sandra Cisneros (published by Vintage Books, a division of Random House, Inc., New York, and originally in hardcover by Random House, Inc.; reprinted by permission of Susan Bergholz Literary Services, New York; all rights reserved); Pat Mora's "Legal Alien" in *Chants* (Houston: Arte Público Press/University of Houston, 1985); Demetria Martínez's "Nativity: For Two Salvadoran Women, 1986–1987" in *Three Times a Woman* (Tempe, Ariz.: Bilingual Press/Editorial Bilingüe, Arizona State University, 1989); and *Borderlands/La Frontera: The New Mestiza,* copyright © 1987 Gloria Anzaldúa (San Francisco: Aunt Lute Books). Material is also reused by permission from the following essays by Sonia Saldívar-Hull: "Feminism on the Border: From Gender Politics to Geopolitics," in *Criticism in the Borderlands; Studies in Chicano Literature, Culture, and Ideology,* edited by Héctor Calderón and José David Saldívar, pp. 203–220, copyright © 1991, Duke University Press (also published in *Tradition and the Talents of Women,* edited by Florence Howe, pp. 292–307, University of Illinois Press); "Helena Maria Viramontes," from *Dictionary of Literary Biography: Chicano Writers, Second Series,* edited by Francisco Lomeli and Carl Shirley, copyright © 1993 Gale Research (all rights reserved); "Political Identities in Contemporary Chicana Literature: Helena Maria Viramontes's Visions of the U.S. Third World," in *Writing Nation, Writing Region,* edited by Theo D'Haen, pp. 156–165, by permission of the Amerika Instituut of the University of Amsterdam; and "Gloria Anzaldúa" and "Helena Maria Viramontes" in Paul Lauter (General Editor), *Heath Anthology of American Literature,* Third Edition, Volume II, copyright © 1998 by Houghton Mifflin Company.

Library of Congress Cataloging-in-Publication Data will be found at the end of the book.

Manufactured in the United States of America

08 07 06 05 04 03 02 01 00
10 9 8 7 6 5 4 3 2 1

The paper used in this publication meets the minimum requirements of ANSI/NISO Z39.48-1992 (R 1997) (*Permanence of Paper*).

Contents

Acknowledgments

I began this project in the late 1980s, when discussions of race, gender, sexuality, and class were under attack. While the Women's Movement and the Movimiento Chicano of the 1970s had shaped my preliminary thoughts about race and gender, they were not being widely discussed in universities. At the University of Texas at Austin, where I was working toward a degree in English, Women's Studies was not even offered as an undergraduate minor. Several American literature and critical theory professors abhorred my venturing into feminist analysis. One even warned that my association with the "unstable" feminists in the English Department would bar me from employment at any respectable institution. Another traditional Americanist said my preliminary work on women's texts exhibited a "circle-the-wagons mentality." From my first year as a graduate student, however, I knew that my intellectual life would center on the emergent writings by Chicanas.

Though I hope this book will contribute to the destabilization of antifeminist prognostications, not much has changed since 1987, when I began the seed essay that became "Feminism on the Border." In fact, the current resurgence of anti-Mexican sentiment in the United States, particularly in Texas and California, creates an intellectual environment where playing it safe is the tactic junior faculty members are urged to adopt. Californians passed the unconstitutional anti-Mexican-immigrant Proposition 187, as well as Proposition 209, the anti–affirmative action initiative that was spawned within the ranks of my own academic institution, the University of California. Nonetheless, I completed this project with the help and encouragement of several colleagues and mentors at the University of California at Los Angeles and at the University of Texas at Austin.

First, I must acknowledge the late Dan Calder, whose tenure as chair of the English Department at UCLA virtually changed the complexion of the department. His expertise and intellectual interests varied widely; his work ranged from the studies he pursued as a renowned medievalist to his emergent discourses on gay and lesbian literatures and theory. Although he no longer chaired the department when I arrived in Los Angeles, this courageous scholar and trusted friend consistently supported my work at the university and ensured that the courses I taught those first years centered on my field of Chicana literature and literary theory. The time we spent discussing and debating theories of intersectionality, Chicana lesbian writers, and Chicana literature in general gave me the confidence to push my early ideas much further. I could not have wished for a more supportive mentor at my first job. Also at UCLA, my colleagues in the English Department, Valerie Smith, King-Kok Cheung, Greg Sarris, Karen Rowe, and Richard Yarbrough, serve as exemplary models of how to negotiate the restrictions of academia, particularly of how to cross the guarded borders of a traditional English department. As my writing, teaching, and university service—indeed, my very presence as a Chicanaist—have contested the boundaries erected by a white male institution, I have turned to these colleagues and learned from their examples. I have gained invaluable insights from my Americanist colleagues Martha Banta, Thomas Wortham, and Eric Sundquist. Katherine King of the Comparative Literature and Women's Studies programs encouraged me to develop my preliminary reading of "Woman Hollering Creek" and continues to be a valued reader and friend. Karen Brodkin and Christine Littleton, in Women's Studies, also merit recognition. Vice Chancellor Raymund Paredes, a fellow Chicanoist, offered guidance on negotiating the labyrinth of the university system and evaluated my manuscript in ways that strengthened my arguments.

My first year at UCLA was one of great political turmoil and intellectual growth within the Chicano Studies Program. The students were demanding a fully funded Department of Chicana and Chicano Studies and expected a faculty that declared its unqualified support. During my first week on campus, representatives of student groups urged me to sign their petitions and publicly declare my support before I even comprehended the complexity of the issues. Fortunately, I had arrived in California armed with lessons and survival strategies learned in Texas, where one of my mentors constantly reminded her students that there is no safe space for resistance workers. In my case, there was no safe time to acclimate to the specificity of the politically charged UCLA campus. Clearly, Chicana and other minority faculty members still do not have the time and space to devote to writing, luxuries that are available to other junior professors.

One contested space that demanded much of my time and energy that first year was the faculty seminar on development of a Chicano Studies curriculum developed and cofacilitated by the chair of the Chicano Studies Program, Vilma Ortiz, and the historian George Sánchez. Their expertise and monumental labor made this seminar an enlightening intellectual experience. For the first time at UCLA, faculty members in Chicano Studies gathered. All were experts in the field, all were working members of the program, all were committed to developing new courses that would revitalize the previously neglected Chicano Studies Program. In the winter of 1991, this group of Latino and Latina scholars met and pondered how to translate our expertise in our individual fields into a truly interdisciplinary curriculum. Vilma and George had a profound effect on the way I perceived critical pedagogy. From their examples I learned how one can effectively work as both administrator and scholar. Together, we all learned the perils of taking on additional university service in conjunction with the traditional obligations to our "home" departments.

Other influential members of that historic seminar also merit recognition. The Tejana film scholar Rosa Linda Fregoso, as a Ford Fellow at the Chicano Studies Research Center, contributed her theoretical expertise and her indomitable spirit. She also initiated this Tejana into the familiar yet unfamiliar ways of Californios. I continue to learn tremendously from her. Daniel Solórzano and José Monleón, with their expertise in pedagogy and critical theory, also contributed to the collective work of the group. Richard Chabran, librarian and scholar at the Chicano Studies Research Library, consistently enhanced my knowledge of a field that he has truly mastered. Additionally, through Vilma Ortiz's leadership at the Chicano Studies Research Center, we acquired funds for a Chicana collective. Vilma helped create a space for feminist humanities at the traditionally male-dominated, social science–

oriented Chicano Studies Research Center. This Nuyoriqueña embodies the spirit of coalition among feminist Latinas, and I thank her for her guidance and support.

The University of California at Los Angeles Academic Senate generously funded my research. The Ford Foundation's postdoctoral Fellowship for Minorities came at a time when the demands of creating a Chicano Studies department consumed all of my time outside the classroom. The Danforth Foundation, through the Dorothy Danforth Compton Fellowship program, funded much of my early work at the University of Texas.

Additionally, I would like to recognize the women who made it possible for me even to think about writing about Chicanas. Both Helena María Viramontes and Sandra Cisneros generously shared early drafts of some of their writing. Meeting Sandra Cisneros at the National Association for Chicano Studies conference in 1984 and hearing her read from her just-published book *The House on Mango Street* altered the trajectory of my life. Years later Sandra was instrumental in helping me put my Chicana feminist theory into practice, leave home, embark on the Tejana intellectual's migration trail to California, and take the academic appointment I had dreamed of having.

At the University of Texas at Austin, I had the good fortune to meet and participate in a Women's Studies course with the noted feminist literary critic and Virginia Woolf scholar Jane Marcus. Her mentorship, above anyone else's, eventually persuaded me to apply to the graduate program, where I became the only Chicana graduate student in English. She subsequently guided my decision to write a dissertation on Chicana authors rather than one on Gertrude Stein. Beverly Stoeltje's knowledge of Chicano folklore and feminist theory also brought focus to my studies on Chicana literature. Jane and Beverly's considerable knowledge is the invisible stitching that helped me design my reinterpretation of contemporary feminist theory.

When these two women left Texas, Barbara Harlow began her influential tenure at the university. Her courses on colonialism and Third World literatures and the countless hours she spent teaching me how to read critically shaped my perception of the world in ways that may surprise her. Were I to expound on how her intellectual acuity and political insights mark my work, I would surely embarrass this erudite and modest activist and scholar. I cannot thank her enough for her patience, her guidance, and the intellectual rigor with which she read my early work. The late Don Américo Paredes graciously encouraged my work on Anzaldúa's *Borderlands,* even when I was reinterpreting his foundational readings of the border. I am privileged to have been taught by these scholars. Additionally, I must thank my early readers at the University of Texas. Douglas Kellner, Wahneema Lubiano, and Warwick Wadlington all contributed to my emergent voice. Because of their encouragement and incisive critiques, this book is much more thorough than its earlier incarnation.

The Chicana critics Norma Alarcón, Norma Cantú, Clara Lomas, María Herrera-Sobek, Teresa McKenna, and Yvonne Yarbro-Bejarano read my work and listened to my presentations at countless academic conferences. They consistently made the time to offer support, reading lists, and gentle suggestions for revisions.

Although the migration from Texas to California was traumatic, the students at UCLA constantly lured me back west from my Texas home-land. It has been an honor to walk into classes in the English Department and the Women's Studies and Chicana/o Studies programs and work with such students as Bert María Cueva, Juan Daniel Mah y Busch, Natalia Molina, Richard Morales, Mona Rivera, Michele Serros, Took Took Thiongthiraj, Jesús Verde, and Richard Villegas, to name just a few brilliant and inspiring undergraduates. Most of these students are now in graduate programs. I also thank Cindy Cruz, a graduate student whose research assistance was pivotal. Tracy Curtis, Justine Hernandez, Jim Lee, David Martinez, Lisa Orr, Karen Thomas Rose, and Omar Valerio-Jiménez made graduate seminars and dissertation projects a pleasure. Theresa Delgadilo and David Zamora merit recognition for exceptional research skills. I must single out a former student and current colleague, Mary Pat Brady, from whom I continue to learn. I additionally owe gratitude to C. Anne Bishop and Linda Garnets.

When I first conceptualized this project, Héctor Calderón recognized some merit in my early studies of Gloria Anzaldúa's *Borderlands*. He graciously took the time to read my early essay, gave it serious thought, and helped me clarify and develop my initial suspicions about the (dis)location and articulation of Chicana feminist theory. With his expert guidance, I published the seed essay of this project as "Feminism on the Border: From Gender Politics to Geopolitics" in the anthology he coedited with José Saldívar, *Criticism in the Borderlands*.

My brothers Ramón and José David consistently encouraged my delayed entry into the field of Chicana and Chicano literatures. Their own struggles at a time when there was even less support for subaltern people crossing fronteras into academia proved to me that it could be done with the double-layered armor of commitment and thick skin.

My unbelievably strong and brilliant sister, Anna María, provided constant encouragement. She motivated me to attempt a task that seemed insurmountable. Anna rearranged her life and co-mothered my son so I could return to school, and in the spirit of true sisterhood she adjusted her undergraduate schedule to allow me to take the necessary graduate seminars. Without her labor and support I could never have found the strength to defy the odds. My son, Marcos Alejandro (a.k.a. Mark), who as a child pointed out that I was spending most of his life in school, at the library, and away at my teaching job, began to understand some of my decisions the year he attended school in Los Angeles. His worldview was indelibly marked by the student rallies demanding a Chicana and Chicano Studies department and the largely working-class community supporters who marched on the UCLA campus. I thank him for knowing when to flash that beautiful smile and when to demand that I recognize that his needs were as crucial as my scholarly work.

Finally, I thank my childhood sweetheart and compañero, Felix. Es un verdadero hijo de Coatlicue, whose Irish great-great-grandfather jumped ship at the Port of Brownsville, married a Chicana, and left him with a mestizaje that in so many ways exemplifies life on the border. Raised to male privilege within the familia, humbled and politicized by his experiences as a mestizo médico, he has negotiated a journey that traces our men's trajectory from the certainty of the land of el puro macho to tentative, tremulous incursions into an emergent Chicano feminism on the border. I thank him for his support.

I dedicate this book to him y a todas las estudiantes en lucha.

I

Reading Tejana,
Reading Chicana

*We are what we do, especially what we do to change what we are:
our identity resides in action and in struggle.*
Eduardo Galeano, "In Defense of the Word"

*It is not individuals who have experience, but subjects who are
constituted through experience.*
Joan W. Scott, "Experience"

In this book I articulate my multiple locations as a Tejana, as a cultural
worker who labors "outside in the teaching machine," to use a phrase
by Gayatri Spivak, who is an advocate of subaltern women. My readings of early Chicana poetry and contemporary Chicana narratives are
informed by my travels from a Brown-town in South Texas to the
corridors of academia. My path hews close to the migration pattern
established by my paternal aunt and uncles who left el valle de Tejas
for economic reasons and settled in California Greater Mexico. Although the goal of my journey, my work as teacher, literary critic, and
feminist theorist, is radically different from that of my gente of the
previous generation, the need to leave el valle for los trabajos remains
the same.[1]

1

Transfrontera Memorias

In the Río Grande Valley of South Texas of the 1950s and 1960s, I was not a Chicana. I am the eldest daughter of working-class parents and the granddaughter, on my mother's side, of migrant workers who returned from their trips "up north" with little cash and many stories about Traverse City, Michigan, and their experiences picking cherries. Early on, my parents exhibited the ambivalence that in my memory still characterizes my life on the border. Traditional ethnic Catholics, yet eager to become fully modernized Americans, they sacrificed to send my older brother and me to a Catholic school, at least until we were properly catechized and made our First Holy Communion. Only then was it safe to send us to regular public school. All seven Saldívar siblings experienced variations of our parents' beliefs about the bridging of a Catholic and a secular education. They agreed in principle with the extended family's rules about a good Catholic education but believed themselves modern enough or, more saliently, *American* enough to come up with a new solution for their children's education. Our father's countless hours working at the shrimp plant and traveling along the coast of Mexico and Central America for the company ensured that my younger brothers and sister, José David, Héctor Antonio, Anna María, and Arnoldo René, could spend more years at Our Lady of Guadalupe School than Ramón had spent at Saint Joseph's Academy or I had spent at la Inmaculada, the Immaculate Conception school.

Intent on realizing their American dream, which our parents believed would materialize with Father's World War II Navy service, if not by birthright as native Tejanos, the Saldívar clan of my youth was in the process of becoming more American than Mexican. The pláticas of Tío Frank, Aunt Armandina, and my parents abound with bitter stories of how they were bombarded with propaganda from what I now understand were the hearings held by Joseph McCarthy as chairman of the Senate's permanent subcommittee on investigations in his relentless search for Communists. In the Rio Grande Valley, it was historically dangerous not to be American. Our Saldívar and García elders had lived the history of Texas Ranger terrorism against Mexicanos. Apá Treviño's disgust with "la pola," the notorious poll tax that kept poor Mexicans from voting, only later made sense to me.

Early on, our parents taught us to consider the border city of Matamoros as a foreign land. While we understood and were fluent in Spanish, we spoke only English at home. Father knew his people had always lived on this side of the Rio Grande; he had no relatives "over there." When his sister-in-law produced the Saldívar genealogy she had long researched, it traced the family to 1811 in the Goliad area of Texas. Our father delighted in this document—indisputable history—as he mercilessly goaded Mother about the unspoken origins of her beloved father, Eleuterio, and her Tía Cándida. My normally obstreperous mother advocated silence only on issues that she believed she could not change. The topic of her paternal Treviño roots in the Tamaulipas ranchitos was the one instance of an uncharacteristic refusal to engage in one of her marathon defenses of her position. Her reticence conveniently erased a past from which neither she nor her hijos could personally profit. Like the teachers I would soon meet in the public elementary school, Mother believed that we could change our identities as easily as the teacher would change our names—expunging the Mexican paternity would ensure her and her children's future as Americans. Nothing would be lost.

My brothers and I speculated that our beloved but clearly unhappy Apá Eleuterio was in hiding because of some covert activities in Mexico. The way he hid the newspapers he acquired in Matamoros led me to assume that he had been involved in the kind of política that my parents avoided. Mother discouraged our curiosity with her anger and would acknowledge only her maternal García Tejano ancestors, whose ranchito in San Pedro made them landowners in her mind. We knew no kin from el otro lado; we were Americans. Nonetheless, in conversations among themselves, the familia, and their compadres, my parents never failed to distinguish themselves from the Anglos whom they unswervingly called los Americanos (always said only in Spanish).

I learned from my parents that Matamoros, and by extension the rest of Mexico, was not "home"; yet as a child I crossed over almost every weekend with my Treviño grandparents, Apá Eleuterio and Amá Alvina, and Tía Lydia, who was more like an older sister than an aunt. We shopped at the parian, sometimes went to the hairdressers, and, as mujeres, always waited at the plaza while Apá visited his barber and argued la política with the other men. Mom and Dad may have insisted on their Americanness, but with my grandparents I constantly crossed back and forth to el otro lado to retrieve the basic necessities of our lives, our cultural molcajetes and jarros de barro para los frijoles, as it were. Where else could we get just the right piñata for my little sister's party? We needed the delicate papier mâché sitting hen to celebrate Anita's birthday properly. With Ramón Jr. and José David manipulating the piñata rope, Hector Anthony and Arnold René required just the right kind of Mexican candy to motivate them to join Anna's little friends in the frenzied quest to demolish the gallinita and liberate the dulces. Even the multicolored ones with the aniseed in the center were prized by the children. The baby, Alfredo Luis, as usual in my arms, would scream with glee. My job was to keep him from getting hit by the broomstick camouflaged with ribbons that the children used to pulverize the piñata.

There was only one salón de novias where we could find just the right arras or lasso or cojines for our Catholic wedding rituals. The First Holy Communion candles, prayer book, and rosary could be found only in Matamoros. And when Tía Lydia was called once again to serve as madrina for a quinceañera, where else could we go but to el otro lado to get the proper dye so her shoes and gloves would match the lavender or perico-green dress that all fourteen damas would wear? I couldn't wait to be asked to a quinceañera or a prom so I too could visit Doña Licha's Casa de Belleza and have my hair shellacked into those lovely gajito curls that would last at least a week if you slept on your stomach, your chin on your hands.

I remember the solemn pilgrimages to Doña Panchita, the holy woman/espiritista who read las cartas, the Tarot, and prayed directly to her god without the need for intermediaries. On those occasions, my normally too American and too unsuperstitious mother would join us. She eased her Catholic guilt by insisting that the gods and goddesses Doña Panchita invoked in her trances were really all the virgins and apostles and saints. If we did not recognize the names, perhaps it was only because she was chanting, as the priests did, in a language we did not know. "Son lenguas antiguas," Amá Alvina would cryptically explain. My admiration for my grandmother only increased when I guessed that she and Doña Panchita communicated in this secret language. These were the special times when Mother made the crossing—how else was she to verify or disregard what the camaroneras were telling her about her husband's long days at the shrimp-processing plant?

But on the numerous occasions when Mother did not cross with us in her late-model Ford, Apá would borrow Tío Juan's shiny 1959 beige

Impala with the fins out to there, a low rider before low riders were fashionable even with the local pachucos. Those earliest memories include feeling a curious mixture of dread and embarrassment as we approached the bridge from Matamoros to Brownsville. We always took "el puente viejo" because my grandparents believed that the Border Patrol agents stationed there were also the viejos who understood that as borderers, they had no need to ask these obviously American Mexicans for proof of citizenship. Yet every time an unfamiliar gringo approached the car, my grandmother would tighten her grip on my hand and anxiously answer her rehearsed "Yes" at the inevitable question, "Ya'll American citizens?" For the following week the outing's success would be remembered and discussed at Amá Alvina's kitchen table in terms of the experience at the puente. If the questions led to a search of the car, Apá would spend the rest of my visit scowling and rattling his Mexican newspapers, invoking the only saint he ever mentioned, San Avabitche, San Avabitche, as he perched on a lawn chair on the front porch, which became off limits to the usually quiet granddaughter playing solitaire jacks with a golf ball on the cool, maroon cement. I attributed his rage to the rinche officer at the bridge. Living on the border, we have our reasons for never differentiating between Texas Rangers and Border Patrol agents.

The crossings over to Matamoros began when I was old enough to declare my citizenship in unaccented English for the border guards; a more formative crossing came at grade 3. Our working-class neighborhood (we said "barrio" only when we were speaking Spanish) was in the border zone between the middle- and upper-class Anglo elementary school, Ebony Heights, and the working-class Mexican American school, Resaca. Would we attend Ebony Heights, where "Ebony" referred to a native tree and certainly not to the hue of the preferred student body, or to Resaca Elementary, named after the stagnant bodies of water peculiar to our southernmost U.S. town? Our parents celebrated when they discovered a quirk in the city school zoning that would allow their children to attain the heights of a privileged public education, and finally assert their claim to the American part of their dual identity.

Much later I learned that only three streets in our neighborhood—Blanche, Velma, and Mildred—were rezoned because this was the Mullen subdivision and the Mullen grandchildren lived on Blanche. Most significant for us, the school bus driver's grandchildren lived on Mildred, and he had been the family retainer of a powerful school board member. Ours was the street in between, Velma. That was one propitious border zone we inhabited.

At Ebony Heights the sections of the third grade were A, B, C, and F. The F section would eventually be termed "Special Education." On registration day, the woman in charge declined to look at my Immaculate Conception School report cards; by virtue of my last name, I belonged in C section at best. My older brother, Ramón, renamed Ray by the Anglo teachers, had crossed over Boca Chica Boulevard to the Anglo part of town two years before. The family accepted that he had actually made my better-than-F-section placement possible with his perfect report cards. To this day he enjoys reminding us that he began his public school education in the F section.

Lining up at the front of the third-grade class with the handful of children my teacher delicately labeled "Spanish," I worked daily on "diction." The fact that we all came from similar backgrounds, with working-class parents, many of whom were fifth-generation borderers and were therefore fluent in English, was ignored by this educator, who felt she was helping us by eradicating all traces of a Spanish accent. By the time the school year ended, the tall, kindly Anglo teacher's Mexican students would proudly pronounce "ship" and not "chip," "Miss" and not "Meese," "chair" and not "share," "shop" and not "chop," "shoe" and not "chew," and so on. I worked my way up the ladder of this educational system until by fifth grade I was in the A section with my Anglo schoolmates. None of them lived in my neighborhood. None of them could come to visit after school. Too far from their neighborhoods, too close to the government projects up the block from our house on Velma Street. I failed to understand why they could never get permission to come, but I was secretly glad because my life at home did not allow playtime for girls. The two granddaughters of the original neighborhood developer were my classmates and we played together during recess, but it never occurred to us to interact back home. We never did. Passing their house on my daily trek to the tendajito, I never saw them outdoors. So that was how they stayed so pale.

While I was proudly fluent in Spanish because of my close ties to my non-English-speaking grandparents, by the end of my elementary school career I affected a British accent, mainly because of my Beatlemania rather than from any ideological leanings. Or so I thought. While I was never physically assaulted for speaking Spanish in the schoolyard, I intuitively assumed the "don't ask, don't tell" version of early-1960s xenophobia in South Texas. If no one challenged my un-accented English, I did not have to acknowledge my fluency in that other language.

Things began to change for me the summer after the Beatles first appeared on the *Ed Sullivan Show*. I was finally asked to be a dama for a quinceañera. As the youngest of the group, I was assigned a cham-berlain from el otro lado who was a family friend of the birthday girl. With my tía and amá's help, my mother began a campaign to ensure that I would not disgrace the family by running off with him. His citizenship canceled out the fact that he came from a relatively wealthy Matamoros family. Ironically, as a not-quite-twelve-year-old, I was more offended by the fact that they could assume my disloyalty to my favorite Beatle and even consider looking at this other boy than out-raged that they had such little faith in my integrity. The bitterness came later, when I realized that for these women in my family, there was no liminal stage of innocent girlhood.

One night, after a late rehearsal for the customary quinceañera pro-cessional and first dance, the young man offered to drive me home. I reacted with extreme suspicion, imagining abduction into slavery or worse in Mexico. The mujeres in my family had succeeded. My unrea-sonable fear of this perfectly well-mannered and actually quite bored young man managed to make the baile an unpleasant duty. To justify her victory, Mother reminded me that quinceañeras were not cele-brated by my Ebony Heights friends. With her proclamation, she si-multaneously rendered them old-fashioned and un-American. Needless to say, when I turned fifteen and the family could not possibly afford such a lavish celebration, I feigned disinterest in that antiquated cus-tom.

Boca Chica, the boulevard that we had negotiated in our commutes to the other side of town, became for me a rarely traveled route that merely shared the name of the beach that we frequented. Boca Chica was our beach, the one our family chose to haunt rather than the more popular Padre Island. The causeway toll of a dollar a carload was ob-viously a factor to my parents and extended family, but as children, we were less concerned about such issues than about the fact that la Boca Chica had better sand dunes. There we began the beach season with an Easter-egg hunt that no one else in my circle could duplicate. The rest of the spring and onto the summer, we could count on Aunt Armandina and Tío Frank to stop by and load some of us seven sib-

lings in their Auto Glass Shop pickup along with their own four children while the rest of us and Tía Lydia piled into family cars to head
out to the playa. We would return well after dark, sunburned and
jellyfish wounded, but with fantastic stories of near drowning and he-
roic rescues. John Lennon's "Twist and Shout" still evokes the smell
of the beach, the taste of sand-dusted hot dogs, pollo asado, and, when
Tío Frank was lucky, taquitos del catch of the day—usually trucha
(trout).

As summer ended, I journeyed to the junior high school to which
my neighborhood belonged and found most of the students Mexican
American. In the few years since we had moved from the notorious
southmost barrio to what some called la Villa Verde (Mom insisted it
was the McDavid neighborhood), new families had followed. Their
children were not part of the Ebony Heights migrants. To me it
seemed as if this barrio de las tarántulas had changed overnight. Suddenly I had friends in the neighborhood with whom I could walk to
school. We spoke Spanish as easily as English. The new girlfriends were
amused by my Ebony Heights pretensions, but as proper borderers,
they understood the unspoken rules, and I needed no excuses or defenses for my crossing to that other school.

Mr. Manzano, the principal of Cummings Junior High, was Mexican American, as was our drama and speech coach, Miss Parra, whom
I credit for encouraging my participation in poetry readings at the
Valley-wide Interscholastic League competitions. Not even my mother
dared confront her about pressing household duties once Miss Parra
decided I was on her team. There I was more than a Mexican, more
than an "American," certainly more than eldest daughter, dishwasher
extraordinaire, and surrogate mother. Surrounded by teachers like Miss
Parra, I could finally indulge in my forbidden passion of reading. Back
home, Mother never tired of reciting the story of her comadre who
had suffered a nervous breakdown after reading the Bible in its entirety.
As a woman of her own time, a product of unresolved conflicts and
ambivalence about her preordained role as a mother and as a woman,
she tried to prohibit me to read because to her the physical inactivity
of reading signified laziness in a girl. Being a full-fledged American and
leaving antiquated Mexican traditions behind did not extend to her
daughter. For me, school became a safe haven from her anger, from
her own disappointments in life. Cummings became a place where I
could indulge my passion for Shakespeare, Austen, Dickens, and the
Brontës under the guidance of marvelous teachers. This unique school

offered a new breed of teachers, Mexican, like Mr. Esparza, and Anglo, like Miss Pugenat, who taught those of us raised on nopales and mesquites how to write and how to appreciate daffodils even if we might never see real ones. The formidable librarian always saved the new books for me to check out first. By the end of seventh grade she had introduced me to Thomas Hardy as well as Margaret Mitchell. Only in hindsight do I wonder exactly why she thought I should read about Tess and Scarlett over the long Christmas vacation. To be fair, she chose other books that offered much more than cautionary tales for this American Mexicana whose Beatlemania now translated into a definite interest in attentive brown-skinned boys. By the time I completed junior high I had read the Austen canon as well as the Brontë sisters' novels. Hemingway, Fitzgerald, and even Faulkner were the more challenging new discoveries that Ramón shared from his high school English classes. School, with its usually abandoned library, was the sanctuary for a girl who loved to read but had more pressing duties at home.

As the Ebony Heights traumas stemming from my outsider status began to fade, negotiating another barrier proved more daunting. At this junior high school, even Mexican girls could be smart, could be the top students and favorites of the legendary librarian. For my mother, however, becoming a full-fledged American never altered her biases against her daughter's attempt to escape traditional gender constraints. The boys in the family could aspire to everything the school system provided, but Mother could not accept a daughter's learning to ride a bike or even to roller-skate. There were vicious arguments in which she proclaimed her fear that I would damage my "female organs." My sputtering response that she was being unfair suffered from the absence of a more forceful language with which to articulate the misogyny of her rules. The brothers could play, read, and study as much as they wanted—indeed, the status of the family somehow hinged on their success—but as a mujercita, I was needed to perform crucial household and child-care tasks. My attempts to read and study were signs of laziness and nothing more. My longing to ride a bike or play baseball with the boys could signify only dangerous propensities to wander, improper desires for a girl. At that time, Mother could not conceive of a different possibility for a daughter.

Contradictions abounded. I was allowed to go to school dances, but only if my older brother agreed to stay by my side. As a result, Ramón and I forged a deep friendship over books and dancing. As best friends we conspired against her rules. If I taught him the latest dances—the jerk, the watusi, the broken hip, even the bolero for the slow dances— we could part at the door of the school gym or the civic center for the big shindigs featuring Kiko and the Dukes, Sonny and the Sunliners, or Little Joe and the Family, and meet up at the end of the dance. We still reminisce about dance lessons to the Beatles' "And I Love Her," as well as that first reading of *Catcher in the Rye*. Unfortunately, not even her eldest son's influence swayed my mother's conviction that I must turn down the editorship of the school newspaper, citing too many demands on my time, since I was also in the band. Since I joined the band for its social benefits, I was possibly the worst clarinetist in Cameron County. She did allow me, however, to contribute to the paper as gossip columnist. I never fully explained that one to my English teacher. Since he was Mexican American as well, I suppose he understood. Unlike Miss Parra, though, he did not challenge the limiting roles my parents had ordained for me.

Growing up on the frontera in Brownsville, Texas, in the 1950s and 1960s taught me to long for something more; yet it also prepared me to accept the limits placed on us. Allowed to excel in junior high, in the town's only public high school I was reunited with my former Anglo and middle-class American Mexican classmates. But this time I noticed that they were all tracked to the college prep classes, regardless of their intellectual capacities. I found it strange that the untouchable "brains" of Ebony Heights were my peers at Brownsville High. In our senior English honors class, they all wrote papers on *The Catcher in the Rye* (the book I had already digested with Ramón when I was in eighth grade) and earned A's, whereas what I now recognize as a proto-feminist paper on "My Last Duchess" enticed the popular Hemingwayesque teacher to lament that while I couldn't write as well as my older brother, at least I had something he did not—shapely legs. It speaks volumes about the late 1960s, a time before the Women's Movement reached our South Texas enclave, that at the end of the school year this master teacher actually wrote with impunity such a blatantly sexist sentiment in my yearbook.

While the White classmates all planned their futures at the University of Texas or other schools as far from the Valley as possible, my girlfriends and I were advised by the senior counselor not to apply to a college. In my case, my indifferent math scores on the entrance exams were more significant than my high scores in English and history. The local junior college, which we disparagingly called Tamale Tech, was all I could aspire to. I had heard of a women's college and attempted to apply to it, but my parents knew nothing of Denton or Texas Women's University and reminded me that the application process was entirely my problem. My boyfriend, who was at the small agricultural college two hours away, warned me that if I went, our relationship was over.

Tamale Tech it would be. I knew that after the tech, I would be married and my life would be complete, anyway. I could not imagine any other way for myself—I knew no other Mexicana from Browntown who had done it differently. There were no other possibilities for young working-class fronteristas, what I now call us frontera dwellers with feminist leanings. All my girlfriends were also being married, and getting good jobs at the phone company or as tellers at the bank. Their employment solution was progress, a step up from our parents' manual labor jobs. As mujeres, we were all considered successful if we graduated from high school and did not end up pregnant and a dishonor to the familia. The fact that we were all smart, a few of us members of the National Honor Society and a handful of us in the top 5 percent of our graduating class of over nine hundred students, did not translate into scholarships to the university.

Little did we know that the world was changing outside the Valley. My older brother, who in spite of his grades could escape no farther than a college in the central Valley, brought back new ideas as well as the long hair and Zapata mustache that Dad hated. His rebellion included leaving behind a full scholarship at that college and our father's rage to venture into the unknown territory of the university at Austin, where we had no family or family history. Judging from my parents' laments at his departure for Austin, sin permiso, it was as if Central Texas were the end of the earth and he would certainly fall into the abyss if he left el valle.

By my first year at the local college, Brown power and women's liberation were beckoning. Too many young Mexican American men who had been my high school classmates or with me in the band returned from Viet Nam "with full military honors." Staying in college to avoid the draft became essential for many of my male friends, in spite of active discouragement by the school counselors. Largely as a result of these first college students, an entire generation identifying as Chicanos soon would produce a body of writing that would speak to our lives on the border, where we existed between Mexican and American, between rich and poor, between the United States and Mexico.

Thinking back on those years when "la frontera" literally signified "the frontier," words such as *marginality, alterity, misogyny*, and *difference* were not concepts available with which we could theorize our subject positions in this land of our ancestors—both the Spanish settlers of Nuevo Santander and the Karankowa or Comanches indigenous to this area. I remember how the significance of my hometown centered on its specific spot on the map. Living in Brownsville, Texas, meant living at the southernmost tip of the United States. When I was a child, the knowledge that we were at the bottom of the U.S. map made sense to me. When we traveled in Mexico, we were called norteños, pochos. Our preference for flour tortillas signified our working-class position; our pochismos also marked us as working class and not real Mexicanos. My grandparents had always been aware of those neighborhoods and certain tiendas in Mexico where we were not welcome. The class bias that we experienced in Matamoros and the rest of Mexico was as powerful as the racism endured in Brownsville. I knew then that I was not Mexican. Armed with these lessons that shaped my subjectivity, if not my political consciousness, I left the Valley.

In my present role as a Chicana cultural worker, I trace the coming to consciousness of my identity to the cultural artifacts, the first Chicana/o poetry I read in the mid-1970s. The act of reading these texts legitimized my experiences as a working-class mujer. The act of reading poetry written by a Chicana complicated and enriched my burgeoning self-consciousness as a feminist Chicana. The feminism on the border I elaborate throughout my study of contemporary writers springs from these preliminary articulations of early Chicano nationalism and the dissatisfaction that so many activist mujeres began to feel in the face of the masculinist notions of that political movement.

I acknowledge the anxiety I share with the cultural critics who warn against conflating the personal lived experience with detached studies of history or with clinical analyses of the class war.[2] As Chicanas, however, our specific experiences as working-class-origin, ethnic women under the law of the fathers undergird our theories. As a female subject of transfrontera culture in the Río Grande Valley of South Texas, I attended college and eventually graduate school only after performing all the requisite roles of a young mujer of the 1960s.[3] Free love and the rejection of materialism did not apply to most of us isolated in the

Valley, under the protection of our fathers and tradiciones. Never imagining that I could do anything other than bask in the reflected glory of a man, I married one year out of high school and dedicated my considerable energies to realizing my husband's career goals. After my second year at college, he began his medical school training. Immediately I left school and went to work, as I had been programmed to do. I knew no other way. No woman in my sphere had ever lived differently. The idea of moving to Houston, where he would study, was ambitious enough for me.

With Ramón completing his graduate degree at Yale and José an undergraduate there as well, I noted no injustice when the extended family gathered at holidays and the talk eventually centered on the men's exciting intellectual work. I welcomed these family reunions as reprieves from my drudgery as an unskilled laborer at a huge Houston hospital. After my husband told his anecdotes about surviving at medical school and mimicked the famous heart surgeon's Louisiana drawl as he expressed his utter contempt for lowly medical students, I attentively listened to my brothers' literary conversations. They knew I was interested, and after an attempt to introduce me to the mysteries of phenomenology and this new critical tool they called deconstruction, the discussion eventually turned to the lack of publications by Chicano writers. I noted that the writers they named were all male (Tomás Rivera, José Montoya, Rolando Hinojosa), and asked if there were any women writing. Included on their impromptu list were Angela de Hoyos, Carmen Tafolla, Inés Hernández, and the young Lorna Dee Cervantes. The brothers promised to send me copies of these women's poems.

We returned to our lives, the brothers to academia, I to my role as supportive wife. My husband and I promised ourselves that we would change the world of el valle when we returned to South Texas armed with his medical degree. His career became *our* causa. We engaged in Chicano political activism in Houston, but only in its emanations in the medical arena. When on a whim I applied for a premed summer program and earned admission, I joined my husband and his family's laughter at how I had fooled the admissions committee into thinking I could participate in such an important field. In a few days I was no longer amused but I nonetheless declined the admission.

The longer I worked at the hospital, the more I found I could accomplish. I soon went from blood collector to medical technician, learned to perform urinalysis, and eventually found myself surrounded by test tubes and beakers and computers in the biochemistry wing of the laboratory, even training first-year medical technology students in the practical aspects of testing blood. My lack of formal training justified low wages, but it was not until the hospital janitors went on strike that I realized that I could not stay at this job. My political sympathies were with the Latino and African American workers, but my college-educated lab colleagues refused to support the strike for fear their "professional status" would suffer if they aligned themselves with "unskilled workers." Illegitimate, skilled, but unschooled, I knew I could no longer work there.

Even in these roles as undereducated, underpaid, almost-white-collar worker and wife of a medical student, I considered myself liberated. I imagined that I too labored for a causa. My early (mis)understanding of "women's liberation" allowed me to contemptuously dismiss my mother as a mere breeder. I congratulated myself on my personal liberation from the familia in the Valley, from the exceptionally strict and profoundly dissatisfied mother skeptical that her daughter could escape her own niche in the working class as mother of seven children. I took pride in my pioneer spirit as I forged what I imagined was a new way.

The medical school welcomed us, the new generation of working-class White women and women of color, with a doctors' wives club that would teach us to appreciate opera, ballet, and the spirit of volunteerism. Ironically, most of us worked to support our husbands and to send money to our parents and younger siblings. That first year I dutifully attended the meetings when my husband insisted that his career would suffer if I dismissed the Ladies of the Distaff. Throughout the medical school years my hospital co-workers warned that med students' wives were commonly dismissed by the young doctors when the M.D. became reality. Even my mother joined in and whispered the fears of the working wives. Her caveat was particularly irritating as she expressed it in the language she had taught me had little value: "Cuídate, te va dejar cuando se reciba." Indeed, many of the wives were handed divorce decrees as the men received their medical diplomas.

In spite of my sense of isolation and insecurity, further fed by night-shift labor at the hospital, my fears dissolved as I devoured the literature that my brothers began to send. José supplied me with the chapbooks the Chicano students at Yale were compiling, as well as copies of Lorna Dee Cervantes's "Mango"; Ramón sent the mimeographed poems by a fellow Tejana, the mestiza Angela de Hoyos. The first poems I read clarified the label *Chicano* for me. I would return to their powerful pages throughout my tenure as a medical student's wife, and soon after, as an obstetrical resident's wife. For now, that was my identity of choice. But something else was happening. I had begun to read and reread the Movimiento poetry my brothers supplied. A new way of thinking began to open up for me.

Tracking History and Subjectivity

By 1975, de Hoyos self-published some of those poems in the collection *Chicano: Poems from the Barrio*. She was an activist during the late 1960s and throughout the 1970s, and her involvement with the Texas Farmworkers Union informed the social vision of her poetry. As Mexicans in South Texas, we identified with the laborers in the fields. If we were not out there ourselves, we had familia who worked the labores. This was the magic valley whose chamber of commerce erased the history of exploitation of the farmworkers by Anglo farm owners. This representation of a "magic" valley whose fields of melons, grapefruit orchards, and cotton fields employed happy peasant workers spurred writers such as Angela de Hoyos to unleash angry voices resonating with poetic and political intensity. Her early poems illustrate the oppositional nature of Chicana cultural production of the late 1960s and 1970s, wherein a quest for a cultural identity set forth a preliminary quest for history. Reading this poetry forced me to think about the intellectual implications of being Chicana alongside my emergent feminist politics.

De Hoyos's poetry provides historical documentation of the Chicano Movement as it exposes the internal contradictions of the Movimiento. On one level, the poetry of the period reflects the awakening of political consciousness among Americans of color. Tejanos knew only too well the fury of armed Texas Rangers when we dared organize protests or strikes. The literature offered different strategies as we articulated rage against Anglo-American domination in forms other than the corrido. In the poetry of women like de Hoyos, we see how an emergent group expanded its struggle from the melon and onion fields to the discursive arena, in this case to the lyric form. These early records, however, remain in obscurity, in out-of-print chapbooks held mainly in personal libraries. Necessity demands that I present the poems in their entirety here.

Hermano

> *"Remember the Alamo"*
> *...and my Spanish ancestors*
> *who had the sense to build it.*

I was born too late
in a land
that no longer belongs to me
(so it says, right here in this Texas History).

Ay mi San Antonio de Bexar
ciudad-reina de la frontera,
the long hand of greed
was destined to seize you!
...Qué nadie te oyó cuando caíste,
cuando esos hombres rudos te hurtaron?...
Blind-folded they led you
to a marriage of means
while your Spanish blood
smoldered within you!

Tu cielo
ya no me pertenece.
Ni el Alamo, ni la Villita,
ni el río que a capricho
por tu mero centro corre.
Ni las misiones
—joyas de tu pasado—
  San Juan de Capistrano
  Concepción
  San José
  La Espada
: They belong to a pilgrim
who arrived here only yesterday
whose racist tongue says to me: I hate
Meskins. You're a Meskin. Why don't you
go back to where you came from?
Yes, amigo...! Why don't I? Why don't I
resurrect the Pinta, the Niña and the Santa María
—and you can scare up your little 'Flor de Mayo'—
so we all sail back
to where we came from: the motherland womb.

I was born too late
or perhaps I was born too soon:
It is not yet my time;
this is not yet my home.

I must wait for the conquering barbarian
to learn the Spanish word for love:

HERMANO

The genesis of revolutionary thought emerges in "Hermano" as the narrative voice scrutinizes the Anglo-American version of Texas and U.S. history. The poem's epigraph, "Remember the Alamo," invokes the battle cry that all White Texas schoolchildren learn to read as their patriotic claim to Texas. The ensuing clause, "and my ancestors who had the sense to build it," immediately undermines that claim of ownership.[4]

When early Chicana writers questioned the accuracy of official Texas history textbooks, through the power of the word they embarked on a process of change. The poetry of that period began a profound transformation as it sparked the recuperation of an erased existence. For the vast majority of readers of Mexican descent from Mexicano Texas, Spanish was the nonstatus, taboo language in which discrimination hid its political agenda. Many of us had never before seen mestiza language with its characteristic code-switching between English and Spanish in print as a legitimate literary discourse. The phrase "Remember the Alamo" may have been verbalized by White bullies on countless Texas schoolyards, but de Hoyos's reappropriation of the phrase allowed many of us to imagine a counterhistory. Movement poems such as "Hermano" gave us our first glimpse of that alternative history.

Conciliatory as the poem now seems, what "Hermano" reflected in the early 1970s was outraged opposition. In the late 1950s and 1960s, when I attended Texas public schools, I never encountered Brown people like me in history texts. The required high school Texas history course ignored crucial oppositional moments such as the Primer Congreso Mexicanista of 1911. Only after the first generation of college-educated Chicanos accessed the archival records did we learn that the 1911 conference was organized by U.S. Mexicanos/as in protest of racial terrorism and economic exploitation. The Congreso denounced segregated public schools and exposed the rampant lynching of Tejanos and Tejanas. The organization, which met in Laredo, Texas, also promoted bilingual education, and according to José Limón, participants such as J. M. Mora called for a "radical working-class ideology." The conference was also revolutionary in its inclusion of women's voices in the proceedings. While the plea for women's education was couched in the rhetoric of the maternal role, nonetheless, as Limón astutely recognizes, the Congreso offered a forum for an emergent feminista politics ("El primer congreso mexicanista," 95).

The poet-activist de Hoyos was in the vanguard of Chicanas who were among the first post-McCarthy-era writers to resist cultural and political domination by Southwestern Anglo America. However, at this early point in what has been termed a contemporary cultural renaissance, de Hoyos's invocation of Spain as the "motherland womb" and the narrator's search for a cultural identity in the Iberian Peninsula point to the entrenched roots of Eurocentrism.[5] Nonetheless, the poem successfully establishes the border as a site of struggle against the political domination by Anglo America. San Antonio, for Mexicanos, emerges as the "border city," the "queen" whose jewels are the Spanish missions that were for many the center of Spanish, or high, culture.

While "Hermano" provides the crucial proto-revolutionary critique that enabled us to develop our identity consciousness, more significantly the narrative allegorizes the obliteration of a racial memory of Tejana/Tejano indigenous ancestry. Without the memory, there is no territory where "Hermano" can address the barbarities of the Spanish conquest. Yet, as we gain access to the elided history, we understand the poet's failure to address the acts of terrorism against Tejanas/Tejanos as well as against Amerindians. The indoctrination of the U.S. Mexican population renders "Hermano" mute with regard to what the European "conquering barbarians" deleted from the historical record. This is how hegemony works.

In the face of the dominating culture's strategies of containment, the poem's late-1960s narrator could not see the Catholic missions as signs of conquest. Not until Antonia Castañeda's groundbreaking work in Chicana history, in such essays as "Sexual Violence in the Politics and Policies of Conquest," did we have access to a record of the missions' roles in the conquest of the indigenous Southwest and West. Louis Althusser's ideological state apparatus, here the Texas public school system, ensured that mestizas would remain ignorant of violence against native women and men in the collusive colonizing projects of the Spanish government and the Catholic Church. When we apply Castañeda's research on the conquest of California to Texas, the northern frontera of "New Spain," where the Catholic missions and forts were points of operation for soldiers who raped and murdered native women, poems such as "Hermano" take on even deeper significance and complexity.[6]

Constrained by an ethnocentric version of history, de Hoyos

mourns the fall of San Antonio to the conquering Anglo. The guiding metaphor of an arranged marriage between a Spanish/Mexican bride and an Anglo legitimizes his lust for the land. The narrative, however, ignores the Spanish soldiers' violence against the native people. The poem ends with the narrator's willingness to "wait for the conquering barbarian / to learn the word for love: / Hermano." Reflecting its historical moment of production, the poem's resisting impulse in this context can only invoke a Hispanic brother. The narrative yearns to claim Europe rather than imagine a new mestiza sibling empowered to embrace an Indigenous heritage, one with the mestiza consciousness to mourn the lost legacy of indigenous languages, as Gloria Anzaldúa would explore in *Borderlands / La Frontera* twenty years after the publication of "Hermano." *Hermano* translates literally as *brother*, and in the rhetoric of the Chicano movement it alludes to the nationalist concept of "carnalismo," the brotherhood of the Movimiento, nationalist yet blatantly patriarchal in practice.[7]

While the technique of code-switching between English and Spanish engages a subversion of literary traditions, ultimately the poem's protest is a cry for the dominant culture's acceptance, a yearning for kinship with Euro-Americans. The poem demonstrates how public institutions indoctrinate children with particular versions of history.

"Hermano" chronicles the political sentiments of the 1960s, and in "Oral History and La Mujer," the historian Vicki Ruiz continues the project of reforming the Chicana subject with the testimony of Rosa Guerrero, a woman from El Paso, Texas, who remembers the obstacles U.S. Mexican children faced in the public school system of the 1940s:

> I remember being punished for speaking Spanish. Nos daban unos coscorrones, pero coscorrones, o nos daban unas zuibandas con un board. Tenían un board of education por hablar español. Yo no entendía lo que me decían, ni jota, ni jota. Pero por eso estoy tan cercana, y mi corazón y mi espíritu al programa bilingüe, porque yo sufrí unas cosas horribles. Yo no fui la única; fueron miles de gentes que sufrieron en Arizona, en Colorado, en Nuevo México, en Texas, en California; que nos estereortipaban horriblemente. "Don't you speak that ugly language, you are American now, you Mexican child." They degraded us horribly, pero uno se hacía valer. (226–27)[8]

Guerrero's testimonio displays the disparity between the ideals of an educational system and the reality of the institutionalized tenets of White supremacy hidden under the cloak of language instruction. Guerrero's experiences in the 1940s echo my own diction lessons in the 1960s. What Anzaldúa calls "linguistic terrorism" continues today. Exclusionary practices long ingrained in the U.S. public school systems are still rampant at this moment of anti–affirmative action fervor. Guerrero and a few people like her may have resisted internalizing what inhumane educators taught us about ourselves, but there are countless others who came to believe they were incapable of learning and left school, and some who thought that they would be the exceptions who would succeed within the parameters established by the dominant group.[9]

If the narrative voice in "Hermano" peers only as far as the Iberian Peninsula, perhaps the reason for this limited perception lies in another of Angela de Hoyos's poems, "Chicano." In twenty-nine brief but eloquent words, the poem offers a Chicano version of W. E. B. Du Bois's double consciousness, "a sense of always looking at oneself through the eyes of others" (*Souls of Black Folk*, 45). In the Chicano context, the doubleness comes from a subject position between Mexican and American, between fluency in English and in citizenship in the United States. Ostensibly a critique of the pressures of assimilation into Anglo culture, "Chicano" presents the ambiguity, the double consciousness that children of Mexican descent experience in an ethnocentric White world:

Chicano:

How to paint
    on this page
        the enigma
that furrows
    your sensitive
        brown face

—a sadness,
    porque te llamas
        Juan y no *John*
as the laws
    of assimilation
        dictate.

Written mainly in English, the poem represents an "enigma" of a child's "sensitive brown face" as he grieves for his existence in that border zone between Juan and John. We can translate the words "y no" in the phrase "porque te llamas *Juan* y no *John*" either as "instead of" or "and not." The Chicano's double vision is thereby reflected in the ambiguity and the multiple possibilities of the translation. Is the child's sadness a result of his desire to be John, an Anglo-American in an Anglo-dominant world? Or is it that the laws of assimilation injure him because the White (or White-identified) teachers in his school have changed his name from the Spanish Juan to the foreign John? In the (mis)translation, those with power to (re)name obliterate his cultural identity. De Hoyos's poem refuses to provide an easy answer, refuses closure. The doubling of Juan/John attests to the existence of the border dweller in at least two places simultaneously. The poem's few lines further capture the tragedy of institutionalized racism against Tejanos caught on the wrong side of the border by the changing tides of political incursions. "Chicano" is the child who endured when, in the words of Américo Paredes, "the border moved—we didn't."[10]

If Juan/John mourns his doubling by assimilationist forces, is there a Chicana, a female subject, in the borderlands poetry of this Movement era whom we can mourn or celebrate? "Mujer Sin Nombre" gives voice to the silences that the women of the Movement family experienced:

Mujer Sin Nombre

Para mí no se hizo el canto
: I drag a nameless grief
like a cloak of thorns upon me
and whither I go
it answers for me
truncating my budding voice
before it has time to bloom.

I inherited from Eve
a satirical apple
: my benign love becomes
a sin
      malignant in the mouths
      of others.

Es que mi suerte
mi enemiga de siempre
          siempre me viste
de tristes colores
: hoja en el viento.
Hija de nadie.
Who knows
from what bed of hungers
I have arisen?

Chicano, amigo mío,
dame de tu aliento
para llevar conmigo
            algo de tí
cuando me devore el tiempo.

In this proto-feminist moment, the narrator reveals herself as a gendered subject who suspects that some authority enforces her silence,
controls her "budding voice." As a woman in the misogynistic Chicano
Movement, she uses the phrase "Para mí no se hizo el canto" as an
indication of her inability to participate in the creation of—or be the
subject of—literature, "el canto." Women's voices were not taken seriously; certainly women's issues were not worthy of inclusion in
Movement poetry performances named after indigenous rituals (such
as Flor y Canto) or in political manifestos. The female narrator of this
poem is a quasi-religious figure upon whose back are juxtaposed the
traditional cloak of the Virgen and the Christ's crown of thorns. What
emerges is a profoundly disturbing vision of the mujer sufrida, the
longsuffering woman, who wears a "cloak of thorns" rather than
merely a crown of thorns. The martyred woman also identifies with
Eve, a figure whom Mexicans on both sides of the border also call La
Malinche, the traitor to the race, who by virtue of her articulations as
translator to Hernán Cortés, the Spaniard to whom she was presented
as a slave, gained infamy in the annals of Mexican and Chicano history
and letters.[11]

While the conquest chronicles have misrepresented this nameless
woman's "benign love" as a sin, a betrayal of her people, the serpent
in the mythic Judeo-Christian tradition serves a different purpose as
evil personified. In indigenous traditions, the serpent represents that
other unnamed, forgotten woman—the Aztec mother of the gods,
Coatlicue. Without access to Chicana or indigenous feminist sources,
the narrator cannot name Coatlicue or any other emancipatory image
for women. Certainly the male-dominated Movement remembered
only the suffering, maternal Guadalupe or Pandora's double, La Malinche.[12] De Hoyos's "mujer sin nombre" anticipates Gloria Anzaldúa's
naming project in Borderlands / La Frontera, as well as Sandra Cisneros's ultimate reclamation ritual at the end of her cuento "Small Mir-
acles, Kept Promises." The nameless woman's anonymity in de Hoyos's
poem points to the way history has obliterated "native women," both
in the Anglo version of Texas/Mexican history and in the androcentric

Chicano nationalist version with its male-centered brotherhood of Aztlán.

The nameless woman's enemies are legion. They insist on dressing her in mourning, relegating her to a colorless existence, doomed to the restrictive stereotype of hija de nadie—nothing daughter, or no one's daughter. Unaware of her stature in an emerging Chicana feminist movement, the nameless woman, ghost sister to Maxine Hong Kingston's defiant, sexual No Name Woman, turns to the authorities, Chicano men. She pleads for the breath of life, for nourishment, from their nationalist politics on her way to inevitable annihilation by time and by history.

What la mujer sin nombre demands in this bleak protest against the insignificance of women in the politics of her time is the signifier *Chicana*, a self-representation that underscores her multiple subjectivity: the complex inextricability of race, class, and gender. As I discuss in the following chapter, mujeres in the Movimiento were indeed sin nombre, anonymous workers and theorists pushed to the background, kept in their places as hijas de La Malinche, Eva, and Guadalupe.

Still without the language of feminist politics, de Hoyos produced yet another chapbook, *Arise, Chicano! And Other Poems*, in 1975. She again returns to the masculine label *Chicano* in her call for a revolutionary coming to consciousness of the colonized Chicano population. As oppositional and richly crafted as Tomás Rivera's better-known novel . . . *Y no se lo tragó la tierra*, the poem "Arise, Chicano!" traces the exploitation and disempowerment of an entire population:

Arise, Chicano!

In your migrant's world of hand-to-mouth days,
your children go smileless to a cold bed;
the bare walls rockaby the same wry song,
a ragged dirge, thin as the air . . .

I have seen you go down
under the shrewd heel of exploit—
your long suns of brutal sweat
with ignoble pittance crowned.

Trapped in the never-ending fields
where you stoop, dreaming of sweeter dawns,
while the mocking whip of slavehood
confiscates your moment of reverie.

Or beneath the stars—offended
by your rude songs of rebellion—
. . . when, at last, you shroud your dreams
and with them, your hymn of hope.

Thus a bitterness in your life:
wherever you turn for solace
there is an embargo.
How to express your anguish
when not even your burning words
are yours, they are borrowed
from the festering barrios of poverty,
and the sadness in your eyes
only reflects the mute pain of your people.

Arise, Chicano!—that divine spark within you
surely says—Wash your wounds
and swathe your agonies.
There is no one to succor you.
You must be your own messiah.

Besides its significance as a poetic rendering of Chicanos' exploitation under the imperialism of the United States, "Arise, Chicano!" serves as a gendered call to arms for the nameless women de Hoyos previously invoked. They are the women who, like the mirrored oppositions of Juan/John, experience multiple disenfranchisement—by the dominant forces of racism and class exploitation and by the androcentric obliteration within the Chicano nationalist movement.

My first reading of the mimeographed "Arise, Chicano!" in the early 1970s evoked memories of the one poem I read in junior high school that I could connect to my family. Edwin Markham's "The Man with a Hoe" was in my mind's eye my Apá Eleuterio bent over his hoe, following the harvest, working the earth in order to feed his family. "Arise, Chicano!" also reminded me of the other cuentos the family had neglected since my Amá Alvina's death from throat cancer. The bitterness of her life culminated in the loss of her voice in the last months of her life. The cancer, which she knew resulted from the pesticide-coated cherries the family picked and ate in the fields of Michigan, had destroyed her vocal cords. I served as her translator in those last days when no one else could decipher her attempts to voice her needs. The poem's seven stanzas crystallize a history of the Chicano in Texas and in the greater borderlands. And in these seven stanzas, the idea of a mujer serving as her "own messiah" was planted in my own mind.

As I look back at these Chicana poems from the 1970s and my own early readings of them, I can see how once we had access to historical archives, reading Chicana identity politics could become more nuanced. The contemporary historians Vicki Ruiz, Antonia Castañeda, Deena González, Ramón Gutiérrez, George J. Sánchez, and Omar Valerio-Jiménez, to name just a few, work with traditional methodologies yet forge the emergent field of Chicana feminist history as they pose questions that earlier historians failed to ask. Turning to feminist theory and cultural studies, the new Chicana/o historians undertake gendered analyses of historical records. Other cultural workers—poets, fiction writers, literary critics—seek innovative methods to uncover and recover that history. The three Chicanas whose texts I examine closely in the following chapters—Gloria Anzaldúa, Sandra Cisneros, and Helena María Viramontes—investigate domestic and other female spaces as they seek additional sources of history. These women, who produced their literary texts in the 1980s, discovered alternative archives in the gossip and rumors for which Chicanas are criticized and through which they are silenced; in the lacunae of family stories that tell of confined grandmothers and abused great-grandmothers; and in the late-night kitchen-table talks with Mexican immigrants to the barrios of the United States.

For Chicanas who once could not imagine our way out of the laws of tradition, learning to read from a Chicana perspective altered the path of our lives. As an insignificant hospital laborer in the early 1970s, I picked up a co-worker's discarded *Ms.* magazine; studied (White) feminist classics to which the magazine alluded; experienced, in the catchphrase of the moment, my own "clicks" and a desire to return to the university; and read the new Chicano nationalist texts. I was a feminist, but I was Chicana feminist. Neither of my recent discoveries—feminism or nationalism—could quench my thirst for a way to discern the complex interconnections between race or ethnicity, class, gender, and sexuality.

One other poem by Angela de Hoyos haunted me as I walked to work at the vast medical center:

Below Zero

No se puede traducir
el aullido del viento:

you can only feel it
piercing your skinny bones
through last year's coat
    papel-de-China

walking to work
from deep in the barrio
una mañana de tantas
    bajo cero.

To my ear, the *o* in *Chicano* struck a dissonant chord. The *o* began to signify that position bajo cero under the o of tradition, costumbres, what *Ms.* instructed me to identify as patriarchal constraints. Below zero was the location of women in the Movement, woman in the family. It was a space that many other mujeres soon would refuse. As I pondered "Mujer Sin Nombre," the poem nurtured a fleeting flash of consciousness, one that eventually grew stronger and achieved its own feminist language. Reading Chicana offered a transfusion of new possibilities. Walking to work, dutiful wife of the Chicano medical student, I drank the lifeblood of Chicana poetry and began to figure how to transform that "cero," and how to name myself as well.

2

Chicana Feminisms

From Ethnic Identity to Global Solidarity

While Chicano historians, political scientists, and literary critics working in the 1960s and 1970s accomplished much in their projects to record the suppressed Chicano experience, too often they made only passing reference to the roles of women in that history spanning the nineteenth and twentieth centuries. If feminist scholars, activists, and writers—who have lived under the *o* in *Chicano*—had to rely on the historical record written by men and male-identified women, Chicanas' roles in history would remain obscured. Contemporary Chicana feminist critics acknowledge the vital preliminary work accomplished by our compañeros, and we applaud and learn from the groundbreaking projects of such men as Américo Paredes, Rodolfo Acuña, and Carlos Muñoz. As feminists, however, we lament that Chicanos have given only a cursory nod to the women who historically labored alongside them in the struggle against Anglo-American domination and exploitation.

While U.S. Latinas attain entry into institutions of higher education at even lower rates than do U.S. Latinos, they have nonetheless published a number of influential texts that direct attention to women's issues within the field of Chicana/o studies (McKenna and Ortiz, 6). Martha Cotera's pioneering texts *Diosa y hembra* (1976) and *The Chicana Feminist* (1977) refuted the stereotype of the Chicana based on the virgin/whore dichotomy. The anthropologist Adelaida del Castillo in "Malintzín Tenépal: A Preliminary Look into a New Perspective" (1977) and the literary critic Norma Alarcón in "Chicana Feminist Lit-

27

erature: A Re-vision through Malintzín: Putting the Flesh Back on the Object" (1981) both exposed the male biases and outright misogyny in the Mexican philosopher Octavio Paz's formulation of La Malinche as la chingada, literally "the fucked one." Malintzín, the historical woman whom Paz calls La Malinche, the Mexican Eve figure, is held responsible for the betrayal of the indigenous people to the Spanish conquerors. In "Mexico's La Malinche: Mother or Whore, Creator or Traitor?" (1988), Liliana Valenzuela reconstructs the misogynist myth through her study of indigenous rituals in Acatlán, where the Indians take a positive view of La Malinche and female sexuality. Norma Alarcón, in "Tradutora, Traditora: A Paradigmatic Figure of Feminism" (1989), offers the most comprehensive analysis of Malintzín thus far.

Clara Lomas is at work recovering the writings of such early twentieth-century Mexican American journalists as Isidra T. de Cárdenas, Andrea Villarreal, Sara Estela Ramírez, Jovita Idar, and Leonor Villegas de Magnón. Lomas's research has uncovered Villegas de Magnón's autobiography, *La Rebelde* (The Rebel), which records women's roles in the Mexican Revolution as well as their political activism on the border. Likewise, Juanita Luna Lawhn has published essays on Mexicana journalists in nineteenth-century San Antonio, and Rosaura Sánchez and Beatriz Pita recovered and republished the nineteenth-century Chicana novel *The Squatter and the Don* (1885) by María Amparo Ruiz de Burton. And María Patricia Fernández-Kelly's *For We Are Sold, I and My People* (1983), on women and the maquiladora system; Patricia Zavella's *Women's Work and Chicano Families* (1987); and Vicki Ruiz's *Cannery Women, Cannery Lives* (1987) restore Chicanas' and Mexicanas' history while they offer insights that shatter convenient stereotypes about the Chicano family. In *Women on the U.S.–Mexico Border*, the historian Vicki Ruiz and the sociologist Susan Tiano present essays on Mexican women on both sides of the border. These essays continue the task of recording and legitimizing female labor: domestic workers, teachers, and agents of a culture that changes as it adjusts to relocation on the U.S. side of the border. Anthologies such as *Third Woman: The Sexuality of Latinas,* edited by Norma Alarcón and her colleagues (1989); *Chicana Lesbians: The Girls Our Mothers Warned Us About,* edited by Carla Trujillo (1991); *Building with Our Hands: New Directions in Chicana Studies,* edited by Adela de la Torre and Beatríz M. Pesquera (1993); *Chicana Critical Issues,* edited by Norma Alarcón (1993); and *Infinite Divisions: An Anthology of Chicana Literature,* edited by Tey Diana Rebolledo and Eliana S. Rivero (1993), add to the growing canon by and about Chicanas and U.S. Latinas. Rebolledo's monumental text *Women Singing in the Snow: A Cultural Analysis of Chicana Literature* (1995) traces Chicana literature from oral traditions to contemporary prose and poetry. Alvina Quintana's *Home Girls: Chicana Literary Voices* (1996), a text firmly grounded in literary criticism and cultural studies, focuses on Sandra Cisneros, Ana Castillo, and Denise Chávez. My work in this book, particularly Chapter 3, on Gloria Anzaldúa, and Chapter 5, on Helena María Viramontes, both relies and builds upon the important work accomplished by the women named above.

Women in Movement: Refusing the Zero

As I began the journey toward renaming myself as a Chicana feminist, a woman who refused the Chicano, I knew too much about women's issues to submit to the local Chicano Movement groups in Houston and serve the male egos coffee along with my intellect, however unschooled it remained. It was time to go beyond the roles of dutiful daughter, sister, and wife, the "mujer sin nombre" of the past. I joined other mujeres in academia who were discovering ways to express their concerns as Chicanas. In "Mexican Women in Organization," Adelaida del Castillo documents how Chicanas in the Movement were "expected by their male peers to involve themselves actively but in subordination" (8). Del Castillo asserts that even when women were de facto leaders of Chicano campus organizations, they were forced to present less active males as their "visible representatives" (8). For these women,

> assuming leadership also meant the risk of having one's personal integrity and emotional stability threatened. The revengeful and denigrative campaigns against women by men were the most effective and successful. Commonly, women in leadership were labeled unfeminine or deviant. At times, women were accused of being sexually perverse or promiscuous, and men were deliberately used to betray them. When a woman leader had a compañero, he was frequently taunted or reprimanded by the other men for failure to keep her under his control. (9)

In her 1977 essay "The Role of the Chicana within the Student Movement," Sonia López states that the Chicano Movement reached its "peak" from 1968 to 1970 (20). In her analysis of the Movement, she discusses the oppressive Mexican and Anglo-American traditions that demand women's passivity and subservience to men. As she delineates the Althusserian ideological state apparatuses, she gives specific examples of how Chicano and Mexican culture use these institutions to enforce women's obedience. López asserts that the family structure is based on masculinist notions that emphasize men's supposedly natural superiority and authority over women. Women's role in the Chicano family is primarily to serve men. She also cites the power of the religious institution, which for Chicanas is primarily the Catholic Church. Through its myths and rules, the church trains men and women to accept patriarchal authority as something ordained by a (male) deity (22). In Mexican culture, López argues, educational institutions serve to steer women to jobs that further promote their dependence on men. She cites proverblike sayings familiar to many Chicanas that question the necessity of education for someone whose ultimate goal in life is marriage, as well as traditional sayings that encourage Chicanas to aspire only to stereotypically female clerical jobs that might result in an advantageous marriage to the boss. Finally, López applies the ideological manipulations of legal institutions to the Chicana situation by pointing out how the legislative and judicial systems perpetuate female dependence through property, divorce, employment, and welfare laws that benefit men (23).

López's essay records the women's role in the Chicano Movement and discusses the contradictions Chicanas faced when they attempted to participate in a liberation movement that urged changes. The changes they wanted were incompatible with their learned perceptions of their roles as women. What resulted was a bitter division between Chicanas and Chicanos. A split also came between traditional, male-identified Chicanas, who refused to recognize women's struggles as legitimate arenas of dispute, and feminist Chicanas, who insisted on liberation from oppressive cultural traditions.

Academic and political conferences were often the sites where these issues and internal divisions played themselves out. As early as the spring of 1969, at the Chicano Youth Conference held in Denver, Colorado, a few vocal Chicana activists raised the issue of the traditional role of the Chicana in the Movement and how it limited her capabilities and her development. The majority of Chicanas participating in the workshop that discussed the role of the Chicana, however, did not feel the same. One Chicana observed that "when the time came for the workshop report to the full conference, the only thing that the representative did say was this—'It was the consensus of the group that the Chicana woman does not want to be liberated' " (24).[1]

López continues analyzing the internal contradictions and political conflicts between Chicanos and Chicanas, noting that women on several California university campuses felt it necessary to organize separate women's groups. The First National Chicana Conference, held in Houston, Texas, in May 1971, drew over six hundred participants (24). Several resolutions were passed, including calls for legalization of abortion; for equal educational opportunities for Chicanas; for the establishment of child-care centers; and for the abolition of traditional marriages as incompatible with women's roles in this nationalist, activist movement. Finally, religion, specifically the Catholic Church, was condemned as "an oppressive institution"—a move that exploded the stereotype of the passively religious Chicana advocated both by Anglo-American culture and by the domineering Chicano men who profit from having passive women around them to promote their own personal agendas. López, however, acknowledges that at least half the women in attendance rejected the resolutions (25). The dissenting women preferred that the conference concentrate on other political issues that did not include gender concerns:

> They felt that the emphasis belonged with the issues that revealed that "our enemy is the 'gavacho' and not the 'macho';" and stressed work in prisons, protesting the Vietnam war, denouncement of immigration laws, and work with the farmworkers struggles. Accordingly they said, if Chicanas are to be politically involved, this involvement must not detract from their family commitment. Chicanas must then make an extra effort to do both jobs, in the home and in the Movement. (25)

López acknowledges the "existence of a hierarchy within the Movement which gave Chicano men superior status within the movement, while at the same time espousing liberation rhetoric" (26).

While López comes close to understanding that one reason the Movement may have failed to survive beyond 1970 was the Chicanos' inability to accommodate sexual politics in conjunction with their nationalist and class politics, she abruptly ends this part of her analysis and instead concentrates on class issues. Furthermore, López stresses class over gender even though her essay originally advocated equal attention to race, class, and gender issues. In addition, López's failure to analyze the men's deployment of "lesbian" as an epithet hurled at any assertive or aggressive Chicana leadership leaves her open to accusations of the homophobia that was prevalent in the Chicano Movement.

Cherríe Moraga, in her genre-exploding mestizaje of a political autobiography/poetry collection, *Loving in the War Years: Lo que nunca pasó por sus labios* (1983), expands the discussion by insisting that the Chicano Movement be held accountable for its flagrant homophobia as well as its more obvious sexism. Moraga further offers a critique of Chicana critics whose writings on feminist issues diminish the importance of the Women's Movement and who insist on separating gender issues from class issues. At the forefront of a Chicana lesbian theory, in her 1983 text Moraga demands that heterosexist critics consider:

> *Who* are they trying to serve? Certainly not the Chicana who is deprived of some very critical information about a ten-year grassroots feminist movement where women of color, including lesbians of color (certainly in the minority and most assuredly encountering "feminist" racism) have been actively involved in reproductive rights, especially sterilization abuse, battered women's shelters, rape crisis centers, welfare advocacy, Third World women's conferences, cultural events, health and self-help clinics and more. (106)

With this probing question, Moraga deconstructs López's uncritical statement that Chicano men accused assertive feminist Chicanas of lesbianism, and she teaches how heterosexist assumptions erase Chicana lesbian subjectivity. López's statement, Moraga argues, "appears without qualification. López makes no value judgment on the inherent homophobia in such a divisive tactic. Without comment, her statement reinforces the idea that lesbianism is not only a white thing, but an insult to be avoided at all costs" (112).

Moraga's objection to the incomplete analysis in critical essays by socialist Chicana feminists continues the Chicana feminist theory that she began articulating with Gloria Anzaldúa in *This Bridge Called My Back*. As she ruptures the inherently heterosexist debates within the Chicano and Chicana communities, addressing the Marxists who insist that feminism itself is a white, self-indulgent stance, she generates a theoretical space for Chicana lesbian feminism and the development of what I identify as "feminism on the border." She points out that Chicanos see no contradiction in citing Marx or Engels, but accuse Chicana feminists of racial betrayal when they cite or build on White feminist theory (106). Moraga also speaks to Chicanas who reject feminism on those same grounds. She proposes that "it is easier for the Chicana to criticize white women who on the face of things could never be familia, than to take issue with or complain, as it were, to a brother, uncle, father" (107).

Chicana theorists such as del Castillo and López insist on examining the Chicano culture in their search for political strategies of liberation. As socialist feminists, these Chicanas agree that class and race analyses are of the utmost importance for the liberation of oppressed and exploited Chicanos and Chicanas—but the analysis cannot stop there. To completely understand the complexities of the Chicana and Chicano subjectivity in the greater borderlands of the United States, discussions of gender and sexuality are central in our oppositional and liberatory projects. In turning to theorists such as Cherríe Moraga, we further learn how to deploy Chicana feminist theory in our readings of texts produced by writers such as Sandra Cisneros.[2]

One would think that in the years since the publication of such crucial anthologies as *Essays on La Mujer* (1977), *Mexican Women in the United States* (1980), and *This Bridge Called My Back* (1981), their essays would have become required reading for anyone studying or working in the field of Chicana and Chicano studies. But more recent celebratory texts on the political movements of the 1960s show that a failure to address women's issues and women's historical participation in the political arena continues. In *Youth, Identity, Power,* Carlos Muñoz attempts to correct the errors and omissions of the historical record in the current texts.[3] Ironically, while Muñoz does accomplish a "critical analysis" of the era, he mirrors the dominating groups' tactics of ideological erasure when he allows women activists only five sentences of acknowledgment in his text. Additionally, Muñoz's memoir mentions no gays or lesbians in his vision of this important political moment. The pressures of historical accuracy, however, force him to conclude his book as follows:

> A vibrant Chicana feminist politics and scholarship have also emerged from the ranks of NACS (National Association for Chicano Studies). Several of the leading feminists have created a journal, *The Third Woman*, based in the Chicano Studies Program at the University of California, Berkeley. Others have created Mujeres Activas en Letras y

Cambios Sociales (MALCS), which is based at the University of California, Davis. Outside the university an increasingly visible Mexican American art and literature continue to grow, and movement artists and poets have achieved national and international recognition for their works. The quest for Mexican American identity and power will continue. (187–88)

In his androcentric version of the history of the Movimiento, Muñoz inadvertently exposes the specific importance of the women's role in history. The women who helped establish NACS, *Third Woman*, and MALCS did not emerge from a historical vacuum. Chicanas too came of political age during the Movimiento and played important roles in earlier history. Today they continue the struggle against domination by those who object to our race, class, gender, or sexual orientation.

The projects I discuss above illustrate the complex and sometimes contradictory position of Chicana feminists. Chicana "feminism on the border" demands that we deal with all these important issues in all their nuances. Life as feminists on the border means recognizing the urgency of dealing with the sexism and homophobia within our culture; our political reality demands that we confront institutionalized racism while we simultaneously struggle against economic exploitation.[4] Chicanas constantly grapple with the demands that our culture places on us as women. The demands include women's compliance with sexist traditions of "respeto," respecting our elders. Further, when we deviate from Mexican/Chicano traditions that oppress and exploit women, other Chicanos/as challenge our identity. In today's conservative climate, little has changed in the popular representation of feminism: for too many people in our communities, feminism in any form—materialist, radical, liberal, lesbian, or heterosexual—is still considered "White."

My project here expands Muñoz's acknowledgment of an emergent literary production led largely by the women who call themselves Chicana feminists. By claiming this identifier, these politically aware and committed women signal their historical class alliances simultaneously. In the historias written by Chicana feminists, we see how the Chicanas' dialectical position as feminists on the border demands different strategies for filling in the gaps of a suppressed history, not only as working-class women of Mexican descent but as women, lesbian and heterosexual.

"Wrestling Your Ally": U.S. Feminists of
Color Negotiate Euro-U.S. White Feminisms

Consider the power of wrestling your ally.
His will is to kill you.
He has nothing against you.
        Lorna Dee Cervantes, *Emplumada*

Even in the face of our active struggle with unreconstructed Chicanos and Eurofeminists who footnote our work but have yet to discover or use our theories *as* theory, we acknowledge the influence of U.S. White feminists in academia. They have made it possible for us women of color who have entered the institution to use our methods to read, teach, and lecture on the emergent literatures. As courses in women's studies came into great demand, many Anglo-American feminists helped create a market for the literatures of women such as Anzaldúa, Cisneros, and Viramontes, all of whom now publish with mainstream or White-controlled publishing houses.

While the presence and struggles of White feminist women in U.S. academia helped promote our literatures, too often the foremost White feminist theorists erased our specificity; indeed, they denied our subject positions as writers, critics, and students of color. Chicanas turned to feminist critics and scholars as our sisters in struggle. We too had read Marxist theory to broaden our understanding of our position as women from the working class. We knew from our experiences within the Movimiento that our specific interests and problems were secondary or even irrelevant to our Marxist compañeras/os. Before long, we had to wonder if we should consider ourselves part of the "sisterhood" called feminism.

In her essay "Feminism, Marxism, Method, and the State," Catharine MacKinnon observes that "sexuality is to feminism what work is to marxism: that which is most one's own yet most taken away" (1). MacKinnon argues that while we can draw parallels between Marxist and feminist methodologies, we must remember not to conflate these two "theories of power and its distribution" (2), that one theory must not be subsumed into the other. She continues: "What if the claims of each theory are taken equally seriously, each on its own terms? Can two social processes be basic at once? Can two groups be subordinated in conflicting ways, or do they merely crosscut? Can two theories, each of which purports to account for the same thing—power as such—be reconciled? Or, is there a connection between the fact that the few have ruled the many and the fact that those few have been men?" (3).

But Chicanas, women with a specific history under racial and sexual and class exploitation, further problematize the feminist/Marxist discussion by adding the complications of race and ethnicity.[5] Our feminist sisters and Marxist compañeras/os urge us to take care of gender and class issues first, and race will naturally take care of itself. Even MacKinnon, thorough as she is, constantly watching that she herself does not recreate a monolithic "woman," uses footnotes to qualify the difference between White women's and African American women's situations. She claims to have checked her statements "to see if women's condition is shared, even when the contexts or magnitudes differ" (6). If her checking revealed an inconsistency, then "the statement is simply wrong and will have to be qualified or the aspiration (or the theory) abandoned" (6).

My project does not suggest that we abandon either the aspiration or the theory. I do urge, however, that our White feminist "sisters" recognize their own blind spots. When MacKinnon uses the "Black" woman as her sign for all dispossessed women, we see the extent to which Chicanas, as well as Asian American, Native American, and Puerto Rican women, for example, have been rendered invisible in a discourse whose explicit agenda is to expose ideological erasure. Chicana readings find color blindness instead of color consciousness in many important feminist essays. These blind spots that socialist feminists scorn as the discourse of liberal feminists indicate the extent to which the issues of race and ethnicity are ignored in feminist and Marxist theories. Theorists such as Rosaura Sánchez, Alma Gómez, Cherríe Moraga, Mariana Romo-Carmona, Gloria Anzaldúa, Sandra Cisneros, and Helena María Viramontes, working collectively as in *Cuentos* and individually as in *Borderlands*, insist on illuminating the complications and intersections of the multiple systems of exploitation: capitalism, patriarchy, heterosexism, and White supremacy.

As Chicanas made their work public, publishing in marginalized journals and with small, underfinanced presses, taking part in conferences and workshops, they realized that the "sisterhood" called feminism professed an ideology that at times came dangerously close to the phallogocentric ideologies of the White male power structure against which all feminists struggle. Rosaura Sánchez, editor of *Crítica*, one of the foremost Chicana/o journals, reminds us of the ideological strategies that the dominant culture manipulates to obscure "the relation between minority cultures and the dominant culture" ("Ethnicity, Ideology, and Academia," 80). She points out that U.S. cultural imperialism extends beyond the geopolitical borders of the country, "but being affected, influenced, and exploited by a culture is one thing and sharing fully in that culture is another" (81). If we extend the analogy to feminism and the totalizing concept of sisterhood, we begin to understand how the specific interests of Anglo-American and other European feminists tend to erase the existence of Chicana, Puerto Rican, Native American, Asian American, and other Third World feminisms. Indeed, feminism as practiced by women of the hegemonic culture oppresses and exploits the Chicana in both subtle and obvious ways.

When White feminists began to categorize the different types of feminisms in the 1980s, we, in turn, began to trace the muting of issues of race and ethnicity under other feminist priorities. Elaine Showalter, in *A Literature of Their Own*, charts the "stages" of writing by women as they progressed through the categories of "feminine, feminist, and female" (13). She first establishes that "all" "literary subcultures, such as black, Jewish, Canadian, Anglo-Indian, or even American," go through phases of imitation, internalization, protest, and finally self-discovery (13). While this ally works in good faith, and accurately depicts some Chicana movements in the recovery of our literary traditions, Showalter, constrained by her historical moment, also creates an ethnocentric, Eurocentric, middle-class history of women's writing.

She creates literary history, and she does not stop with British women. In "The Feminist Critical Revolution" she maps out "phases," this time of feminist criticism (1985). In Showalter's program, feminist criticism progresses from critiques of sexist texts by men to the rediscovery of the female literary tradition, then, finally, to the revision of literary theories, taking into account women's own interpretations in a type of essentialism that assumes the universality of Woman's experience. When we look at a Chicana literary project such as Helena María Viramontes's "The Cariboo Cafe," in *The Moths and Other Stories,* published at the same historical moment as Showalter's essay, we can see that her model cannot contain Chicana writers or Chicana agendas. While some Chicana literary critics, such as Norma Alarcón, employ French feminist theory and selectively employ theories that help tease out the complexities of Chicana texts, they never ignore historical and material specificity.

Liberal, Anglo-American feminists such as Showalter are not alone in the re-creation and re-presentation (colonization) of women's literary history. In "Women's Time," Julia Kristeva also defines a hierarchy of feminism, which sounds alarmingly like a version of the anthropologist Lewis Henry Morgan's familiar categories of savagery, barbarism, and civilization, which he used to structure the evolution of societies. The most "primitive" would be the position that women in the United States would call liberal feminism. While not denying the political importance of this phase—the struggle for universal suffrage, equal pay for equal work, abortion rights, and so on—Kristeva nonetheless sees its ahistorical, universalist, globalizing limits. Next on the evolutionary scale is the radical feminist phase, a reductive, essentialist feminism in which women "demand recognition of an irreducible identity, without equal in the opposite sex and, as such, exploded, plural, fluid" (37). A mixture of these two feminisms, Kristeva explains, constitutes the dominant European feminism. She ultimately privileges the final "signifying space." Extremely premature in her optimism that a real change in sexist institutions of power has occurred, she abandons "the very dichotomy man/woman as an opposition between two rival entities" (51). This dichotomy, she claims, belongs to the metaphysical: "What can 'identity,' even 'sexual identity,' mean in a new theoretical and scientific space where the very notion of identity is challenged?" (52–53).

While Kristeva defines her first three categories politically, the category she advocates for herself is political in its "apolitical" pretensions, and it is unapologetically ahistorical. Even if we accept that Kristeva specifies European feminisms, her own category assumes a universalist privilege. Nowhere in Kristeva's essay is there a sense that she even considers women of color in her theories.

Toril Moi, in a text that was used as the primer for introductory feminist theory courses in the 1980s, polarizes Anglo-American feminism against European feminism. She goes to great lengths to critique various Anglo-American feminists, often charging that they have not gone far enough in their politics: "The central paradox of Anglo-American feminist criticism is thus that despite its strong, explicit political engagement, it is *in the end* not quite political enough; not in the sense that it fails to go *far* enough along the political spectrum, but in the sense that its radical analysis of sexual politics still remains entangled with depoliticizing theoretical paradigms" (*Sexual/Textual*

Politics, 87–88; Moi's emphasis). Only one paragraph earlier, however, Moi issued an apologia for omitting "black or lesbian (or black-lesbian) feminist criticism in America" (87). Not only does she assume that she can conflate the concerns of all women of color in the United States as "black" or "lesbian" or a reductionist combination of the two, she continues to show her bias against non-European feminist theory by stating that *"in so far as textual theory is concerned* there is no discernible difference between these three fields [Anglo-American, 'black,' and lesbian criticism]" (86; Moi's emphasis). After homogenizing all women of color as black and/or lesbian, and doing it all in a single paragraph, Moi chastises further Anglo-American, heterosexual, middle-class women who have made their concerns universal. Moi's neglect of race or ethnic specificity in the United States mirrors the way White supremacy institutes its racist ideology; her feminism becomes hegemonic feminism.

Ultimately, neither Kristeva nor Moi acknowledges that feminists in the United States, for the most part, have worked within academic institutions where their ability to publish and teach feminist ideologies depended on their struggles to change a White male institution. European feminists, particularly the women of the French feminist school, consisted of women such as Kristeva and Luce Irigaray, who, along with their university affiliations, had private practices in the community. If we are to engage in a judicious examination of the different branches of Eurofeminism and U.S. feminisms, we must formulate different political strategies.

When the leading European and Anglo-American feminists working in the 1970s and 1980s displaced, misplaced, or outright ignored Chicana feminisms and other feminisms articulated by U.S. women of color, they inadvertently colonized the very terms *feminism* and *politics.* The strategies of containment practiced against feminists of color include a feminist theory that does not recognize race as a component of women's identity. The feminism advocated by women of color recenters the concerns of U.S. women who identify as racialized women committed to working-class politics and, to use Cherríe Moraga's words, to a spirituality that "inspires activism and, similarly, politics which move the spirit" (*Loving in the War Years,* 130). While the men worried that Chicana feminism meant becoming White-influenced, leftist feminists feared that a racialized feminism could only mean indulgence in the concerns of a privatized self. Even the term *politics* became contested.

In her essay "Homelands of the Mind: Jewish Feminism and Identity Politics" (1987), Jenny Bourne examines what she considers legitimate political work and what she sees as a mere nostalgic search for the private self. She centers her argument on the proposition that Jewish feminists should question "how, out of our particular history and experience of oppression, we can, as progressive feminists, construct an identity and a politics which confronts all the material issues, including Israel itself" (19). Bourne attempts to untangle the personal from the political issues in feminist identity politics. After the popular slogan "the personal is political" brought many women to feminism, Bourne observes, for many feminists "the personal" devolved into a "separatist, individualistic, and inward-looking" feminism (2). For Bourne, a return to a feminism that grew out of a commitment to a radical politics that is "anti-racist, anti-imperialist or anti-fascist" (1) would mean that Jewish feminists could reject Zionism, critique the occupation of Palestinian territory, and not be accused of being anti-Semitic. For U.S. feminists of color whose individual histories as Amerindians, as descendants of slaves, or as fronterizas left them, in the manner of the Palestinians, deterritorialized in "Occupied America," the objection to Bourne's essay is not based on her advocacy of Palestinian self-rule; what concerns us is how Bourne limits the definition of politics.

In the opening lines of this essay, first published in *Race and Class: A Journal for Black and Third World Liberation,* Bourne dismisses "identity politics" as a legitimate locus of struggle. Focusing her agenda clearly against the women she perceives as unwilling to critique Israeli exploitation and colonization of Palestinians, she dismisses other women's struggles, such as the struggle engaged in by the women of the Combahee River Collective. In refocusing attention on the history and power of the Israeli state and its treatment of Palestinians, Bourne finds herself attacking the U.S. women of color who survived the turbulence of the Civil Rights movements of the 1960s and refused to allow internal gender conflicts to derail their political commitments. When Bourne maps out her definition of politics and implicitly presents it as the only legitimate method of contestation for "Black and Third World Liberation," she misreads and dismisses the historically based, materialist, feminist politics of U.S. women of color. While her target is Jewish feminism and what she considers Jewish feminists' inability to grapple with the contradictions of Israel and the Palestinian struggle, Bourne casts her disparaging net to "the Blacks, the Women, the Gays," whose central agendas, she believes, lack praxis. In her words, "what is to be done has been replaced by who I am" (1).

In an otherwise instructive essay that provides crucial information about the Palestinian struggles in the 1980s, Bourne's misreading of the Combahee River Collective's "Black Feminist Statement" exemplifies why it is a mistake to dismiss "identity politics" as political methodology. For U.S. women of color, identity politics was a tool of material and theoretical engagement. Bourne's inability to read the political documents by women of color (or to read them *as* political) exposes her failure to understand race and gender within the specific historical contexts of these women. When she critiques the Combahee River Collective's statement, an early Black feminist political manifesto that called for human rights for all people of color, Bourne's leftist politics again betrays the inability of otherwise progressive allies to consider seriously the material conditions of U.S. people of color.

Bourne believes that her desire for a new brand of feminist politics has not materialized. Yet the Chicana feminists who forged alliances with other women of color with the publication of *This Bridge Called My Back*, particularly with the Black feminists of the Combahee River Collective, breathe life into what Bourne conceptualizes as a dead or, at best, self-indulgent notion of feminism. The U.S. women of color in *Bridge*, together with the African American feminists who collaborated on the Combahee statement, challenge Bourne's skepticism about feminism as a viable politics. They construct "an identity and a politics" with which they confront a different history—as racialized women, as mestizas, literally as peoples of "mixed blood"—and all that mestizaje implies in sexual, historical, and material terms in the United States.

When Bourne takes the Combahee's "Black Feminist Statement" out of context—critiques it as merely an attempt "to find one's true identity" and stops there—she omits everything that the politically active Combahee River Collective advocated. She understands when the collective reclaims their specific historical positions apart from the White feminist "universal sisterhood"—but she then quotes only one phrase from the statement to illustrate how U.S. feminists derailed "liberatory socialist principles":

> The venue for this change of direction in our politics already existed in a strain of radical feminism that began to emerge in the USA in the late 1970s among black feminists as a way of grappling with the issues (of race, class, and power) which threatened the feminist view of a universal sisterhood. "The most profound and potentially the most radical politics

come," said the Combahee River Collective, "directly out of our own identity as opposed to working to end somebody else's oppression." It was a politics which Jewish feminists would soon be taking up. (2)

What Bourne omits from her indictment of this "strain" of U.S. feminism, however, is the historical context in which these women were writing and theorizing.

Even a cursory examination of the 1977 document reveals its historicity. A note in the reprint of the "Black Feminist Statement" in *Bridge* gives the historical and political genesis of the Combahee River Collective: "The Combahee River Collective is a Black feminist group in Boston whose name comes from the guerrilla action conceptualized and led by Harriet Tubman on June 2, 1863, in the Port Royal region of South Carolina. This action freed more than 750 slaves and is the only military campaign in American history planned and led by a woman" (210). An early articulation of the theory of "interlocking oppressions" of women of color, the manifesto is grounded in the historical legacy of slavery and in the spirit of activist women. It presents how Black women's sexual identity—inextricable from their racial identity—urges them to develop what in the early 1970s was, indeed, a new and radical theory of feminism.

Like the Chicanas who refused the Chican*o*, the Combahee women identify with the Black liberation struggles of the 1960s and 1970s and claim their participation in the Civil Rights, Black nationalist, and Black Panther movements, but cite their disillusionment with the sexist practices of these groups. As they came to consciousness as women, they developed the collective's new antiracist and antisexist political theories.

Bourne's mid-1980s interpretation of the Combahee statement is exactly what the collective was attempting to redress in the mid-1970s. Her injudicious reading of the statement through inattention to the historical legacy of racism in the United States symptomizes socialist feminists' critiques of publications by materialist U.S. women of color. Rather than focus on an individualist "personal consciousness," as Bourne suggests that the Combahee River Collective advocates, the manifesto clearly links the collective's politics to the material, historical positions endured by the majority of African Americans:

> Our development must also be tied to the contemporary economic and political position of Black people. The post World War II generation of Black youth was the first to be able to partake of certain educational and employment options previously closed completely to Black people.

Although our economic position is still at the bottom of the American capitalistic economy, a handful of us have been able to gain certain tools as a result of tokenism in education and employment which potentially enable us to more effectively fight our oppression. (*Bridge,* 212)

Clearly, the Combahee River Collective ignored neither its class position nor its relationship to American history. The "Black Feminist Statement" calls attention to its authors' positions as intellectuals, but acknowledges their privileged status as educated African American women. As they articulate their politics, they emerge as organic intellectuals. And in the spirit of Antonio Gramsci's radical philosophy, their politics aims beyond interpreting the world; their aim is to change it.[6]

When the women of the collective do articulate their feminist theory, they cite identity politics as one means by which they will remedy the sexism of Black nationalism and the racism in feminist theory as articulated by White women in the United States. They underscore the context of their manifesto by stating that they intend to focus "upon our own oppression," their collective voice clearly articulating their struggle for human rights and their subjectivity as women, descendants of slaves, confined to the working class and to the subproletariat. This is the "identity" of which they speak:

The most profound and potentially the most radical politics come directly out of our own identity, as opposed to working to end somebody else's oppression. In the case of Black women this is a particularly repugnant, dangerous, threatening, and therefore revolutionary concept because it is obvious from looking at all the political movements that have preceded us that anyone is more worthy of liberation than ourselves. We reject pedestals, queenhood, and walking ten paces behind. To be recognized as human, levelly human, is enough. (212)

Unfortunately, the veracity of the Combahee River Collective "Black Feminist Statement" is proven by Bourne's implicit argument that the Palestinian situation is somehow more relevant, more urgent, more political than the ongoing African American women's political struggle for human rights in the United States. In the final section of the statement, "Black Feminist Issues and Projects," the women of the collective identify themselves as Third World women and delineate their praxis as political activists.

Had Jenny Bourne considered the text within its historical and material context, perhaps it would have been clear to her that for these

African American feminists, "what is to be done"—including their work against sterilization abuse, for abortion rights, and as advocates for battered women—was not replaced innocently by "who I am," but was determined by their historical identities as U.S. Third World Black feminists. Limited readings that peer only at single issues, such as class, violate the spirit and politics of the Combahee River Collective "Black Feminist Statement." Denigrating the urgent need for African American women to assert their subjectivities as gendered, as women of color, as working class, as separate from Black men before the law ignores the specific political theory the statement presents. Bourne then dismisses it as an example of self-indulgent identity politics characteristic of a generic feminism.[7]

Theory out of Lived Experience:
Chicana / Third World Feminisms

In her essay "Chicana Feminism: In the Tracks of 'the' Native Woman," Norma Alarcón shows the benefits of using Western feminist theory to underwrite projects on Chicana subjectivity. In the process, she translates French feminist theory into Chicana theory. Alarcón's deployment of what some might call "high" feminist theory, however, never subsumes her central project on Chicana, Mexicana, or other subaltern women. What Alarcón tracks in her work is "the" native woman's rightful place in the realm of theorizing as well as her place in the material world. Her ironic use of *the* to signify mestiza women as native women serves to remind readers that Chicanas, like our indigenous American kin, stride across multiple worlds as U.S. Mexicanas. Rather than monolithize diverse Native American communities both in the United States and in the other Americas as a group apart from mestiza Chicanas who dare precarious incursions that are restricted for other indigenous women in the Americas, Alarcón ironically brackets "the." In Alarcón's theory, the political signifier *Chicana* remains a useful self-referent for those of us who refuse to ride the hyphen between Mexican and American for the sake of expediency. When we do ride the hyphen, it serves as the new space, the bridge, to borrow from Cherríe Moraga and Gloria Anzaldúa, across which those whom Sandra Cisneros calls "Mericans," and whom my Treviño grandparents called "mejicanos de este lado," can negotiate an empow-

ering racial, gendered, working-class, political terrain we also call mestizaje.

Chicana counters the objections of U.S. Hispanics who insist that
the identifier articulates outdated concerns of old-style 1960s radical
men. In "Why the Term 'Hispanic'?"—an apologia on how, in the early
1970s, the term *Hispanic* became the official designation for a population considered a new minority—Grace Flores-Hughes describes how
"the Office of Education (O.E.), an agency within the U.S. Department of Health, Education, and Welfare (H.E.W.), commissioned and
released a study that addressed important education issues affecting
America's Hispanic and Native American populations." The meeting's
original agenda was quickly displaced when representatives of both ethnic groups objected to the "report's ethnic identification categories."
Out of that contentious debate, the O.E. "decided to form an inter-
departmental task force to address the issue of racial/ethnic identification." In 1973, Flores-Hughes served on the committee that rejected
the term *Latino* for fear it would include people who were not "historically discriminated against," as defined in the Civil Rights Act of
1964. According to Flores-Hughes, "I proposed and fully supported
the term Hispanic because it denoted only those peoples who were of
Spanish lineage" (64). Flores-Hughes, for all her good intentions, ignores crucial class issues. To paraphrase Alarcón, since there is no recognized nation-state "Chicana" or "Chicano," when we invoke *Chicana*
as a self-identifier, we invoke race and ethnicity, class, and gender in
their simultaneity and in their complexity ("Chicana Feminism," 250).
Alarcón's essay presents a different approach to the identity politics of
the early women's movement and goes well beyond the facile decisions
of government bureaucrats. In "Chicana Feminism" and other essays,
she shows how to effectively merge identity politics and political praxis.

The writers whose works I examine present themselves as Chicana
feminists, all conscious of their working-class origins. They all reside
in that other borderland between professional writer, seasonally employed academician, and community activist. As mestizas, they acknowledge their political and ethnic relationship to African American
feminists as well as their indigenous ties to Native American traditions.
They find the term *Latina* acceptable because of its implicit solidarity
with other similarly politically oriented Spanish-speaking people in the
United States.

My own training as a Chicana feminist (I entered graduate school
only when I came to the conclusion that the emergent literature by

Chicanas published in the early 1980s was indeed a legitimate field of study in American literature) informs my decision to call myself and the Chicana writers I discuss women of color. I read Alice Walker, Toni Morrison, Maxine Hong Kingston, and Leslie Marmon Silko before works by Anzaldúa, Cisneros, and Viramontes were published. For Chicanas, *women of color* is a *political* designation that expresses our solidarity with Asian American, African American, and Native American women who share similarities in our histories under racism, class exploitation, and cultural domination in the United States—a kinship that extends beyond sharing a national language. Finally, as we read the literatures emerging from other Third World countries, the connection between women in those countries and Chicana feminists not only is strengthened by essays written by social or literary critics but also becomes the thematic material that the writers themselves address. As a result, through their search for a feminist critical discourse that adequately takes into account their position as women under multiple oppressions, Chicana feminists are finding their own organic intellectuals.

Because our work has been ignored by the men and women in charge of the modes of cultural production, we must be innovative in our search. Hegemony has so constructed the ideas of method and theory that often we cannot recognize anything that is different from what the dominant discourse constructs. As a consequence, we have to look in nontraditional places for our theories: in the prefaces to anthologies, in the interstices of autobiographies, in our cultural artifacts (the cuentos), and, if we are fortunate enough to have access to a good library, in the essays published in marginalized journals not widely distributed by the dominant institutions. While Chicana scholars do publish feminist essays in journals such as *Crítica, The Americas Review* (formerly *Revista Chicano-Riqueña*), and *Third Woman*, as I discussed earlier, I will focus on a specific type of Chicana feminism that deconstructs the borders erected by Eurocentric feminism as it extends the borders of what is considered legitimately political.

The prefatory testimonio to *Cuentos: Stories by Latinas* (1983)—collectively written by the editors, Alma Gómez, a Nuyorican; Cherríe Moraga, a Chicana; and Mariana Romo-Carmona, a Chilena—offers such a site of Chicana and Latina "theory." The collaborators identify themselves and each other as "U.S. Third World women," writers whose efforts shatter the tradition of silence imposed on them by the pressures of a culture that works against the viability of an oral tradition. Romo-Carmona begins the testimonio by locating the site of a Latina cultural production: the domestic space, with her grandmother in the kitchen and her mother pondering the economic difficulties facing the extended family. "There were those centers in our lives," Romo-Carmona relates, "but when you read the stories [produced by the literary institution], none of that was there" (vii). Her statement elaborates what Ramón Saldívar sees as "the nature of the economy of the domestic, its *oikonomia*, its public and private spheres" (*Chicano Narrative*, 303).

The material realities of life in the urban barrio or ghetto cannot sustain, as the *Cuentos* collaborators state, "a tradition which relies so heavily on close family networks and [is] dependent upon generations of people living in the same town or barrio" (vii). The economic realities faced by women of color under capitalism in the United States now urge Latina women to write what was once spoken. As the editors testify, what was once a communal production of Latino culture can no longer be sustained under such pressures, because the "way of life that kept Latina tales re-told," they assert,

> is falling apart; for they have taken the story-tellers and scattered us all over the world. The written word, then, becomes essential for communication when face-to-face contact is not possible. Particularly for so many Latinas who can no longer claim our own country, or even the domain of our own homes—barely holding la tierra [the earth] below our feet—we need una literatura [a literature] that testifies to our lives, provides acknowledgment of who we are: an exiled people, a migrant people, mujeres en lucha [women in struggle]. (vii)

These U.S. Latinas, however, speak of much more than a cultural diaspora; in identifying their preface as a *testimonio*, they express their solidarity with such women as Domitila Barrios de Chungara, Rigoberta Menchú, and Elvia Alvarado, whose own testimonios expose the exploitation and massacre of their people in Bolivia, Guatemala, and Honduras. Moreover, with their testimonio, these border feminists contextualize themselves within a global literary history.[8] The U.S. Latinas speak of their specific histories: for the Chicana, the history of the absorption of the Mexican territories by the United States; for the Nuyorican and the Chilena, their different histories as exiles, as people forced to emigrate to the United States from homelands—one Puerto

Rico, which remains a colony of the United States, and the other Chile, devastated by economic and military wars financed and led by U.S. economic interests.

Additionally, the Gómez, Moraga, and Romo-Carmona project explodes many hegemonic feminist assumptions about women's writing. As women whose daily existence confronts institutionalized racism, class exploitation, sexism, and homophobia, U.S. Third World women do not enjoy the luxury of privileging one oppression over another. While recognizing that Latinas are not a homogeneous group, the editors do acknowledge that "as Latinas in the US, our experience is different [from that of White people]. Because living here means throwing in our lot with other people of color" (x).

Elaine Showalter's important text *A Literature of Their Own* (1977) insists that the first stage of feminist criticism looks back to find a literary tradition; the collaborators of *Cuentos,* however, believe that if we are to forge a new affiliation among working-class people of color in the United States who share a kinship of exploitation, looking to a romanticized past is a luxury in which we cannot indulge. Such a quest is what Gayatri Spivak calls "an 'essentialist' search for lost origins," which cannot solve the "problem of the muted subject of the subaltern woman" ("Can the Subaltern Speak?" 295). Instead, the stories the Latinas present are tied to the specific historical imperatives of the working class and subaltern women of color.

Expanding on her collaboration with other U.S. Latinas in *Cuentos,* Cherríe Moraga wrote a new foreword to the second edition of the breakthrough anthology *This Bridge Called My Back: Writings by Radical Women of Color* (1983). Her theoretical approach in this foreword transforms her previous brand of radical feminism. She bridges the chasm between radical women and exploited men, acknowledging that if the volume had been written in 1983 rather than in 1979, "it would speak much more directly. . . to the relations between women and men of color, both gay and heterosexual." Four years after the first edition, Moraga envisioned a more internationalist *Bridge* that affirms the connections between U.S. people of color and the people she calls "refugees of a world on fire."

Further expanding the Chicana feminist agenda around issues of gender, race, class, ethnicity, and sexual orientation, Moraga expressed solidarity with the Third World people struggling against the hegemony of the United States. Chicana feminist theories present material geopolitical issues that redirect feminist discourse, again pointing to a theory of feminism that addresses a multiplicity of experiences, what I call "feminism on the border." Though the details have changed, the issues that Moraga first presented in 1983 remain urgent even in the twenty-first century:

> The United States is training troops in Honduras to overthrow the Nicaraguan people's government.

> Human rights violations continue on a massive scale in Guatemala and El Salvador (and as in this country, those hit the hardest are often the indigenous peoples of those lands).

> Thousands of unarmed people are slaughtered in the Middle East. The United States government daily drains us of nearly every political gain made by the feminist, Third World, and anti-war work of the late '60s and early '70s.

Even now the assault continues against the subproletariat, the working poor, people of color, and women. The Central American civil wars are not over and, in fact, have spread to Chiapas in Mexico as indigenous peoples throughout the Americas join forces in protest of genocide.[9] Death squads continue to control resistance in Central America, and while South Africa is successfully recovering from the devastation of the apartheid system, the Palestinian struggle continues.

Following on her initial theories in *This Bridge Called My Back,* Cherríe Moraga presents a comprehensive articulation of Chicana / Third World feminism in *Loving in the War Years: Lo que nunca pasó por sus labios* (1983). It is this text that critics such as Bourne need to read and take seriously as political theory. In her mestizaje of a text that anticipates Anzaldúa's genre-exploding *Borderlands,* Moraga presents feminist theory along with autobiography, memoir, and poetry. She names her writing Chicana theory and links Chicana feminism with Third World feminism. Throughout, the Chicana feminism that Moraga theorizes is a global theory of power for women. In the long section of the book titled "Lo que nunca pasó por sus labios" she links her brand of feminism to the politics she learned from the Combahee River Collective's "Black Feminist Statement" (108, 132–34). In the section "Feeding People in All Their Hungers," Moraga recontextualizes and reconceptualizes spirituality, rejecting it as an abstraction used by organized religion to manipulate women into adhering to patriarchal customs, using it as a vehicle for political action. Consistently drawing from the example of activist African American women in the Civil

Rights Movement, Moraga transforms spirituality into praxis. As well as gleaning political theory from the "Black Feminist Statement," Moraga finds articulations of U.S. Third World feminist theory in literature by African American women:

> In Toni Cade Bambara's novel, *The Salt Eaters*, the curandera asks, "Can you afford to be whole?" This line represents the question that has burned within me for years and years through my growing politicization. *What would a movement bent on the freedom of women of color look like?* In other words, what are the implications of not only looking outside our culture, but into our culture and ourselves and from that place beginning to develop a strategy for a movement that could challenge the bedrock of oppressive systems of belief globally? (109)

This desire for wholeness leads Moraga to theorize lesbian politics and center on sexuality as a legitimate site of theory. As a Chicana lesbian, asserting a sexuality that rejects the Chicano traditions of compulsory heterosexuality, Moraga risks being "outcast" from her "culture." In the early 1970s, "with no visible Third World feminist movement in sight," Moraga felt that "to be a Chicana lesbian put me far beyond hope of salvation" (125).

In articulating her Chicana lesbian politics, Moraga insists on her relationship with women of color or "poor and Third World women" (129) rather than with White separatist radical feminists. Her critique of the privilege that separatist feminists invoke leads Moraga to theorize Third World feminism. She acknowledges, however, that the lesbian and gay liberation movements of the 1970s gave women like her a space to develop as critical thinkers. The reaction by neoconservatives in the Reagan 1980s, however, made it imperative that liberation movements no longer invoke "the family and, therefore, homophobia, as the righteous *causa* without linking themselves with the most reactionary, and by definition, the most racist political sectors of this country" (131). The result was the development of a theory of Third World feminism that, according to Moraga, has its genesis in the "Civil Rights Movement in its culturally-based, anti-separatist, and 'humanist' (not to be confused with liberal) approach to political change" (131). Ultimately, it is in her discussion of sexuality and spirituality that Moraga conceives her call for a Third World feminist theory:

> Simply put, if the spirit and sex have been linked in our oppression, then they must also be linked in the strategy for our liberation.
> To date, no liberation movement has been willing to take on the

task. To walk a freedom road that is both material and metaphysical. Sexual and spiritual. Third World feminism is about feeding people in all their hungers. (132)

At this juncture, Moraga again credits Black feminists for presenting her and Chicanas like her a vision of and a possibility for liberation as women of color. In reply to the critics who do not consider sexuality a legitimate site of struggle, Moraga insists that we integrate it alongside other issues specific to women in our liberatory struggles to ensure whole human rights:

> To be concerned about the sexuality of women of color was an insult to women in the Third World literally starving to death. But the only hunger I have ever known was the hunger for sex and the hunger for freedom and somehow, in my mind and heart, they were related and certainly not mutually exclusive. If I could not use the source of my hunger as the source of my activism, how then was I to be politically effective? But finally here was a movement, first voiced by U.S. Black women, which promised to deal with the oppression that occurred *under* the skin as well, and by virtue of the fact that that skin was female and colored. For the damage that has been done to us sexually has penetrated our minds as well as our bodies. The existence of rape, the veil, genital mutilation, violence against lesbians, have bludgeoned our entire perception of ourselves as female beings. (133)

Moraga's assertions bring to mind the testimonio of Elvia Alvarado, a Honduran activist in the struggle for the land rights of indigenous Americans. With Moraga's theory of a Third World feminism that addresses all of women's hungers as legitimate political arenas, we can read Alvarado's text in its multiple dimensions.

As Moraga made clear in her foreword to the second edition of *This Bridge Called My Back*, forging a Third World feminism was certainly easier in theory—that is, between the covers of a text—than in the real world. Moraga points to homophobia in heterosexual women of color as well as "racism among us cross-culturally" as the two major obstacles in the face of coalition building. She urges that we educate ourselves about each other's cultures and histories—particularly in the face of a shared oppression—in order to build resistance strategies for our mutual liberation.

Moraga ends *Loving in the War Years* by acknowledging her project as an attempt to "develop some kind of Chicana feminist theory" (136). What exactly has she accomplished? She linked the genesis of Chicana and Third World feminisms to the Civil Rights movements and to Black feminist theory as articulated by the Combahee River Collective. She asserted sexuality, specifically lesbian sexuality, as a legitimate site of political struggle. And she urged heterosexual women, especially other Chicanas, to attend to their heterosexual privileges.

The publication of *Loving in the War Years* in 1983 provided a major theoretical statement on Chicana feminism:

> A political commitment to women must involve, by definition, a political commitment to lesbians as well. To refuse to allow the Chicana lesbian the right to the free expression of her own sexuality, and her politicization of it, is in the deepest sense to deny one's own self the right to the same. I guarantee you, there will be no change in heterosexual relations as long as the Chicano community keeps us lesbians and gay men political prisoners among our own people. Any movement built on the fear and loathing of anyone is a failed movement. (139–40)

For Chicana border feminists, academia is another site of struggle. In "Ethnicity, Ideology, and Academia" (1987), Rosaura Sánchez calls for a counterdiscourse that practices an active resistance against attempts by the mainstream discourse to silence, incorporate, or ignore the voices of oppressed and exploited people living within the borders of the United States. Likewise, Gayatri Spivak's work on subaltern women intersects with Sánchez's work in her call for strategies to resist the forces of a dominant ideology. "In seeking to learn to speak to (rather than listen to or speak for) the historically muted subject of the subaltern woman," Spivak asserts, "the postcolonial intellectual *systematically* 'unlearns' female privilege. This systematic unlearning involves learning to critique postcolonial discourse with the best tools it can provide and not simply substituting the lost figure of the colonized" (295).

In other words, as academic women of color working on projects that threaten to wrest control from the elite, from the traditional academic, we find it appropriate to use the master's tools to dismantle the master's house. My own formulation here does not break with Audre Lorde's warning in the title of her essay "The Master's Tools Will Never Dismantle the Master's House" (in *This Bridge Called My Back*); rather, it builds upon Lorde's insistence that White academic feminists acknowledge "differences of race, sexuality, and age" (98). To Lorde's original categories, Chicana feminism appends the differences of class and historical specificity.

Chicana academics working in the U.S. academy build a counter-hegemonic project upon the foundation compañeras/os in Latin America and the Caribbean provide. This project puts Lorde's assertions yet another way: using the Cuban theorist Roberto Fernández Retamar's "Calibán" as their model, the dominated groups learn the master's language not just to curse him, but to defeat him and his privilege.[10]

It is possible for Chicanas, African Americans, Asian Americans, Indigenous Americans—in short, the muted cultures of the United States—to form a "family of resemblance" with each other as well as with other exploited and oppressed groups resisting incorporation by dominant cultures throughout the globe. We can look to the enclaves of activist women in Mexico, for example, who have developed a "feminismo popular," and to the masses of people in India whose histories are researched by the Subaltern Studies group in that country. While Chicanas and the subaltern peoples of India have distinct histories, the Subaltern Studies group's project to recover histories from nonofficial documents and any other sources is similar to the way Chicanas must garner their own histories. Chicanos have retrieved history from the resistance ballads, los corridos, from oral testimonies, and from written documents. Chicanas are currently looking into these same sources, but also into the gaps, lapses, and absences in the masculinist discourses that have written women out of their historical agency. Contemporary Chicana feminist writers are playing an important role in contributing to this historical project. Both groups examine what Edward Said describes as the "constitutive role of an enormous mass of subaltern Indians, the urban poor and the peasants, who throughout the nineteenth century and earlier, resisted British rules in terms and modes that were quite distinct from those employed by the elite" (*Selected Subaltern Studies,* vi).

When Chicana writers such as Sandra Cisneros, Helena María Viramontes, and Gloria Anzaldúa, as well as Chicana critics such as Cherríe Moraga, Rosaura Sánchez, Yvonne Yarbro-Bejarano, and Norma Alarcón, resist dominant discourse in their respective counterhegemonic projects, they take what they have learned in the U.S. educational system—in which some of them now work—and relentlessly resist what Althusser called "the rules of order established by class domination" ("Ideology and the State," 132). If we are to use the "master's tools" and speak Prospero's tongue, however, Sánchez urges that the Chicana/o academic remain alert to the way in which the dominant ideology seems to make room for dissent when, in reality, it diffuses praxis. As she points out, when Chicana/o academics

> produce the dominant ideology, our articles and books are seen strictly as evidence of intellectual ability and research capacity, but, if we dare present another perspective, our work is seen as being totally biased and ideological. Ethnic Studies faculty [and Women's Studies faculty, I might add] continue to struggle to demonstrate the legitimacy of their research and to attain "Quality," that mythic element so prevalent in the discourse of the dominant academicians whose criteria is assumed to be nonsubjective and based on the highest standards. ("Ethnicity, Ideology, and Academia," 87)

As relatively privileged intellectuals, writers, and critics—many employed by what Ruth Behar in *Translated Woman* calls "academic corporations"—we are compelled to probe the significance of our self-interpellation as "Chicanas," a label that emerged out of the liberation struggles of the 1960s but was not always accepted by the vast majority of U.S. peoples of Mexican descent.

In the same way that we must break with traditional (hegemonic) concepts of genre to read Chicana feminist theory, working-class women of color in other Third World countries also articulate their feminisms in nontraditional ways and forms. Chicana feminists acknowledge the vast historical, class, racial, and ethnic differences among women living on the border. Further dividing them is the nature of hegemony practiced by the united powers of patriarchy, capitalism, imperialism, and White supremacy, which promotes the illusion of an irreconcilable split between feminists confined within national borders. We must first examine the First versus Third World dichotomy before we accept this opposition as an inevitable fissure that separates women who are politically committed in different ways from coming together for any common cause.

In my final chapter, I will give a brief examination of how some Third World Latin American women, speaking to us through their testimonios, see themselves as women engaged in liberation struggles. The feminism on the border that I have begun to discuss is more than a theoretical position; it is also an articulation of political solidarity between Third World women in the United States and women such as the Bolivian Domitila Barrios de Chungara, Rigoberta Menchú of Guatemala, and Elvia Alvarado from Honduras.

I can now name myself a Chicana feminist scholar—a Third World woman raised at the periphery of the First World, the border region of South Texas. I use *Third World feminism* to indicate how our histories as Chicana/Latina feminists force us to examine geopolitics as well as gender politics. As our alignment with women of the Third World indicates, our subject position exists in the interstices of national borders. More to the point, we are aligned as women whose specific needs have largely been ignored by most of our own male theorists as well as by many Euro-American feminists. We now engage with other people whose experiences mirror our own. It is currently fashionable for scholars, even White feminist scholars, to dismiss race issues as essentialist. I do not claim an essentialist privilege based on my own ethnicity or childhood class background or gender position. As a now middle-class academic who is fair-skinned and married to a Chicano with a name that opens doors only until "they" confront his brown skin, I nevertheless claim unequivocally the right to *engage* in the discussions—theoretical, historical, or otherwise. We Chicanas, along with other previously unlistened-to subaltern women, now insist on our agency to speak for ourselves. The question remains—who will listen and how well equipped with relevant information is that audience? When Chicana feminists align themselves with Third World Latin American women whose liberation struggles must confront the dominant group's oppression of subaltern men as well as women, they are often seen as having an "underdeveloped" sense of feminism. In the last chapter of this book, my discussion of Rigoberta Menchú, Domitila Barrios de Chungara, and Elvia Alvarado begins a study of a popular, internationalist feminism that these Latin American women practice.

In the following chapters, I explore how Sandra Cisneros's feminism on the border aligns itself with inquiries that concern U.S. Latinas and Mexican immigrants to the United States and how her concern with a practical feminism approaches the "feminismo popular" of Mexico. Helena María Viramontes's story "The Cariboo Cafe," clearly articulates feminism on the border as a political connection with the Salvadoran refugees in the border cities of California. Finally, Gloria Anzaldúa, in *Borderlands / La Frontera*, cites the geographical region of the Southwest as one site of Third World struggles within the First World:

> The US–Mexico border es una herida abierta [an open wound] where the Third World grates against the first and bleeds. And before a scab forms it hemorrhages again, the lifeblood of two worlds merging to form a third country—a border culture. Borders are set up to define the places that are safe and unsafe, to distinguish *us* from *them*. . . . Gringos

in the US Southwest consider the inhabitants of the borderlands trans-
gressors, aliens—whether they possess documents or not, whether
they're Chicanos, Indians, or Blacks. Do not enter, trespassers will be
raped, maimed, strangled, gassed, shot. (3)

While it remains imperative that First World feminists distinguish
their concerns from those of Third World women, by recognizing the
specific struggles of women across geopolitical borders, feminism can
forge new bridges and continue to grow as a politically relevant system
of ideas.

Familia de Mujeres

I said earlier that before "the" subaltern woman can be
heard, there must be an audience "prepared" (in every sense of the
word) to hear her. Part of my formulation of "feminism on the border"
addresses the ways in which Chicana feminism participates on the "border" between U.S. feminism and Latin American feminism, and alongside the feminisms of other women of color in the United States. Reading Chicana feminism, then, makes certain demands on the audience.
We ask the reader to learn our histories, to read our literature, and,
finally, to understand that we have established arenas of discussion
within a Chicana/o and Latina/o context. That is, we have been discussing these issues among ourselves in our own journals, anthologies,
and forums. As literary and cultural critics, we must address all of our
different audiences; nonetheless, they must understand that we also
have internal issues about which we have been in dialogue among ourselves.

This situation is similar to the African Americanist position within
literary institutions. When addressing an audience that may not have
the necessary information to contextualize the reading of an African
American text, the critic is pressured perhaps to oversimplify complex
issues in the interest of providing quick overviews. As Wahneema Lubiano observes, no scholar writing on contemporary British literature
is obliged first to present a complete history of British literature or life.
The scholar of "minority" literatures, however, is expected to reinvent
the wheel at every turn. In her essay "Constructing and Re-constructing Afro-American Texts," Lubiano points out that

unlike other specialists, critics of Afro-American literature must try to
speak to each other even as they must realize that they are also address-

ing other interested readers who may not feel, or may never have felt, that it is within the scope of their own critical or pedagogic agendas to know very much about current debates within Afro-American literature. Du Bois's "double consciousness" returns with a vengeance: we critics of Afro-American literature feel the need to speak to each other with the uninformed audience constantly in mind, a dilemma that often results in producing criticism that of necessity reinvents certain wheels of our discourse instead of focusing on the complexities of history and interpretation. (432–33)

As Eliana Ortega and Nancy Saporta Sternbach state in their essay "At the Threshold of the Unnamed," the emergence of Latina writers at a moment when the field of women's studies is enjoying a "honeymoon between women's literature and the publishing industry" (11) has certainly helped Latina writings to flourish. That such Chicana texts as Denise Chávez's *Face of an Angel* and Sandra Cisneros's *House on Mango Street* have been issued by East Coast publishing houses (Farrar, Straus & Giroux and Random House, respectively)[11] reflects Ortega and Sternbach's assertion that

editorial decisions [are] influenced by the fluctuations of the market according to the laws of supply and demand, incorporating the trends of imposed tastes for the consumption of reading lists with "new and worthy books." In spite of the vicissitudes experienced by women's studies programs and departments in the academy, in the publishing world women's literature is a "commodity," particularly when it is the production of a group often depicted as "exotic." What the academy marginalizes as "other," the market exploits as profit. (11)

We have reached the political juncture where we must question whether or not we want to position ourselves within the U.S. literary tradition, proving that our work is "equal" in complexity and "quality" to mainstream U.S. literary production. If we do, what exactly do we sacrifice? Whose ends do we serve? What "authority" have we given to a literary establishment against which we contend, or the terms of which we resist? If we locate ourselves as Third World women who have more in common with women and their literary production south of the U.S. border, will we ensure that we are banished from English departments and course syllabi? My work attempts to address these issues by locating a Chicana feminist literary production flourishing on the border between academic departments, between geopolitical locations.

3

Mestiza Consciousness
and Politics

Gloria Anzaldúa's Borderlands / La Frontera

Who, me confused? Ambivalent? Not so. Only your labels split me.
Gloria Anzaldúa, "La Prieta,"
in *This Bridge Called My Back*

In *Borderlands / La Frontera: The New Mestiza* (1987),
Gloria Anzaldúa presents an explicit articulation of the politics of feminism on the border. Soon after the publication of this text, "the border" quickly became a fashionable metaphor used by many feminist
Chicana/o studies and cultural studies critics and scholars.[1] Anzaldúa's
theoretical statements illustrate the dialectical position in which feminists on the border "find themselves," in every sense of the phrase. Her
theory of "Mestiza Consciousness" recenters her brand of Chicana feminism in the concrete, material locations of working-class-identified
women whose ethnicity and sexuality further dislocate and displace
them. The multiple and often contradictory identity issues that I discussed in the preceding chapters converge in this text's form, language,
identity politics, feminist proclamations, class analyses, and historical
reconstructions. For Anzaldúa, the multiple issues that informed her
radical political awareness finally culminate in what she calls "a new
consciousness" for the women who dare examine and question the
restrictions placed on them in the borderlands of the United States. In
Anzaldúa's political manifesto, a "New Mestiza" can emerge only after
she develops an oppositional consciousness.[2]

The Politics of Mestiza Consciousness

Entering into Anzaldúa's borderlands, the unprepared reader can lose herself in what Yvonne Yarbro-Bejarano eloquently labels the "serpentine movement" of the text ("Anzaldúa's *Borderlands / La Frontera*," 17). In my experience teaching this demanding and rich text to both Chicana studies majors and English majors with their varying degrees of knowledge of frontera history and culture, I have found it useful to enter the text at its center, Chapter 7, "La conciencia de la mestiza: Towards a New Consciousness." This final chapter in the prose section of the book deploys a mestiza methodology required to decipher the rest of this fronterista (border feminist) text.[3]

Anzaldúa grounds this methodology in the history of the Americas, urging that Chicanas turn to the preconquest histories and traditions to recover an indigenous heritage. By the end of the conquest, in 1521, the Spanish imperialist project had not only destroyed all the great temples and sites of indigenous worship, but also erased the memory of an entire civilization. The noted semiotician Walter Mignolo, in his monumental study of language, memory, and space in the pre-Cortesian Americas, *The Darker Side of the Renaissance*, calls this process the "colonization of memory." Doris Heyden and Luis Francisco Villaseñor, in *The Great Temple and the Aztec Gods* (5), further inform us that with the razing of the Templo Mayor, the Great Temple in the center of Tenochtitlán, what we now call Mexico City, much more than art and architecture was demolished by the conquering Spaniards. For the next several centuries, in Mexico as in the Chicana borderlands/frontera, it was not acceptable to claim indigenous heritage. Only recently have archaeological projects been funded by the Mexican government.

Anzaldúa's methodology brings to light (to borrow from Mignolo) strategies for unearthing a razed indigenous history as a process of coming to consciousness as political agents of change. Mestizas can turn to the Templo Major to recover women's place in a satanized past and learn about the centrality of female deities rendered passive with the interruption of Western androcentric ideology. The mestiza/o Aztec legacy idealized by Chicano nationalists focuses only on the blood sacrifices of this military power and further obscures the other indigenous tribal traditions that Aztec hegemony absorbed. Anzaldúa's reclamation of Aztec deities and traditions begins a reformulation of Aztlán from a male nation-state to a feminist site of resistance.

For Anzaldúa, feminism and lesbian politics emerge as the forces that give voice to her political agenda as a "New Mestiza," which claims much more than an essentialist "mixed blood." After an analysis of this important chapter where Anzaldúa clearly presents her political ideology, we can return to the first six chapters with a deeper understanding of the history of the borderlands she reconstructs.

The New Mestiza challenges the dualisms that underpin the power structure of the United States. In "Una lucha de fronteras / A Struggle of Borders," Anzaldúa expresses the multiple consciousness of feminists whose gender politics are lived simultaneously with race, class, and sexual awareness. Her many-faceted identity as a working-class-origin lesbian of color allows her to broaden her analysis to include other internal struggles she experiences. She also pushes Du Bois's theory of double consciousness much further. There are warring ideologies within the border dweller, and Anzaldúa, as a mestiza, asserts that she must

> continually walk out of one culture
> and into another,
> because I am in all cultures at the same time,
> *alma entre dos mundos, tres, cuatro,*
> *me zumba la cabeza con todo lo contradictorio.*
> *Estoy norteada por todas las voces que me hablan*
> *simultáneamente.* (77)

Gloria Anzaldúa's political, feminist position takes as its primary premise the fact of Chicana history across two cultures, Mexican and American, and in the interstices of two worlds: First and Third. In her analysis of the power system, she ventures into the mechanisms of the way the dominant group enforces its domination. When she asserts that "reaction," or resistance, is limited by and dependent on what it is reacting against, she is engaging in the political theory based on the works of Antonio Gramsci and Raymond Williams. What she describes in "Struggle of Borders" is how hegemony and counterhegemony work.

Ultimately, the New Mestiza vision is utopian. As she presents her agenda for a new political awareness, she seems to be willing to accommodate a coalition with the dominant group: "At some point on our way to a new consciousness, we will have to leave the opposite bank, the split between the two mortal combatants somehow healed so that we are on both shores at once, see through serpent and eagle eyes. Or perhaps we will decide to disengage from the dominant culture, write it off altogether as a lost cause, and cross the border into a wholly new and separate territory" (78–79). As she continues her critique, however, the utopian moment of possible integration with the dominant culture is fleeting. While at this point of the analysis, Anzaldúa appears to open up the borderlands as a pathological, psychological state of uncertainty and insecurity, she quickly moves to a plan of action that includes the possibility of revolution. With the understanding that Latinas/os will soon be a majority population in the Southwest, she concludes: "The possibilities are endless once we decide to act and not react" (79).

The multiple consciousness that forms feminist mestizaje brings with it a "tolerance for ambiguity." She notes how mestiza consciousness breaks down dualisms that keep fronteristas from praxis. The border consciousness she ultimately develops produces a new, revolutionary theory of politics. Anzaldúa creates a new culture, a new way of being that will entail a global healing and freedom from violence. Her desire to see with "serpent and eagle eyes" invokes the New Mestiza who claims the heritage of Aztec imagery. The serpent is the female, Coatlicue legacy and the eagle is the masculinist impulse of the dominating Aztec tribe. Anzaldúa proposes an identity that merges the two warring traditions, the female and the male, into a new unity.

In "The Crossroads," Anzaldúa's mythmaking constructs the image of the cornstalk to denote strength from indigenous ties to the earth. She describes the border dwellers as a dark people whose labors under the sun produce a capacity for new world visions. As a lesbian and a feminist, Anzaldúa also recognizes that the traditional Chicano culture does not claim her, so she considers herself "cultureless." But rather than lament that condition, she creates alternative myth systems: "I am cultured because I am participating in the creation of yet another culture, a new story to explain the world and our participation in it, a new value system with images and symbols that connect us to each other and to the planet. *Soy un amasamiento,* I am an act of kneading, of uniting and joining that has not only produced a creature of darkness and a creature of light, but also a creature that questions the definitions of light and dark and gives them new meaning" (81). The image of indigenous women kneading corn at the metate produces the type of dissonance that nurtures New Mestiza revolutionary theory.

The power of these political articulations lies in the deployment of feminist language that reclaims for dark women the right to theorize and create new world visions as well as to celebrate the traditions of their foremothers, the indigenous women who endured like the molcajete and metate they used to grind the spices and maize for the survival of the border people. The New Mestiza, for Anzaldúa, has her genesis in the bodies of grandmothers and mothers who literally forced survival from the earth. In poetry form, Anzaldúa credits the women who ensured the survival of borderers:

> We are the porous rock in the stone *metate*
> squatting on the ground.
> We are the rolling pin, *el maíz y agua,*
> *la masa harina. Somos el amasijo.*
> *Somos lo molido en el metate.*
> We are the *comal* sizzling hot,
> the hot *tortilla,* the hungry mouth.
> We are a coarse rock.
> We are the grinding motion,
> the mixed potion, *somos el molcajete.*
> We are the pestle, the *comino, ajo, pimienta,*
> We are the *chile colorado,*
> the green shoot that cracks the rock.
> We will abide. (81–82)

The New Mestiza's Aztlán:
From Nation-State to Coatlicue State

In "The Mestiza Way" Anzaldúan Chicana theory provides a methodology for a new consciousness based on recovering history and women's place in that erased history: "She puts history through a sieve, winnows out the lies, looks at the forces that we as a race, as women, have been a part of" (82). Along with providing a historical and lyrical document of the nameless women who ensured our survival under the conquest and under occupation, in *Borderlands / La Frontera,* Anzaldúa creates a new story with a revision of patriarchal appropriations of indigenous icons. As the theorist formulates the questions to be asked by the feminist historian, she accomplishes a "conscious rupture with all oppressive traditions of all cultures and traditions" (82), which signals the feminist basis of her theory. The

New Mestiza's charge is as a feminist historian whose most important task is to "document the struggle" and "reinterpret history": by "using new symbols, she shapes new myths" (82). The New Mestiza locates an alternative to la Virgen de Guadalupe: the indigenous mother of all gods, Coatlicue. New Mestizaje legitimizes a new language, Chicano Spanish. The New Mestiza also embraces a new consciousness about resistance strategies. Ultimately, Anzaldúa ends her outline for new political consciousness with a return to feminism: "The struggle of the mestiza is above all a feminist one" (84). Though the text often has been dismissed as indulging in a quest for lost origins or criticized for appropriating an indigenous heritage that does not belong to Chicanas, I propose that even in its most mystical, spiritual moments, the text circles back to a political consciousness with a specific political agenda that identifies not with the patriarchal nation-state Aztlán but with the feminist state, Coatlicue.

Again, her understanding of history is what prevents Anzaldúa's escape into the "self," into the personal, and away from the collective analysis. The only history previously available to contemporary Chicana lesbians, however, was the history of the Chicanos' oppression by the U.S. imperialist forces in their conquest of South Texas, by the Spanish conquest over the indigenous cultures, and by the destruction of female goddesses in those increasingly androcentric indigenous cultures before the disaster of Cortés's crusade. Even with her critique of the conquest, Anzaldúa refuses to romanticize an Aztec history in which male domination "drove the powerful female deities underground by giving them monstrous attributes and by substituting male deities in their place" (27).

When the New Mestiza historian invokes Aztlán, the mythical homeland of the preconquest Aztecs located in what we now know as the U.S. Southwest, it is an Aztlán transformed by a mestiza feminist sensibility. While she engages in the debate with Chicano nationalists who unequivocally claim the U.S. Southwest as the Chicano homeland, her claim to this "origin" is a strategic move that aligns her, a lesbian feminist, with the undeniably homophobic, often misogynist nationalist Chicano movement. Her dialectical position as a feminist on the border, however, allows her to move between Chicano nationalism and socialist feminism.[4]

Anzaldúa manages to do justice to both nationalist and socialist feminist tendencies as she reconceptualizes both impulses. While she has been accused of escaping into essentialism in her probing into the psy-

che of the lesbian mestiza and in her insistence on discussing indigenous goddesses, her working-class experience always pulls her back to
concrete analysis.[5]

Both Yvonne Yarbro-Bejarano in "Anzaldúa's *Borderlands / La Frontera*" and Norma Alarcón in "Anzaldúa's *Frontera*" provide extensive
discussions on Anzaldúa's Coatlicue State and her formulation of the
Shadow Beast. I would like to relocate these two images as central
strategies in the material recovery work Anzaldúa accomplishes as a
mestiza historian, a creator of counterdiscourses of New Mestiza myths
upon which we can build a counter-Aztlán, a Coatlicue "state."

In the chapter "Entering into the Serpent," the storyteller takes us
into the cuentos border families tell their children. For the narrator of
this section, Prieta, the story of the snake that slithers into a woman's
uterus and impregnates her provides the link to her "serpentine" feminist theory.[6] If the New Mestiza's task is to "winnow out the lies,"
then she will provide an alternative metaphor to the ones promoted by
androcentric psychologists and priests. Anzaldúa invokes Olmec myth
when she asserts that "Earth is a coiled Serpent" (26) and rewrites the
origin of the Catholic Guadalupe, empowering her as a pre-Columbian
"*Coatlalopeuh*, She Who Has Dominion Over Serpents" (27). In this
chapter's subtopic, Anzaldúa claims the earth as a female, feminist deity
in all her emanations. Like the constantly shifting identities of the Chicana in the contemporary world, the deities Anzaldúa unearths and
names become a pantheon of potential feminist icons. Through these
icons mestizas can unlearn the masculinist versions of history, religion,
and myth. The New Mestiza methodology unravels how both the
"male-dominated Azteca-Mexica culture" and the postconquest church
established the dichotomy of the virgen/puta when they split Coatlal-
opeuh/Coatlicue/Tonantsi/Tlazolteotl/Cihuacoatl into good and evil,
light and dark, sexual and asexual beings. Guadalupe, then, is Coatlalopeuh with "the serpent/sexuality out of her" (27).

In her mestiza feminist project to "use new symbols" and "shape
new myths," the New Mestiza theorist presents the traditional Virgen
de Guadalupe story both in Spanish (28) and in English (29). Then
she consciously "ruptures" the old cuentos with the sections on Aztlán
and La Llorona (31–33). Throughout her revisions she intertwines the
familiar stories with new feminist threads so that her insistence on the
recuperation of the feminist—the serpent—produces a tapestry at once
familiar and radically new. While "la facultad" can be interpreted as a
spiritual extrasensory perception, what New Mestizaje has in fact de-

veloped is the ability to rupture the belief systems that have been presented as ancient truths and accurate histories.

"La herencia de Coatlicue," in Chapter 4, is where history ultimately leads us. With *Borderlands / La Frontera*, for the first time Chicanas—mestizas—can turn to a document that offers a female-centered heritage. Undoing the dichotomy, which Alarcón accurately sees as the project of the Coatlicue State ("Chicana Feminism"), entails recovering the history of female serpent worship as well as writing new myths. While I do not want to ignore the psychological and philosophical aspects of these complex *Borderlands* chapters, I will focus on the material project with which the New Mestiza theorist also comes to grips.

As a mestiza historian with a mestiza political consciousness, Anzaldúa presents "the cluster in what I call the Coatlicue State" that are the pre-Columbian female deities she once again names: "Coatlicue, Cihuacoatl, and Tlazolteotl" (42). Armed with her new myths and symbols of female power, she confronts and tells the "terrible secret" of her childhood menstrual blood, which she calls "*la seña*" and "the mark of the beast," an abnormality that magnifies her alien status. This alienating mark is what Western medicine calls "precocious menarche" (43).[7] If her secret is embedded in female physiology, it is multiply encoded in obscure passages on her many names and fears. In her work as a mestiza historian, Anzaldúa has already offered us the multiple names of female deities, but now she has to complete her metamorphosis into a mestiza with a feminist, oppositional, political consciousness. Once she presents her "fear that she has no names / that she has many names / that she doesn't know her names" (43), she tells, in Spanish, how that fear is the outcome of dominant ideology: internalized racism. And as Yvonne Yarbro-Bejarano notes, "the mark of the Beast, earlier associated with internalized racism and homophobia, is here linked with physical abnormality and multiplicity" (21). In "Anzaldúa's *Frontera:* Inscribing Gynetics," Norma Alarcón asserts that the Shadow Beast figures as Anzaldúa's New Mestiza, *the* native of the Americas, as well as "the sign of savagery—the feminine as a sign of chaos." And through chaos, or rather non-Western, non-linear-thinking, New Mestiza consciousness, illuminates how to enact a (border) crossing from marginalized other to whole woman who constantly shifts, crosses, and gains power from contradiction and ambiguity.

What the Shadow Beast finally leads to is knowledge, a mestiza political hermeneutics that makes Chicanas finally aware of exploitation and oppression. Once she begins to understand that her power lies in her ability to define by asking questions and providing new answers, the New Mestiza crosses over with an acute consciousness: "I am no longer the same person I was before" (48). Anzaldúa presents what and who she is with birth imagery: a woman who delivers with an inner power, the "entity that is the sum total of all my reincarnations, the godwoman in me I call *Antigua, mi Diosa*, the divine within" (50). Indeed, the New Mestiza historian and creator of neomyth divines the recovered names of Coatlicue in all her emanations; the politically conscious mestiza historian and mythmaker comes armed with the power of knowledge.

A New Mestiza Discourse

Using both Western and non-Western theoretical and philosophical approaches in her work, Anzaldúa is an academic completing a doctoral degree at the University of California at Santa Cruz, as well as a spiritualist who crosses over to philosophical traditions deemed illegitimate by U.S. academia and self-indulgent by traditional leftist scholars. Anzaldúa's feminism exists in a borderland grounded in but not limited to geographic space; it resides in a space not acknowledged by the dominant culture. She uses the border as an organizing metaphor for Chicanas living in multiple worlds, multiple cultures, and employs border discourse to describe the borderlands' inhabitants: "*Los atravesados* live here: the squint-eyed, the perverse, the queer, the troublesome, the mongrel, the mulato, the half-breed, the half-dead; in short, those who cross over, pass over or go through the confines of the 'normal' " (3). By invoking racist, homophobic epithets, Anzaldúa obliterates the dominant culture's power over what is "normal" or acceptable. She uses the Spanish word *atravesados* to capture the multiple meanings the bilingual border speaker understands; *atravesado* also invokes the meaning of continuous resistance against a person or power.

Anzaldúa uses this border discourse throughout her text. It is a mestizaje of English, Spanish, Chicana/o dialect, and even some Nahuatl, the Aztec mother tongue. Throughout, Anzaldúa insists on the legitimacy of her border language:

> For a people who are neither Spanish nor live in a country in which Spanish is the first language; for a people who live in a country in which

English is the reigning tongue but who are not Anglo; for a people who cannot entirely identify with either standard (formal, Castillian) Spanish nor standard English, what recourse is left to them but to create their own language? A language which they can connect their identity to, one capable of communicating the realities and values true to themselves—a language with terms that are neither *español ni inglés*, but both. We speak a patois, a forked tongue, a variation of two languages. (55)

In this important chapter, "How to Tame a Wild Tongue," Anzaldúa reclaims language for the fronteristas de este lado. The Spanish dialect she names as a "living language" (55) emerges in this chapter as a tongue that she wants to reclaim and legitimize yet simultaneously critique as a language that enforces the codes of silence imposed by border patriarchs. For the New Mestiza linguist, an analysis of border discourse echoes her analysis of the mestizas' multiple identities: we have many languages just as we have many names. Anzaldúa's list of border languages travels from "Standard English" to norteño "Mexican Spanish dialect" (55). The vernacular of South Texas Chicanas figures as a central "homeland" as well. Her discussions of pochismos and of pachuco discourse are possible only after she has undertaken the political and psychological work of the previous chapters. Once she confronts the internalized racism of the Shadow Beast and reclaims Coatlicue, a feminist strength through the recovery of (feminist) history, the New Mestiza as linguist can now reconsider how language has been one more arena of contestation for borderers.

In her essay "Chicano Spanish," Anzaldúa once more exhibits a New Mestiza consciousness. She guides the reader through a Chicano Spanish–language lesson that includes the way South Texas Chicanas pronounce words with two adjacent vowels and offers a history that legitimizes the Chicanas' use of "archaisms." In a brilliant rhetorical move, Anzaldúa deconstructs the elitist disregard with which other (standard) Spanish speakers react to Chicano Spanish. She chooses the words borderers use that are most often mocked—*semos* [*somos*], *truje* [*traje*], *ansina* [*así*], *naiden* [*nadie*]—and implies that they are "pure" in the sense of their origins in sixteenth-century Spanish (57). The New Mestiza etymologist offers a counterhistory of language that battles the Shadow Beast criticizing Chicanas/os for their illegitimate use of Spanish:

Due to geography, Chicanos from the Valley of South Texas were cut off linguistically from other Spanish speakers. We tend to use words that the Spaniards brought over from Medieval Spain. The majority of

Spanish colonizers in Mexico and the Southwest came from Extremadura—Hernán Cortés was one of them—and Andalucía. Andalucians pronounce *ll* like a *y,* and their *d*'s tend to be absorbed by adjacent vowels: *tirado* becomes *tirao.* They brought *el lenguaje popular, dialectos y regionalismos.* (57)

In the section titled "Linguistic Terrorism," Anzaldúa herself becomes the terrorist as she unloads the ultimate irony for Chicanas: we are punished for speaking Spanish in "American" classrooms and playgrounds, yet we are mocked by other native Spanish speakers for the version of Spanish we have managed to retain. She refuses to give in to either hegemonic impulse; thus her strategy of using Chicana mestiza discourse in the text itself: the chapter titles and subtitles in *Borderlands / La Frontera* are in English and then Spanish, or vice versa, a reflection of the duality of the mestiza experience.

New Mestiza History of the Border

Whereas the earlier works of women such as Angela de Hoyos articulate Chicano nationalist issues, Anzaldúa makes the leap from the history of colonization by the United States to the history of colonization as a mestiza, a Native American woman. And although some Chicana critics reject the internal colony model because, as María Linda Apodaca states, "when the land was conquered, the Mexican population in the Southwest was small given the total land mass" ("Double-Edged Sword," 110), the specific history of the Tejana/o urges us to remember that there is not one monolithic Chicano/a experience in the United States. Apodaca's assumptions fail to acknowledge the historical specificity of the Tejanas/os who were forced to live under a reign of terror in post-1845 Texas.

In the poem "Hermano," which I discussed in Chapter 1, Angela de Hoyos taunts the Anglo usurper by reminding him of his own immigrant status. He is told to "scare up your little 'Flor de Mayo'— / so *we* can all sail back / to where we came from" (13; emphasis added). While de Hoyos identifies with her European heritage—the *Pinta,* the *Niña,* and the *Santa María* of the Spanish conquerors—Anzaldúa, in opposition, insists on identifying with the indigenous Indian tribes and the African slaves who mixed with the conquerors to produce the mestiza/o. She bases her political, feminist position on the Chicanas' history within multiple cultures: indigenous Mexican, African, and always "grounded on the Indian woman's history of resistance" (21).

In this border world, the Chicana is no different from the undocumented worker: "the only 'legitimate' inhabitants are those in power, the whites and those who align themselves with whites" (4). Anzaldúa immediately proceeds to present the history of the conquest of the Americas, linking the Chicana in kinship with North American Indians to "form an even greater mestizaje" (5).

Anzaldúa's text itself is a mestizaje: a postmodernist mixture of autobiography, historical document, and poetry collection. Like the "atravesados" whose lives it chronicles, *Borderlands* resists genre boundaries as well as geopolitical borders. The text's opening epigraph is an excerpt from a song by the conjunto Los Tigres del Norte. But if Anzaldúa's historical ties are closer to the corrido tradition than to the historical imperatives of postmodern theory, she is creating a new corrido of the mestiza with a political analysis of what it means to live as a woman in a borderland.

Through issues of gender politics, Anzaldúa locates personal history within a history of the border people. Legitimacy belongs to the Anglo hegemony; the indigenous population is nothing more than an aberrant species. To the White power structure, the mojado (wetback) is the same as the Mexicano de este lado (Mexican from the U.S. side). As she records the history of the new mestiza, Anzaldúa explores issues of gender and sexual orientation that most Chicano historians have not adequately addressed.

Presenting the other history of Texas that Anglo-Texans such as J. Frank Dobie and Walter Prescott Webb never mention, Anzaldúa further merges autobiography with historical document. Her family history becomes the history of the Chicana/o experience in South Texas after colonization and occupation by U.S. forces. The Texas Rangers lynched those who dared resist.

She speaks of how the Tejanas/os "were jerked out by the roots, truncated, disemboweled, dispossessed, and separated from [their] identity and [their] history" (8). "My grandmother," Anzaldúa recounts, "lost all her cattle / they stole her land." The history of dispossession is transmitted orally from one generation to the next; Anzaldúa's mother tells the story of her widowed mother who was cheated by the Anglo usurper. In this narrative, we get the Tejano/a version of a history that such writers as Larry McMurtry in *Lonesome Dove* or James Michener in *Texas* have not recognized:

"Drought hit South Texas," my mother tells me. "*La tierra se puso bien seca y los animales comenzaron a morirse de se'. Mi papá se murió de un* heart attack *dejando a mamá* pregnant *y con ocho huercos,* with eight kids and one on the way. *Yo fuí la mayor, tenía diez años.* The next year the drought continued *y el ganado* got hoof and mouth. *Se calleron* in droves *en las pastas y el* brushland, *pansas blancas* ballooning to the skies. *El siguiente año* still no rain. *Mi pobre madre viuda perdió* two-thirds of her *ganado.* A smart *gabacho* lawyer took the land away *mamá* hadn't paid taxes. No *hablaba inglés,* she didn't know how to ask for time to raise the money." (8)

The woman's border discourse, comfortably switching between English and Spanish, further emphasizes the historia that Tejanas articulate as opposed to the monolingual, monolithic version that Anglo-Texans or Anglo-Americans impose.

As it constantly shifts from personal story to collective historia, Anzaldúa's autobiography as presented in *Borderlands* reflects a Chicana positionality on the border. For the New Mestiza, autobiography *is* the history of the colonization of indigenous Southwestern people by Anglo-American imperialists intent on their Manifest Destiny. Texas history, in Anzaldúa's revision, is incomplete without the presentation of the Mexican woman who dares to cross the border. She is the one who is the most easily exploited, physically as well as sexually. The coyote can enslave her after raping her. If she is lucky enough to make it to the U.S. side, she can look forward to laboring as a maid "for as little as $15.00 a week" (12).

Traitorous Cultures / Rebellious Movements: Mestiza Feminism

Once she establishes a working definition of the mestiza/o border culture with which she identifies, Anzaldúa begins her internal critique of that world. Because she is so much a part of it, she can penetrate its inner dynamics and understand the oppressions that it uses to control women within that culture. When Anzaldúa tells how she rebelled, we can see the intense power that the Chicano culture holds over women: "*Repele. Hable pa' 'tras. Fuí muy hocicona. Era indiferente a muchos valores de mi cultura. No me dejé de los hombres. No fuí buena ni obediente.* [I argued. I talked back. I was quite a bigmouth. I was indifferent to many of my culture's values. I did not let the men push me around. I was not good or obedient]" (15; my translation).

The ideal woman of the borderland is one who stands behind her man in silence and passivity. If she refuses her female role as house-keeper, she is considered lazy. To study, read, paint, or write is not a legitimate choice for a mestiza. Anzaldúa's testimony rings true for many Chicanas who struggle against their gender indoctrination. That her history exists for us to study is a testament to her resistance: "Every bit of self-faith I'd painstakingly gathered took a beating daily. Nothing in my culture approved of me. *Había agarrado malos pasos* [I had taken the wrong path]. Something was 'wrong' with me. *Estaba más allá de la tradición* [I was beyond the tradition]" (16; my translation). "Cultural tyranny" is an additional power against which the Chicana feminist struggles. She must not only contend with the racism of Anglo-American restraints but also resist the oppressive yoke of the sexist Chicano culture.

In addition to her study of colonialism and capitalism in *Borderlands,* Anzaldúa examines how patriarchy is inextricably linked to these two forces and how all three transcend geopolitical borders. She has shown how the men in the preconquest Americas invoked patriarchal privilege to displace the female deities. We now get an analysis, through self-writing, of how the family as an institution empowers imperialism, capitalism, and patriarchy across geopolitical boundaries. Gender politics emerge in her assertions that "culture is made by those in power—men. Males make the rules and laws; women transmit them. How many times have I heard mothers and mothers-in-law tell their sons to beat their wives for not obeying them, for being *hociconas* (bigmouths), for being *callejeras* (going to visit and gossip with neighbors), for expecting their husbands to help with the rearing of children and the housework, for wanting to be something other than housewives?" (16). Anzaldúa's gender politics are always aware of the women who are complicit agents of the patriarchy.

But gender politics is never her only concern. When she examines how Chicanas have traditionally been limited to roles as nuns, prostitutes, or mothers, she discusses the liberating potential of an education for women. She recognizes, however, that this last possibility is available to very few Chicanas. For Anzaldúa, feminist possibilities are always intertwined with class issues: "As working class people, our chief activity is to put food in our mouths, a roof over our heads and clothes on our backs. Educating our children is out of reach for most of us.

Educated or not, the onus is still on woman to be a wife/mother—
only the nun can escape motherhood. Women are made to feel total
failures if they don't marry and have children" (17). Anzaldúa consistently links gender analysis with class analysis. Ultimately for Chicana
feminists, there can be no separation of race, class, sexuality, and gender
issues.

The New Mestiza refuses to wait patiently for the men to liberate
her. Given her history as a woman of a culture that insists that its
women be submissive, Anzaldúa "refuses to glorify those aspects of
[her] culture which have injured [her] in the name of protecting [her]"
(22). As she puts it, "I abhor some of my culture's ways, how it cripples
its women, *como burras* [like asses], our strengths used against us, lowly
burras bearing humility with dignity. The ability to serve, claim the
males, is our highest virtue. I abhor how my culture makes *macho*
caricatures of its men" (21).

Anzaldúa's project problematizes further still the traditions of Chicanismo, when, as a lesbian Chicana, she forces the homophobes of
Chicano communities to see their prejudice. If heterosexual Chicanas
are ostracized from their culture for transgressing its rules of behavior,
for the Chicana lesbian, "the ultimate rebellion she can make against
her native culture is through her sexual behavior" (19). She makes "the
choice to be queer" and as a result feels the ultimate exile from her
homeland, cultural as well as geographic. She transforms the bourgeois
concepts of "safety" and "home" into concepts she can carry with her
along with her political commitments. As a Chicana "totally immersed"
in her culture, she can choose to reject the crippling aspects of
traditions that oppress women and silence homosexual men and
women. Her refusal to "glorify those aspects of my culture which have
injured me and which have injured me in the name of protecting me"
signals the agenda for the New Mestiza, the border feminist (22). The
feminista that Anzaldúa presents is a woman comfortable with new
affiliations that subvert old ways of being, rejecting the homophobic,
sexist, racist, imperialist, and nationalist.

New Mestiza Political Poetry

The second half of *Borderlands* rearticulates Anzaldúa's
theories in poetry form. The poem "Immaculate, Inviolate: *Como Ella*"

retells the story of her grandmother, whose economic exploitation was exacerbated by the fact that her husband had children by another woman:

> Sometimes when I get too close to the fire
> and my face and chest catch the heat,
> I can almost see Mamagrande's face
> watching him leave
> taking her two eldest
> to play with his other children
> watching her sons *y los de la otra* [and those of his other woman]
> grow up together. (110)

Anzaldúa's anger is palpable when she writes of her grandmother Locha:

> I can almost see that look
> settle on her face
> then hide behind parchment skin
> and clouds of smoke.
> *Pobre doña Locha,* so much dignity,
> everyone said she had
> and pride. (110)

Like the Bolivian feminist Domitila Barrios de Chungara, Gloria Anzaldúa presents powerful women's testimony. Unlike Barrios de Chungara, however, Anzaldúa, as a Chicana, a Third World woman in the First World, cannot ignore how women have toiled beside men, how women were lynched alongside men, and how, ultimately, they are still condemned to hard labor with little access to power within the Chicano culture. Through her relentless critique, Anzaldúa makes the border feminist's dialectical position clear: patriarchal traditions become co-conspirators with capitalism, imperialism, and White supremacy to keep the Chicana exploited, oppressed, and silent.

In addition to the gender transgressions that Anzaldúa's New Mestiza introduces, new subject matter for poetry is an "aberration" she presents. African Americanists from Ida B. Wells to Hazel Carby and Wahneema Lubiano have explored the terroristic method by which the dominant culture kept the African Americans under control: the law of the rope. Likewise, Chicanas/os, particularly in Texas, have lived under the threat of lynching. The historian Arnoldo De León has investigated lynching as an institutionalized threat against Tejanos, but it takes Anzaldúa's poem "We Call Them Greasers" to flesh out the ramifications of the lynch law for Chicanas. In the poem whose title pays tribute to De León's history *They Called Them Greasers*, the connection between the oppression of nineteenth-century African slaves and ex-slaves and nineteenth-century mestizos/Chicanos emerges.

Narrated by the Anglo usurper, this example of what Barbara Harlow has called resistance literature speaks of how Tejanos lost their lands and, often, their lives. The Anglo narrator assumes the role of deity as he forces the Tejanos to place their hats "over their hearts" and lower their eyes in his presence. He rejects their collective farming techniques, cultural remnants of indigenous tribal traditions of the mestizo.

He sneers, "They didn't even own the land but shared it." The Tejano "troublemakers" who actually have "land grants and appealed to the courts" are laughingstocks, "them not even knowing English" (134). For the Anglo-American imperialist, literacy in Spanish or any other nonstatus language is illiteracy. The women, in particular, suffer additional violence before they are murdered by the gringo.

While Chicano (male) historians have done much to expose the realities of violent acts against the Tejanos, they have, to a great extent, been reluctant to voice the perhaps unspeakable violence against Tejanas. Even Américo Paredes (considered the dean of border studies) in his breakthrough text *With His Pistol in His Hand* cannot articulate the violence that Gregorio Cortez's wife, Leonor Díaz Cortez, must have suffered in the four months she spent in a Texas jail, incarcerated for her husband's alleged crime (87). During the Rangers' manhunt for Cortez, a Mexican woman is alleged to have given information to the sheriff leading to Cortez's capture. Paredes states: "The woman, whoever she was, at first refused to talk, but 'under pressure' told Glover where Cortez was going, so that Glover knew his destination before Cortez reached it. What sort of pressure Glover used, whether it was physical or psychological, there is no way of telling" (68).

Precisely because "there is no way" for a nonfeminist historian to tell the history of the Chicana, it takes Anzaldúa's voice to articulate the violence against nineteenth-century Tejanas. In "We Call Them Greasers," rape is an institutionalized strategy in the war to disempower Chicano men. While the Tejano is tied to a mesquite tree, the Chicano version of the African American hanging tree, the gringo rapes the Tejana.

> She lay under me whimpering.
> I plowed into her hard
> kept thrusting and thrusting

> felt him watching from the mesquite tree
> heard him keening like a wild animal
> in that instant I felt such contempt for her
> round face and beady black eyes like an Indian's.
> Afterwards I sat on her face until
> her arms stopped flailing,
> didn't want to waste a bullet on her.
> The boys wouldn't look me in the eyes.
> I walked up to where I had tied her man to the tree
> and spat in his face. Lynch him, I told the boys. (134–35)

Once the rapist gains total control over the Tejano through the violation of "his" woman, the rapist can feel only contempt for her. Within the hierarchy of powerlessness, the woman occupies a position below the already inferior Brown man. De León chronicles how Anglo-American occupiers made their conquests and massacres more bearable by comparing their victims to animals; similarly, by emphasizing the mestiza's *Indian* features, the imperialist further relegates the Chicana to the "savagery" of the Native American (14–23). The White-supremacist Texans in the poem can discern no difference between the "dark blood" of Amerindians and that of Chicanas/os. Indeed, mestiza Chicanas and Native Americans suffer a kinship under institutionalized racism. Anzaldúa's reluctance to condemn the passive observers in the poem, "the boys," does not stem from misguided loyalty to men or gringos. Rather, she implicitly recognizes the power of class structure even in nineteenth-century Texas, where the rich land barons controlled all of their workers, regardless of gender, race, or ethnicity.

To the history of Anglo agribusiness in the 1930s Anzaldúa juxtaposes her father's history as a sharecropper in South Texas. We begin to understand her need to search for her Aztec, preconquest pantheon of goddesses. If history for the Chicana Tejana is the history of "blood feuds, lynchings, burnings, rape, pillage," then we must allow for Anzaldúa's "escape" into the self as her way of recreating her history. If she dwells on the rediscovery of indigenous goddesses, it is because of her tribal memories:

> I remember my father scanning the sky for a rain that would end the drought, looking up into the sky, day after day, while the corn withered on its stalk. My father has been dead for 29 years, having worked himself to death. The life of a Mexican farm laborer is 56—he lived to be 38. It shocks me that I am older than he. I, too, search the sky for rain. Like the ancients, I worship the rain god and the maize goddess, but unlike

my father I have recovered their names. Now for rain (irrigation) one offers not a sacrifice of blood, but of money. (90)

In poems like "Sus plumas el viento," "Cultures," and "Sobre piedras con lagartijos," Anzaldúa reasserts her solidarity with the exploited women and men along the greater border. "El sonavabitche" protests the exploitation of undocumented farmworkers in places such as Muncie, Indiana. The poem exposes the methods by which unscrupulous farm owners create a modern-day slave system. Hiring undocumented Mexican laborers to work their fields, they tip off the Immigration and Naturalization Service (INS) for a raid just before payday. The Chicano narrator expresses solidarity with his undocumented compañero when he refuses to work for the "sonavabitche" who colludes with the INS as part of his business strategy:

> *Como le estaba diciendo,*
> today was payday.
> You saw them, *la migra* came busting in
> waving their *pinche pistolas*.
> Said someone made a call,
> what you call it? Anonymous.
> Guess who? That *sonavabitche,* who else?
> Done this three times since we've been coming here
> *Sepa Dios* how many times in between.
> > Wets, free labor, *esclavos.*
> > *Pobres jijos de la chingada.*
> > This is the last time we work for him
> > no matter how *fregados* we are
> > he said, shaking his head,
> > spitting at the ground.
> > *Vámonos, mujer, empaca el mugrero.* (126–27)

In the poetry and prose of *Borderlands* Anzaldúa redefines feminism. She complicates issues of First World versus Third World in ways that link the Chicanas' struggles with the struggles of women in other nations in the Americas. In the long narrative poem "En el nombre de todas las madres que han perdido sus hijos en la guerra" (In the name of all mothers who have lost children to war), written entirely in Spanish, Anzaldúa rewrites the Llorona legend. The indigenous woman who narrates the poem ("Soy una pobre india") laments the child who has been machine-gunned in her arms by fair-skinned soldiers. But her lament quickly becomes more than powerless weeping. She clearly identifies the oppressors who have murdered two other sons and one daughter in their war. In her grief she wants to die, but she also expresses her despair with a militancy that seeks revenge on the men responsible for her children's murders. The Weeping Woman in this poem will not wander the earth searching for the children she killed — she will engage in active resistance against the military forces intent on massacring the indigenous peoples of the Americas.

Finally, it is in the poem "To Live in the Borderlands Means You" that Anzaldúa sums up her definition of the New Mestiza, the feminist on the border. She is one who "carries five races" on her back, not Hispanic, Indian, African, Spanish, or Anglo, but the mixture of the five, which results in the mestiza, the mulata. She is also a "new gender . . . both woman and man, neither" (194). While not rejecting any part of herself, Anzaldúa's New Mestiza becomes a survivor because of her ability to "live sin fronteras (without borders) / be a crossroads" (195).

While Anzaldúa transgresses aesthetic boundaries in her text; transgresses gender boundaries with her "choice" to be a lesbian; transgresses ethnicity and race in her formulation of the New Mestiza combining Indian, Spanish, African, and even Anglo "blood" to form a mestizaje, her project is nonetheless articulated within the vital history of the Texas Chicana. If history is what forces Anzaldúa's escape into identity politics, it is because the only history previously available to Chicanas in Texas was the history of the mestiza's colonization by both the Spanish conquerors and the Anglo-American imperialists in their conquest of South Texas.

Once the Chicana feminist has learned the history of the border people, she can turn to other urgent concerns. María Patricia Fernández-Kelly's *For We Are Sold, I and My People* presents a history of the mestiza laboring in the exploitative maquiladora (factory) system that Anzaldúa alludes to in her own work. Anzaldúa also calls attention to the unwritten *historia* of the mestizas in the colonias of South Texas and in border cities such as El Paso and Ciudad Juárez. In these homelands of victims of U.S. multinational corporations, these people are being poisoned by the water they are forced to store in chemical drums that once held carcinogens.

Anzaldúa's feminist theory and methodology in *Borderlands* is ideological analysis, materialist historical research, as well as race, class, and gender analysis. It is never an ahistorical "politics of equal oppressions," to use Jenny Bourne's phrase ("Homelands of the Mind," 16), because Chicana feminism on the border develops from an awareness of specific material experience of the historical moment. Unlike the feminism of sisterhood, which Bourne defines as "feminism which is separatist, individualistic and inward-looking" (2), Chicana border feminists look inward in moments of self-exploration and see themselves as daughters of non-Western, indigenous tribes. Anzaldúa's feminist discourse leads her to look inward and claim a dual spirituality, one that culminates in a deeper understanding of a larger erased history and in a crossing of borders in solidarity with the indigenous peoples of the Americas.

4

Mujeres en Lucha /
Mujeres de Fuerza

*Women in Struggle / Women of Strength
in Sandra Cisneros's Border Narratives*

In the spring of 1984, the National Association of Chicano Studies (NACS) held its annual conference at the University of
Texas at Austin. At that conference, the publisher Nicolás Kanellos
organized readings by four Chicanas whose works Arte Público Press
had just published: Evangelina Vigil, Pat Mora, Ana Castillo, and Sandra Cisneros. The women electrified the audience with their performances. In addition to Chicano and Chicana academics, many Chicanas
working in the Austin community were drawn to the conference because of its theme, "Voces de la Mujer" (Chicana Voices).

Evangelina Vigil, reading from her book of poetry *Thirty an' Seen
a Lot*, represented a Chicana/Mexicana waiting for the bus at a crowded
corner on Quitman Street, in a Houston barrio. As she read the poem
"¡Es Todo!" she brought to the Lyndon Baines Johnson Auditorium
"mujeres mexicanas! with. . .skinny ankles / and muscular chamorros."
Vigil's poetry allowed working-class Mexican women front-door entrance to a Texas university that historically relegated Mexicanas to
roles as faceless women pushing the broom carts, mopping the corridors, and cleaning the bathrooms. As someone who had grown up in
South Texas with the knowledge that the university did not welcome
Mexicans de este lado, "from this side" of the border, watching the
performance and listening to Chicanas as *subjects* of a literary discourse
as well as *agents* of this discourse, I began to formulate new possibilities
for academic studies.

The poet Pat Mora, from El Paso, read from her *Chants,* once again reminding us of our indigenous ties to the Southwestern landscape. Appropriately addressing her audience of Chicana/o academics and other people from the community, Mora insisted that we recall our status as "legal aliens" in the United States even as we move to middle-class occupations:

> able to sit in a paneled office
> drafting memos in smooth English,
> able to order in fluent Spanish
> at a Mexican restaurant,
> American but hyphenated,
> viewed by Anglos as perhaps exotic,
> perhaps inferior, definitely different,
> viewed by Mexicans as alien,
> (their eyes say, "You may speak Spanish but you're
> not like me")
> an American to Mexicans
> a Mexican to Americans. (52)

Ana Castillo voiced distinctly feminist concerns as she read from *Women Are Not Roses*, prompting me to think that perhaps a place needed to be made in a university such as this one for someone to teach and write about this new literature. Castillo's poem "1975" signaled that Chicana feminism included race and class issues, chronicling "proletariat talks / during laid-off hours / cursing and cussing / complaining of unpaid bills / and bigoted unions / that refuse to let us in" (49).

But it was Sandra Cisneros, reading from her just-published *House on Mango Street,* with its Chicago Chicana perspective, that convinced me—finally—that I had found a literature I could work on that would speak to me in a way that Jane Austen, Charlotte Brontë, or even Virginia Woolf could not.

Since that day in 1984, *The House on Mango Street* has sold nearly 1.2 million copies and was awarded the Before Columbus American Book Award in 1985.[1] The book lost a large segment of its potential college and university audience when Arte Público placed it in the "Young Readers" section of its catalog, but since its publication by Random House it has become a basic text in many women's studies and American literature courses. In the same way that it brought me back to the university, this book also offers its readers, particularly its Chicana readers, a vision that allows them to believe that they too can speak and write their own versions of *Mango Street. The House on*

Mango Street is a book that speaks to U.S. working-class women of color as it ultimately allows them to theorize about the "undoing" of the intellectual's privilege with the return of the organic intellectual.

Transgressing Boundaries

Sandra Cisneros, faced with a triple alienation as a working-class woman of color in an elitist writing program in the Midwest, devised resistance tactics to avoid incorporation by what she calls the "mainstream."[2] As the sole Chicana in her graduate program at the University of Iowa Writer's Workshop, Cisneros was alien because of her race and ethnicity, alien as a working-class woman—alien, that is, as a product of her specific history. Her resistance strategies for survival included writing counter to what was expected of her. She describes her "conscientization"[3] as a writer "obsessed," driven by her own history to record a previously muted world through her stories:

> Until Iowa [and the Writer's Workshop] I had never felt my home, my family, and neighborhood unique or worthy of writing about. I took for granted the homes around me, the women sitting at their windows, the strange speech of my neighbors, the extraordinary lives of my family and relatives which was nothing like the family in "Father Knows Best." I only knew that for the first time I felt "other." What could I write about that my classmates, cultivated in the finest schools in the country like hot house orchids, could not? My second-rate imitations of mainstream voices wouldn't do.... What did I know except third-floor flats. ... That's precisely what I chose to write: about third-floor flats, and fear of rats, and drunk husbands sending rocks through windows, anything as far from the poetic as possible. ("From a Writer's Notebook," 72–73)

As Gloria Anzaldúa asserts in her critique of patriarchal Chicano culture, the Chicana's position within her own community often depends on her willingness to sacrifice herself for the sake of antiquated cultural "traditions." But what happens when a Chicana writer dares enter a room that houses Chicano "tradition" and finds herself in a house of horrors that threatens her life? When Chicana feminist writers begin to examine Chicano "tradition" and criticize wife battering, child abuse, "drunk husbands," the misogyny that is embedded in the culture, they are branded "vendidas," sellouts, who betray their people and contribute to the damaging stereotypes of Mexicans and Mexican Americans that Anglo America already believes.

In *The House on Mango Street,* the reader is led into a borderland that defies stereotype. Set in an urban city (most probably Cisneros's own hometown of Chicago), Mango Street is an urban barrio surrounded by privilege but excluded from it. The sexual, racial, and geopolitical emerge in the *Mango Street* characters' lived experiences as working-class people of color in the borderlands of Greater Mexico.[4]

Juan Rodríguez, editor of the notoriously sexist Chicano newsletter *Carta Abierta* and one of the first critics to review *Mango Street*, is representative of (Chicano) readers unprepared to recognize female domestic space as a legitimate site of struggle. Rodríguez's review of this feminist text reveals much about the androcentric Chicano attitudes toward women's issues that Cisneros exposes in *Mango Street*. For Rodríguez, the novel's controlling image of the house appears simple because the narrator and characters seem to be bourgeois and steeped in the ideology of the American Dream. While Rodríguez does recognize that "poverty and limited opportunities in the barrio" are more than "mere inconveniences" to the Mango Street residents, he does not believe that its inhabitants can escape their imprisonment "except as characters in a piece of fiction." Rodríguez continues his (mis)reading: "That Esperanza chooses to leave Mango Street, chooses to move away from her social/cultural base to become more 'Anglicized,' more individualistic; that she chooses to move from the real to the fantasy plane of the world as the only means of accepting and surviving the limited and limiting conditions of her barrio becomes problematic to the more serious reader" (*Austin Chronicle*, Aug. 10, 1984). But "serious readers" who remove the ideologically charged blinders of male supremacy and view the text in terms of gender as well as race and class analyses observe in Cisneros's narrator and characters a far greater complexity than Rodríguez allows them. Rodríguez is a noted Marxist scholar whose work helped establish Chicano literature and literary history in academia. His appeal to the "serious reader" seems paradoxical. His reluctance in 1984 to consider an oppositional feminist theory as "serious" resistance work begs us to question his need to enlist an elitist category of sophistication.

When Rodríguez refers to Cisneros's text as "poetically-charged prose sketches" without further discussing the complexity of genre, he denies *Mango Street* the legitimacy of "serious" literature. While it may be tempting to label *Mango Street* a novel, in the same way that

Tomás Rivera's. . . *Y no se lo tragó la tierra/And the Earth Did Not Part*
is a novel by the genre's usual broad definition, I agree with Pedro
Gutiérrez-Revuelta that what we can label "chapters" are also historias.[5]
Just as the word *testimonio* loses the overt political agenda of the genre
when we translate it simply as *testimony, historia* loses its mestiza power
when it is translated as either *story* or *history*. The text is a mestizaje,
like Moraga's *Loving in the War Years* and Anzaldúa's *Borderlands*, a
mixture of fiction and history. *Mango Street* provides literary stories as
well as politically charged histories of people often ignored in official
histories and canonical literature. In this manner, *Mango Street* is a
project not unlike the Subaltern Studies group's version of an "alternative discourse," to apply Edward Said's term (*Selected Subaltern Studies*, vi). The *Mango Street* historias are distinct from the official Anglo,
Chicano nationalist, and Chicano (male) versions of history.

Attempting to fit *Mango Street* into a manageable genre, Gutiérrez-
Revuelta considers Cisneros's own description of her text as "stories
from the barrio." He ultimately agrees with Rodríguez that *Mango
Street* never transcends an individualistic quest for material comforts,
but he does approve of Cisneros's "definition" of these barrio histories,
"ya que opuestamente a cuentos o leyendas, las *historias* (historias del
barrio) llevan implícito un carácter de historicidad, de realismo; de lo
que, aunque no aparezca ni en los libros de historia ni en los noticieros
ni en los periódicos, es parte de la verdadera y diaria historia del barrio.
Convirtiéndose así la autora no simplemente en creadora de fábulas o
leyendas sino en testigo de lo ocurrido en el barrio y transmisora de
las voces *sin voz* de sus habitantes" (51). ("Now in opposition to stories
or legends, the *stories* [stories of the barrio] implicitly carry a type of
historicity, of realism; which, while it may not appear in history books
or in newscasts or in newspapers, is part of the truthful and daily history of the barrio. The author is thus transformed, not simply as creator
of fables or legends but as witness to what happened in the barrio and
as transmitter of the voicelessness of its inhabitants" [my translation].)

As scholars of Third World literature understand, one of the distin-
guishing characteristics of the literature is its resistance to incorporation
by Western literary conventions.[6] But is the novel itself a "foreign
body" or an "acculturated form" in the Third World? Gutiérrez-
Revuelta concedes that the difficulty critics have faced in categorizing
Mango Street is that it may well belong to "un género nuevo," a new
genre, possibly postmodernism (51). While postmodernism may address the stylistic and aesthetic characteristics of *Mango Street,* its prac-

titioners have not yet adequately addressed the specific sociopolitical issues that Chicana feminist texts display.[7]

George Lipsitz, for example, in "Cruising around the Historical Bloc—Postmodernism and Popular Music in East Los Angeles," attempts to show how the music of the Chicano "postmodern" band Los Lobos "reflects the decentered and fragmented nature of contemporary human experience" (160). He argues that Chicanos successfully "used the techniques and sensibilities of postmodernism to build a 'historical bloc' of oppositional groups united in ideas and intentions if not experience" (160). While Lipsitz's essay succeeds in showing how Chicano artists such as Los Lobos resist domination in the United States, he concludes that ultimately they practice a "cultural politics that seeks inclusion in the American mainstream by transforming it" (177).

Lipsitz, however, neglects to elaborate on what he means by "transformation" and "inclusion." His otherwise insightful analysis seems overly confident in the largesse of cultural pluralism. Los Lobos' production cries out for a discussion of what "inclusion" implies to historically muted groups such as Chicanas/os. Unfortunately, Lipsitz's optimism that Los Lobos can influence "mainstream" culture extends only to their English-language songs. When the band subsequently recorded traditional Mexican/Chicano music in "Con la pistola y el corazón," the album that followed the mainstream success of "La Bamba," it received negligible air play on mainstream radio stations. Would cultural critics' universalizing use of "postmodern" apply to Los Lobos' "Con la pistola y el corazón," or is "Pistola" merely an exercise in foreign-language/traditional Mexican music that has little relevance to U.S. cultural critics? Could it be instead that Los Lobos' project in this album is not one of postmodern skepticism, or an attempt to be included through transformation, but rather an example of conscious cultural opposition? If we listen to Los Lobos within their historical context as Chicanos whose use of the corrido form and of Spanish are expressions of political and cultural resistance, the music presents a much more complex study for cultural critics.[8]

Likewise, while *The House on Mango Street* can, on one level, be read for its postmodern aesthetic attributes, it resists easy generic categorization because it is a border text. This text emerged from the geographic regions between the United States and Mexico, from the working class, and contains elements of both "high" culture and popular culture. Cisneros's mestiza text is both lyrical and realist; it has the rhythms of poetry and the narrative power of fiction. It participates in (borders on) a variety of genres—historia, testimonio, and poetry, as well as working-class, U.S. feminist fiction closely allied to Tillie Olsen's novel of the 1930s, *Yonnondio.*

Sandra Cisneros's personal background is that of a border feminist, a product of Chicago's urban barrios whose family "constantly move[ed] back and forth between Chicago and Mexico City due to [her] father's compulsive 'homesickness' " ("From a Writer's Notebook," 69). Cisneros begins to deconstruct the opposition between the intellectual and struggling subaltern women, women imprisoned in their homes by patriarchy as well as by a system that depends on passive participants to reproduce its surplus army of labor. Instead of dwelling on what Rodríguez insists is a "fantasy plane," Cisneros writes of undocumented workers and of men who "wake up tired in the dark." She writes of women who refuse to learn to speak English because they have no desire to remain in a country that does not want Brown immigrants from countries whose dictators the United States often supports.

Narrated by a child, Esperanza Cordero, who hopes to leave the barrio and own a house of her own, *The House on Mango Street* is a set of short narratives of life at the periphery. Cisneros offers us a glimpse of a mass of people ruled by what Said has termed "coercive or sometimes mainly ideological domination from above" (*Selected Subaltern Studies,* vi). Esperanza's naive dream of a house is informed by the image of what her parents have promised will be hers:

> They always told us that one day we would move into a house, a real house that would be ours for always so we wouldn't have to move each year. And our house would have running water and pipes that worked. And inside it would have real stairs, not hallway stairs, but stairs inside like the houses on T.V.. . . Our house would be white with trees around it, a great big yard and grass growing without a fence. This was the house Papa talked about when he held a lottery ticket and this was the house Mama dreamed up in the stories she told us before we went to bed. (7–8)

Lacking only the white picket fence to complete the stereotype of the bourgeois American woman's dream, the image of "house" that Esperanza and her family hope to have one day is a product of ideological manipulation from above. In her essay "Ethnicity, Ideology, and Academia," Rosaura Sánchez reminds us that "it is the very nature of ideology to provide an account of the world which will allow those of us who live in this society to continue to perform our roles and duties while ignoring the real conditions of our existence" (80). Lottery tickets and highly publicized tales of the overnight transformation of factory workers into multimillionaires serve as additional ideological manipulation to obscure the injustices of a system built on the labor of the marginalized. The reality of Esperanza's Mango Street house is, in the child's words, "not the way they told it at all. It's small and red with tight little steps in front and windows so small you'd think they were holding their breath. Bricks are crumbling in places, and the front door is so swollen you have to push hard to get in. There is no front yard, only four little elms the city planted by the curb" (8). Esperanza is disillusioned with the house not only because of its location in the midst of the barrio and because it is small and crumbling. Certainly the narrator desires possessions, but her implicit critique of the ideological domination from above extends beyond a crass desire for upward mobility.

In this same introductory chapter, *Mango Street* critiques the Catholic Church as an ideological state apparatus, in Althusserian terms, whose aim is to maintain the status quo of the ruling class. Esperanza remembers how a nun from her school observed the Cordero house when they lived on another barrio street and, in her reaction to the poverty, made the child "feel like nothing" (9). The nun here becomes the traditional intellectual who is in fact a "functionary," what Antonio Gramsci calls the "dominant group's 'deputies' exercising the subaltern functions of social hegemony and political government" (*Selections from the Prison Notebooks,* 12). Esperanza's reaction to the nun's actions becomes symptomatic of how the dominated are controlled. As a result of the nun's pronouncement, the child responds:

> I had to look to where she pointed—the third floor, the paint peeling, wooden bars Papa had nailed on the windows so we wouldn't fall out. You live *there?* The way she said it made me feel like nothing. *There.* I lived *there.* I nodded.
>
> I knew then I had to have a house. A real house. One I could point to. But this isn't it. The house on Mango Street isn't it. For the time being, Mama said. Temporary, said Papa. But I know how those things go. (9)

While Esperanza's desires and her parents' response resonate with the earlier European immigrant tradition, the need to "wait till our ship comes in," this ideology of delayed gratification assumes that all right-thinking people want to be integrated and that their needs are only material. Esperanza's particular situation, however, further emphasizes the historical specificity of the Chicana's position. Unlike European immigrants to the United States, many of the Chicanos in the Midwest are descendants of Tejanos or Californios—that is, of people who were not immigrants to the United States but whose homelands were conquered and absorbed by nineteenth-century U.S. imperialism. As Rodolfo Acuña documents in *Occupied America*, the Immigration and Naturalization Service has a long history of collusion with farmers in the Southwest. In 1953–55, for example, when the growers demanded the cheap, surplus labor that Mexican nationals could provide in order to break strikes by Chicano farmworkers, the INS would oblige by allowing illegal immigration. One result of this practice was the migration of Chicanos to the Midwest and other areas of the United States (156). Acuña traces the beginnings of Chicano and Mexican settlement in the Chicago area to the 1920s and on through the 1970s. These people established distinctly Chicano barrios in South Chicago, Back of the Yards, and the Pilsen areas (353). Chicanos, Acuña points out, were "attracted by the higher paying jobs in the heavy industries of that region. High unemployment in the Southwest drove Chicanos further north" (408).

We learn of Esperanza's father's family in Mexico in "Papa Who Wakes Up Tired in the Dark," when he returns to Mexico for his father's funeral. In "A Smart Cookie," the mother's revelation that she "quit school" because she did not have "nice clothes" (83) implies that she is at least a first-generation Chicana. Esperanza's neighbors and good friends, Lucy and Rachael, have "immigrated" from Texas: "We come from Texas, Lucy says and grins. Her was born here, but me I'm Texas" (17).[9]

Even in her innocence, Esperanza seems to know of the ideological manipulation of the ruled, of how the masses are pacified by the promise of a winning lottery ticket or a dream house. The child's understanding of "how those things go" is an implicit comment on Gramsci's critique of the state, of how the masses are "kept happy by means of moralizing sermons, emotional stimuli, and messianic myths of an awaited golden age, in which all present contradictions and miseries will be automatically resolved and made well" (150).

In *The Bluest Eye* Toni Morrison presents another way of understanding U.S. Third World women's desire for a place of their own. As Morrison discusses the concept of "outdoors"—the literal dispossession of homeless people of color, and this includes slavery for African Americans—she further problematizes issues of ownership and private property. Commenting on the "peripheral existence" of African Americans within the dominant culture, Morrison dramatizes life "on the hem of life," historicizing their fight for survival with dignity:

> Knowing that there was such a thing as outdoors bred in us a hunger for property, for ownership. The firm possession of a yard, a porch, a grape arbor. Propertied black people spent all their energies, all their love, on their nests. . . . And these houses loomed like hothouse sunflowers among the rows of weeds that were the rented houses. Renting blacks cast furtive glances at these owned yards and porches, and made firmer commitments to buy themselves "some nice little old place." In the meantime, they saved, and scratched, and piled away what they could in the rented hovels, looking forward to the day of property. (18)

What separates the African American and Mexican American experience and desire for "property" and a "real house" from that of immigrant groups is *how* these two groups became "American." The specific histories of slavery for African Americans and imperialistic absorption for Mexican Americans demand that issues of "private property" and "ownership" require a nuanced analysis rather than a reductionist Marxist methodology that focuses only on class. The history of Chicana/os and African Americans insists that when we look at passages like the one above, we remember that the property these women desire is property denied them through terroristic methods employed by the Ku Klux Klan and the Texas Rangers.

Body (W)Rites on the Border

I ain't single no longer, she sighed. From now on I'm nuthin but an old married lady. Cricket's ball and chain. His ole lady. For better or worse. Till death do us part. Ain't no longer gonna come home to this house, to the smell of my Ma's good food. Nor to my bed that sags in the middle, she lamented. Starting tonight I'm gonna be wiz my honey. My husband.

Mary Helen Ponce, *The Wedding*

The House on Mango Street also explores a world where women are betrayed by the ideology of family, of "home," of sexuality, and of national language. In Esperanza's world, women learn to believe that marriage to "the right man" can liberate them from poverty and the rule of fathers. In her world, girls learn to fear sexuality because the realities of rape and incest complicate still further the fact of living below the poverty line. Cisneros analyzes the role of tradition in the Chicano culture, a tradition that hegemony so imposes on Chicanas that they cannot transgress class and gender constraints. The houses that betray "women leaning their sadness on an elbow" also hide the realities of wife/daughter battering. Echoing the oppressive patriarchal traditions that transcend national and ethnic borders, traditions that Maxine Hong Kingston, for example, also examines in *The Woman Warrior*, Esperanza tells the story of her great-grandmother, a woman who shared her name—in English, Hope. Establishing affiliations with the Asian women who are condemned for their gender, Esperanza places her namesake within that larger family of resemblance: "She was a horse woman too, born like me in the Chinese year of the horse—which is supposed to be bad luck if you're born female—but I think this is a Chinese lie because the Chinese, like the Mexicans, don't like their women strong" (12). But while Kingston's No Name Woman is punished by the community for "crimes" of her sexuality and even has her name erased from the family memory, Esperanza's ancestor, as well as her story, does, at least for now, survive her punishment for being born female. Through the oral tradition, the cuentos and historias that serve as counterhistories, Esperanza hears the discourses of Mexican women who were abducted by men and incarcerated in the house, the domestic site that women are supposed to see as the "safe space."

In an inversion of the more widely disseminated whitemale story of Anglo women's abduction by Indians, Esperanza tells a captivity tale that exposes the difference between life on la frontera for Mexican women and on the frontier for White women:

> My great-grandmother. I would've liked to have known her, a wild horse of a woman, so wild she wouldn't marry until my great-grandfather threw a sack over her head and carried her off. Just like that, as if she were a fancy chandelier. That's the way he did it.
>
> And the story goes she never forgave him. She looked out the window all her life, the way so many women sit their sadness on an elbow. I wonder if she made the best with what she got or was she sorry because she couldn't be all the things she wanted to be. (12)

In *The Land before Her* Annette Kolodny began the project of recovering women's experiences on the "American frontier," acknowledging that she restricts her analysis to middle-class, English-speaking White women. Kolodny's pioneering research shows that some of these women, regardless of their initial unwillingness to journey to the "wilderness," nevertheless "claimed the frontiers as a potential sanctuary for an idealized domesticity" (xiii). For others, however, "the dream of a domestic Eden had become a nightmare of domestic captivity" (9). Through captivity narratives, however, these women's suppressed anger against the men who often forced them to venture into an "inhospitable environment" was displaced by female readers onto the Indian (33).

Esperanza's historia prods us to seek another, more inclusive version of seventeenth-, eighteenth-, and nineteenth-century women's experiences. This missing counterhistory alerts Esperanza to the need to deconstruct the concept of "home" for women of her class and culture and to understand it as something other than a safe haven. She struggles to fill in the gaps, the silences of her great-grandmother's life. Suspecting the worst, a domestic confinement that resisted the label of imprisonment or indentured servitude, Esperanza resolves a different script for herself: "Esperanza. I have inherited her name, but I don't want to inherit her place by the window" (12).

Esperanza's struggles to comprehend the lesson of her great-grandmother's story serve as a model for reading the gaps in Chicana history. Are we to read the great-grandmother's historia as a cautionary tale that the women of her family pass on, warning succeeding generations of the consequences for women who passively accept men's rules? Or is the story instead a master narrative that the women take up as their own, thereby unwittingly reproducing their own oppression and exploitation by their men? Esperanza resolves not to duplicate her great-grandmother's history; she fills in the gaps, the story's political unconscious, and guides the reader through the Mango Street neighborhood to illustrate contemporary repetitions of her great-grandmother's historia.

Cisneros's feminist critique of the domestic reminds us of how sexism can also cut across race and class lines. As Nina Baym argues in *Women's Fiction*, in the "cult of domesticity" women are urged "to find fulfillment in marriage and motherhood" (26). But in her study of Anglo-American women's novels between 1820 and 1870, she finds that what these women actually wrote contradicted the domestic ideal. Instead, "home life is presented, overwhelmingly, as unhappy. There are very few intact families in this literature, and those that are intact are unstable or locked into routines of misery" (27).

Charlotte Perkins Gilman, in one of the earliest, most lucid critiques of the institutionalization of domesticity, *The Home: Its Work and Influence* (1903), presents a rhetorically charged analysis of how women of her race and class were restricted by the ideology of housewifery. Unfortunately, her intended audience was limited to middle-class White women.

On first reading, Gilman's text would seem to offer an early model that Chicanas might use to examine their own experiences as women. Gilman warns: "To the girl who marries all too hastily as a means of escape . . . and to the woman—the thousands upon thousands of women, who work while life lasts to serve that sanctuary by night and day—to all these it may not be unwelcome to suggest that the home need neither be a prison, a workhouse, nor a consuming power" (13). Instead, Gilman envisions a concept of home that liberates women from unnecessary, unpaid labor; she proposes the transformation of the private sphere into a collective environment. She astutely makes the connection between the domestic and the "theory of private property rights" (21), asserting that the maternal duties that initially confine women to the home are quickly transformed into "the custom of ownership in women." The woman "belonged to the man, as did the house; it was one property group" (22), she says, an issue she had addressed earlier in *Women and Economics* (1898). Gilman called for "a room of one's own" twenty-six years before Virginia Woolf; but unlike Woolf, Gilman explicitly excludes the "lower" classes from her gender analysis. In fact, one of Gilman's rhetorical devices is to urge the dismantling of the home as an institution to avoid the need to deal with "ignorant" servants. Her appeal to the class bias of her readers reminds us of other nineteenth-century feminist appeals to White women's racism in the struggle for (White) women's suffrage.[10]

In his work on nineteenth-century Mexican women, the historian Richard Griswold del Castillo documents that

> the traditional domestic life for a large number of working-class Mexican-American women was only a dream. Increasingly they found themselves as heads of families with small children without a spouse for support, whether through abandonment, temporary long-term absences, death, or separation. By the late nineteenth century, almost 30 percent of all Hispanic families in the urban areas of the Southwest

were headed by women. A significant proportion of these women heading husbandless families were forced to work for wages as laundresses, seamstresses, maids, servants, vendors, and in other insecure occupations. For them the morality of domesticity offered little help in raising their families or in putting food on the table. ("Commentary," 44–45)

Therefore, while the tendency even within Chicano traditions has been to idealize the home as the sacred abode of la familia, *The House on Mango Street* exposes what that enclosure, the house, hides from public view. If the image of mangos evoked by the title conjures images of the exotic, of a lush paradise, the underside of the image plays on the fragility of the mango—how easily it bruises. When Cisneros transposes the tropical fruit to the frigid landscape of Chicago, she unearths a different garden for the women of Mango Street. The Mango Street neighborhood is filled with women imprisoned in the domestic space by patriarchal and economic constraints.

Cisneros is at her demographic best when she shows the ethnic diversity of a Latino community of women that includes women from other U.S. island colonies. Acuña's historiography of an "occupied America" indicates that the term *Latino* fits the population of the Midwest, since Chicanos there lived in close proximity to the Puerto Ricans who migrated in great numbers after World War II (408). *Mango Street* brings history to life in the portrait of the young Puerto Rican woman Marin, who works for an aunt caring for the younger cousins.[11] Marin believes that if she stays in the city, she can get a "real job downtown that's where the best jobs are, since you get to look beautiful and get to wear nice clothes and can meet someone in the subway who might marry and take you to live in a big house far away" (27). But Marin is ill equipped to see the contradictions inherent in her fantasy. She aspires to the image of bourgeois womanhood, career, husband, and dream house, but she remains in her aunt's house, which she cannot leave "until her aunt comes home from work, and even then, she can only stay out in front" (12).

Trapped by the undereducation imposed on women and men of her class and ethnicity, Marin can imagine no other solution to her situation. Esperanza imagines a static Marin, "under the streetlight, dancing by herself. . . singing the same song somewhere. . . waiting for a car to stop, a star to fall, someone to change her life. Anybody" (28). Dependent as she is on her kinship ties for economic survival, Marin acquiesces in the traditional expectations for women, what Rosaura Sánchez calls a "guarantee of economic and social security" ("Chicana

Labor Force," 6). Since Latinas in the United States are excluded from the benefits of education and other privileges provided to mainstream America, these women "face the future with dread and anxiety." They mistakenly "view the lack of husband and children as a lack of insurance against total destitution" (6).

Mango Street also houses women who, out of fear of economic dependency, reproduce their own exploitation. "Minerva Writes Poems" scrutinizes the perpetuation of mother-to-daughter exploitation. Minerva, only a few years older than Esperanza, has two children and "a husband who left" (80). A woman who raises children alone and without an economic base, she duplicates her own mother's situation: "Her mother raised her kids alone and it looks like her daughters will go that way too" (80). Unable at this point to theorize how traditional concepts of familia contribute to her exploitation by her husband, Minerva has only one explanation for her victimization at her husband's fists—"her luck is unlucky." Minerva writes poems, aspires to a life of the intellect, but cannot imagine another possibility for her life. For her, the domestic dream is instead a nightmare in which the home is vulnerable to the "big rock" her violent husband hurls through the window.

Rosa Vargas is yet another woman who seems to validate the myth that families without a male are doomed to turn out "bad." Playing on the children's story of the old woman who lived in a shoe, Cisneros writes, "Rosa Vargas' kids are too many and too much" (30). Her husband has left her "without even leaving a dollar for bologna or a note explaining how come" (30). If the Vargas kids are "bad," Cisneros insists on showing the situation in which the single parent raises the children:

> After a while you get tired of being worried about kids who aren't even yours. One day they are playing chicken on Mr. Benny's roof.
>
> Mr. Benny says, hey ain't you kids know better than to be swinging up there. Come down, you come down right now, and then they just spit. See. That's just what I mean. No wonder everybody gave up. Just stopped looking out when little Efren chipped his buck tooth on a parking meter. . . and nobody looked up not once the day Angel Vargas learned to fly and dropped from the sky like a sugar donut, just like a flying star, and exploded down to earth without even an "Oh." (30–31)

Women like Minerva and Rosa Vargas, who contend with their positions as sole heads of their households, further explode the stereotype of Chicano family unity as a phenomenon that is often romanticized by Chicano men and dominant institutions attempting to diffuse responsibility for the perpetuation of exploitation. The stereotype, as Rosaura Sánchez writes, "projects an image of families which, although poor, are willing to accept their divorced or separated daughters, as well as their grandchildren, back into the home. All too often these divorced women are encouraged by their families to seek remarriage rather than remain in their parents' home with three or four children and no means of support. Separation or divorce often implies a transfer of dependency from husband to father or to the Welfare Department" ("Chicana Labor Force," 6).

On Mango Street, however, the husbands who stay are often not much better than the ones who leave. Rafaela, who in Esperanza's eyes is "still young but getting old from leaning out the window so much, gets locked indoors because her husband is afraid Rafaela will run away since she is too beautiful to look at" (76).

Physical beauty for these women becomes one more factor that adds to their exchange value in the world of Mango Street. Esperanza and her girlhood friends learn the lessons of their sexuality at an early age. Anticipating their impending womanhood, the girls play with the high-heeled shoes a neighbor gives them. They both fear and desire female sexuality; "the truth is," confides Esperanza, "it is scary to look down at your foot that is no longer yours and see attached a long long leg" (38). The danger comes when they parade their now transformed legs, once "skinny and spotted with satin scars where scabs were picked," but now "all our own, good to look at, and long" (38). Once they are subjected to the male gaze of Mr. Benny, the neighborhood grocer, they are warned of the danger of being women in a phallogocentric world: "Them are dangerous, he says. You girls are too young to be wearing shoes like that. Take them shoes off before I call the cops" (38). They ignore Mr. Benny but cannot ignore the "bum man" who emerges from a bar to leer and claim the young girls' sexuality. The message they get from his attempt to buy a kiss for a dollar is quite clear: women are open targets on streets beyond Mango Street, and perhaps their fathers are correct—to be beautiful, to be a woman, is dangerous.

That frightening episode notwithstanding, Esperanza and the girls of Mango Street manage to salvage some aspects of the female body as their own. While legs and beautiful faces may be fetishized by men, Cisneros "writes the body" for her readers to see arms and legs and hips as agents of power, fighting back, dancing, running away. Condemned by her thoughtless mother to attend a baptismal party wearing "the old saddle shoes I wear to school, brown and white, the kind I get every September because they last long and they do," Esperanza feels her adolescent body awkward, her feet "grow[ing] bigger and bigger" (45). She refuses to dance with a boy her age but dances with her uncle, in spite of "feet [that] swell big and heavy like plungers" (46). Momentarily losing herself in the exhilaration of a new dance, Esperanza "forget[s] that [she] is wearing only ordinary shoes, brown and white, the kind my mother buys each year for school" (46).

The legs that the "bum man" and Mr. Benny differently sexualize, but sexualize all the same, are reappropriated by Esperanza into feet in plain shoes that allow her to express herself through dance, through her body. She is aware, however, that a boy watches her dance all night and that female sexuality is an issue with which she eventually must contend. The Mango Street girls perceive their sexuality and how, through ideological socialization, women's sexuality is mediated by the male gaze.[12]

Cisneros further problematizes women's (hetero)sexuality—how it empowers the women of the barrio as well as how, in conjunction with the economic pressures, it also betrays them. In the lyrical chapter "Hips," the girls' songs are full of speculations about female reproductive organs. In the singsong of jump-rope chants, the reader hears how the female body functions for the girls: "One day you wake up and they are there. Ready and waiting like a new Buick with the keys in the ignition. Ready to take you where?" (47). They locate the center of production and reproduction in the hips, proclaim that the hips are centers of difference between the sexes. Taking their game a step further, they proceed to produce new meanings for their bodies, something other than making babies. What they produce is poetry, song, and dance:

> You gotta get the rhythm, and Lucy begins to dance. . . .
> It's gotta be just so, I say. Not too fast and not too slow. . . .
> I want to shake like hoochi-coochie, Lucy says. She is crazy.
> I want to move like heebie-jeebie, I say picking up on the cue.
> I want to be Tahiti. Or *merengue*. Or electricity. Or *tembleque!*
> Yes, *tembleque*. That's a good one. (48)

As the young barrio poets jump the rope and flaunt their innocent physicality, they celebrate their ability to play with words and with the multiple languages available to them as women of the Chicana borderlands. To different degrees of success, they create mestiza rhythms. Esperanza practices her ethnopoetics on the streets:

I take a little while before my turn, take a breath, and dive in:

> *Some are skinny like chicken lips.*
> *Some are baggy like soggy band-aids*
> *after you get out of the bathtub.*
> *I don't care what kind I get.*
> *Just as long as I get hips.* (48–49)

At this point in their sexual development, the girls transform their bodies into a source of creativity. In this way Cisneros offers some optimism that for the girls of Mango Street, the female body and female sexuality need not be all bad.

In spite of betrayals like the forced kiss by an older man at her first job, Esperanza anticipates her impending maturity and experiences the first stirrings of desire. Sire, the young man her parents call "punk," looks at her "like that"; it makes her "blood freeze to have somebody look at [her] like that" (69). It is she, however, who watches Sire and his girlfriend, Lois, and imagines what they do together. Her mother's disapproval of Sire and Lois means nothing to Esperanza, who articulates her desires in a child's language: "Everything is holding its breath inside me. Everything is waiting to explode like Christmas. I want to be all new and shiny. I want to sit out bad at night, a boy around my neck and the wind under my skirt. Not this way, every evening talking to the trees as I lean way out my window imagining what I can't see" (70).[13]

In the Mango Street world, however, women are limited by the conventions of male rule. Figures of female sexuality, in Esperanza's experience, can take only the dualistic forms represented by such cultural icons as the Virgen de Guadalupe. In her aunt Lupe, Esperanza witnesses the (dis)embodiment of a once-vital woman with "swimmers legs" into a bedridden invalid betrayed by her body.

At the other end of the virgen/puta dichotomy, Esperanza's young friend Sally is the exemplar of all the imprisoned and exploited women of Mango Street. She represents the polar opposite of the paralyzed, blind Aunt Lupe. Sally is "the girl with the eyes like Egypt and nylons the color of smoke. . . . Her father says to be this beautiful is trouble" (77). Restricted and defined by rules of the father, Sally rebels by wearing her makeup at school and afterward being careful to "pull [her] skirt straight [and] rub the blue paint off [her] eyelids" before "entering

the house [she] cannot come out from" (78). While Sally and Esperanza imagine that the makeup and tight skirts signify Sally's refusal to
submit to the patriarchal contract, those markings on her young body
brand her as a man's possession in the same way that her bruises from
her father's beatings signal his proprietary interest in her body. If Sally's
only mischosen venue for protest results in her marriage to yet another
father figure/jailer, it is because the Chicanas of Mango Street cannot
imagine any other way to exist. To a certain degree even Sally accepts
her father's violence because it is a legacy from the sins of an aunt who
disgraced the family by running away. In a tradition that values a
young woman's virginity and recognizes females' value only as property, a young woman's expression of her sexuality and her desire to act
on her sexual impulses end in violence.

Sally's father's inappropriate reactions to her sexuality hint at an
incestuous impulse. Obsessed with her virginity, he beats her "like a
dog. . . like if I was an animal. . . . Just because I'm a daughter" (85).
When the Cordero family takes Sally in after a particularly brutal beating, her penitent father quickly fetches her home. The truce is short-
lived, however, and when he catches her talking to a boy, he loses
control: "he just went crazy, he just forgot he was her father between
the buckle and the belt" (85–86). The leather belt with which he beats
Sally signifies paternal power; the image of the buckle and belt hint at
the father's phallus as another weapon for possession of the daughter.

In *Mejor sola que mal acompañada: For the Latina in an Abusive Relationship* (1985), Myrna Zambrano notes that the profile of the abusive
male is not restricted by class or ethnicity. She asserts that "our society
suffers from sexual inequality, which puts men in positions of power;
male violence often is used as a way to maintain that power" (154). For
the Latino male immigrant to the United States, however, the fact that
he may be in exile from a war-torn country adds to an oppression that
"can strip men of their pride and integrity." Their resulting powerlessness as aliens in the United States tends to reinforce their desire to
claim power and complete control in their homes. According to Zambrano, "they may not be respected in the outside world, but in their
home they will demand it" (156).

The houses of Mango Street are clearly the domains of the men
Zambrano describes. Hidden behind the drawn curtains, women and
men perform the deadly dance from which the women's battle-scarred
bodies ultimately emerge, displaying the unequal distribution of power
between them and their angry men. Rather than the prison camp that

Sally's house represents, the home Esperanza imagines for her friend is a space far from the reality of Mango Street. Esperanza's dream house for Sally is one with "big windows" that perhaps would expose more to the public eye and protect Sally from her father's abuse. Esperanza desires for Sally a space where "no one could yell at you if they saw you out in the dark leaning against a car, leaning against somebody without someone thinking you are bad" (78–79). But Sally's fate is overdetermined by her gender and class position. She gets married "before the eighth grade" to a man much like her abusive father. Instead of living in Esperanza's dream house, Sally ends up even more isolated and trapped, with a violent man who cuts her off from outside communication and "doesn't let her look out the window" (95).

Mujeres en Lucha Leave
Mango Street to Return

In spite of the overwhelming number of imprisoned women surrounding her, Esperanza decides to fight back and have a life different from theirs. The lessons of the female body have convinced her that beauty invites brutality at the hands of men and that sexuality can only lead to the body's betrayal, like Rosa Vargas's multiple pregnancies or Sally's punishment in marriage. Esperanza asserts liberation because she is "an ugly daughter. . . one nobody comes for" (82). Armed with her youthful innocence, Esperanza determines to escape men's brutality by training herself in male strategies of resistance: "I have begun my own quiet war. Simple. Sure. I am the one who leaves the table like a man, without putting back the chair or picking up the plate" (82). Unlike Sally's silent mother, Esperanza's mother encourages her to refocus her ambitions. She encourages Esperanza's intellectual endeavors and urges the child not to depend on a man for financial security. In addition to what is fundamentally a feminist analysis, Esperanza's mother tells her daughters her own story as a precautionary tale against dropping out of school. She admonishes her daughters about the vanity and folly of allowing "shame" at not having "nice clothes" to keep them from completing school (84). These well-meaning words come from a creative woman who sings arias from operas and who draws, but she cannot take a subway train downtown, cannot articulate the economic inequities imposed on her, and cannot draw an analysis without limiting it to a judgment of personal folly; as the system wants her to do, she blames herself.

Ultimately, in spite of her guerrilla efforts, Esperanza too experiences violence at the hands of men. She is assaulted at the local carnival by a man who calls her "Spanish girl" and who professes love as he rapes her. Even at her young age, Esperanza learns to discard the lying tales of romance and love, "all the books and magazines, everything that told it wrong. Only his dirty fingernails against my skin, only his sour smell again" (94).

In contrast to all the Mango Street women who submit to patriarchal imperatives, another Mango Street friend, Alicia, suggests different solutions, different resistance strategies in the face of exploitation by fathers and state institutions. In spite of a father who believes that women should not aspire to higher education, Alicia attends the university at great personal sacrifice. It is difficult to make time to study because, as a motherless eldest daughter, she must care for her siblings as well as her father. To get to the university, she takes "two trains and a bus, because she doesn't want to spend her whole life in a factory or behind a rolling pin" (32). Alicia urges Esperanza to examine her Mango Street surroundings and understand the importance of her position in the barrio. Esperanza's impulse is to flee the neighborhood, which offers only confinement for women, but Alicia teaches her how to accept her identity formation as a Mango Street female: "Like it or not, you are Mango Street and one day you'll come back too" (99). When Esperanza refuses to return "until somebody makes it better," Alicia voices the organic intellectual's understanding that it is up to women like themselves to change the barrio.

The theory of change, of action, that women like Alicia suggest points to *The House on Mango Street* as a primer for the political New Mestiza consciousness advocated by Chicana theorists like Anzaldúa and Moraga. Cisneros expands her feminist concerns in such chapters as "No Speak English," where the resisting woman endures verbal abuse from her husband when she refuses to give in to the dominant language. Contrary to what the Immigration and Naturalization Service would have us believe, many immigrants to the United States would prefer to remain in their own countries, but because of the U.S. government's economic policies, the underdevelopment of Third World countries forces the underemployed and the politically persecuted to seek solutions in the United States.

The woman's refusal to accept the United States as her new home belies the myth of the descending Brown hordes from Latin America who want a so-called free ride from the U.S. government and its tax-payers. We see ideological warfare in action when the reluctant immigrant finds her baby boy singing "the Pepsi commercial he heard on TV" (74). The ideological state apparatus in this case consists of the electronic media, whose commercials program consumers to believe that having access to products like Pepsi and Colgate undoes the underlying material inequities. To cite Rosaura Sánchez, "being affected, influenced, and exploited by a culture is one thing, and sharing fully in that culture is another" ("Ethnicity, Ideology, and Academia," 81).

In a similar act of resistance, Esperanza comes to the conclusion that education will perhaps break the bondage of ignorance, exploitation, and domination for Mango Street women. She realizes, however, that her oppositional tactics entail leaving the barrio itself. Her feminist instincts inform her that the Chicana's escape from the prison house of Mango Street requires rejection of traditions and customs that shackle the mind as well as the body. Her solution, an education, does not have to be a bourgeois escape to an academic ivory tower, but is one option that allows the Chicana working-class intellectual the possibility of a return "for the ones who cannot out" (102). Like Anzaldúa in her urge to return to South Texas to continue her work on the border, Cisneros presents the young Esperanza with a consciousness that the task of Chicana activist, feminist intellectuals involves transforming the role of the traditional intellectual. Instead of serving as functionaries for the dominant class and gender, Alicia and Esperanza threaten to become "new intellectuals" who confront and defy the dangers of Mango Street and engage in real sociopolitical and cultural confrontations by speaking to their own people.

The return, of course, is the book itself. The house Esperanza seeks is found in the pages of *The House on Mango Street*, a site that offers countless Chicanas and other women a mirror of their own lives under Chicano (male) rule and signals how it is possible to resist and to build new structures as women. With the publication of this Chicana feminist text in 1984, Sandra Cisneros transformed the concept of home from mere private space to a site that includes a broader concept of community. The imprisoned women of Mango Street are trapped only when they remain isolated from one another, an isolation that perpetuates domination by patriarchy as well as by other ideological forces.

Mujeres de Fuerza
in "Woman Hollering Creek"

I can shoot back at a man with a gun. But as for the
[wo]man with a pencil, watch out for [her].

Américo Paredes, *With His Pistol in His Hand*
(adapted)

Sandra Cisneros's *House on Mango Street* and *Woman Hollering Creek and Other Stories* offer us exemplary texts for thinking theoretically about Chicana literature. Characteristic of feminism on the border, feminism with a political consciousness, the texts themselves give us the theory with which we may begin to analyze them. The sexual, racial, and geopolitical emerge in the characters' lived experiences, which are based on Cisneros's own experiences as a working-class woman of color from the borderlands of Greater Mexico.

Both texts problematize static notions of identity and complicate a simple dichotomy of the metropolitan opposed to the rural. Simultaneously, they address the reductionist opposition of First versus Third World. For marginalized people in the United States, the contradiction of living in poverty in the wealthiest country in the world affects their perception of themselves as part of the country yet apart from it. Further, their existence on the borders of the mainstream informs their perception of the possibilities available to them. At different levels, then, and in different ways, the barrio people of Mango Street perceive the barriers imposed on them by their dual existence as people whom Pat Mora describes in "legal aliens," as "American to Mexicans/Mexican to Americans." In *Woman Hollering Creek and Other Stories*, Cisneros questions the hegemonic definition of American in "Mericans" and continues the Anzaldúan project of mestiza consciousness as a political methodology that breaks down dualistic thinking. Cisneros's "Remember the Alamo" acknowledges that the borderland inhabitants include gays and lesbians. In "Never Marry a Mexican," she offers a biting satire on feministas falsas who wreak havoc on lovers' lives as well as their own.[14]

In "Woman Hollering Creek," the short story written seven years after *The House on Mango Street*, Cisneros further problematizes the dichotomy between gender conditions in the United States and those in Mexico by juxtaposing the collision of two cultures and two countries in the rural Texas town of Seguin. As the story's protagonist travels from Mexico to the United States, it becomes obvious that the material conditions of domination and exploitation imposed on Mexican women in the United States are similar to those they seek to escape in the pueblos of Mexico.

In different ways and to different degrees, the women and men Sandra Cisneros portrays in her texts struggle to resist incorporation by the dominant class and culture. Additionally, the women of Mango Street and the women "hollering" their defiance against patriarchal constraints offer resistance strategies in the face of domination by Chicano and Mexicano men, as well as by the ruling class and dominant race. The configurations found in Cisneros's work elaborate in simple yet elegantly poetic language a theory of praxis in which activist Chicanas situate themselves as materialist feminists of color.

The stories in the collection present an explicit indication of Chicana feminismo popular, "popular feminism," a political position that moves beyond abstractions to praxis. Whereas critics of *Mango Street*, such as Rodríguez and Gutiérrez-Revuelta, have seen Cisneros as projecting her own fantasies through the adolescent Esperanza, in "Woman Hollering Creek" we see the scope of her overt political commitments.

As Gisela Espinosa Damián discusses in her essay "Feminism and Social Struggle in Mexico," the feminism of the 1970s simply did not address the situations of working-class and peasant women in Mexico and other Third World countries. Limited, for the most part, to bourgeois and petit bourgeois women, the feminist movement in Mexico was "isolated, ridiculed, and satanized" even though feminists had succeeded in calling attention to women's specific oppressions under capitalism (31). In the 1980s, however, the Women's Movement made a huge impact on working-class women when feminist activists went into the factories to discuss women's specific problems in the workplace. The tremors that reverberated from this new alliance between working-class, peasant, and "traditional" feminists ironically came as a result of the 1985 earthquake in Mexico City. Espinosa Damián chronicles the moment when "there emerged a movement of women whose wretched working conditions and high level of exploitation were revealed from the rubble of their workshops and factories: the dressmakers" (33). Out of the chaos and suffering endured by the masses in the aftermath of the earthquake, the Mexicanas organized as gendered workers with specific problems who required new ways of formulating their needs: "The opening-up of the women's question among poor and working class communities gave feminism a new dimension. If in the 1970s feminists were relentlessly denouncing the problem of the sexes, in the 1980s women from the exploited classes [were] seeking to incorporate demands and struggles, arising from their own particular forms of exploitation and oppression, into the popular movement in general, creating their own areas for discussion and new forms of organisation" (33).

The Mexican usage of the term *popular* underscores what Lynn Stephen, in "Popular Feminism in Mexico," calls "common marginalization," a label employed by several opposition movements. Stephen reports that

> Mexican women who are struggling to define popular feminism for themselves are looking to the harsh realities of their daily lives—economic problems in the household, long days of domestic work made worse by a lack of services and infrastructure, domestic violence, poor health and lack of control over their own bodies, and a life of work which has remained invisible—for tactics and strategies to develop a unified struggle around gender and class, without subordinating one to the other. Most women begin participating in Mexico's urban popular movement because of an awareness of their own economic condition and lack of material resources, not in relation to their oppression as women. (102)

The invisible "life of work" that Chicanas and Mexicanas share on both sides of the Mexico/U.S. border brings to light a new formulation of Chicana feminism. Cisneros makes the invisible discernible in "Woman Hollering Creek" as she writes about the struggles of these women as they come to consciousness about their oppression and exploitation in the domestic sphere. "Woman Hollering Creek" changes the subject of dominant discourse as a Mexican woman travels from passive victim who accepts the plots and heroines of romances to a woman who claims her agency as creator of stories and becomes what Norma Alarcón, in "Conjugating Subjects: The Heteroglossia of Essence and Resistance," calls a "speaking subject," or a feminist "subject in process."

After her own migrations as guest lecturer and visiting writer in residence at various universities in the late 1980s, Cisneros lived in Central Texas, mainly in San Antonio and Austin. Surrounded by Chicana community activists, writers, and artists, Cisneros identified with a group of Chicana "popular feminists" who struggled to change the literary scene as well as the lives of less privileged women around them.

In an informal interview, Cisneros told how these women indeed became "mujeres de fuerza" as they, in fact, ran an underground railroad for women, both Chicanas and recent Mexican immigrants, victimized by their men and by the economic collusion between the United States and Mexico on both sides of the border.[15]

"Woman Hollering Creek" is one outcome of Cisneros's commitment to popular feminism. The story offers several reasons why working-class and subproletariat women confined to the house are omitted by and subsequently remove themselves from feminist influence. In the cuento, ideological manipulation through mass media—the romance novel, the fotonovela (photo novel), and the telenovela (soap opera)—as well as through the male constructions of woman in the folk figure of La Llorona collude to keep women submissive.

When Gómez, Moraga, and Romo-Carmona, in their introduction to *Cuentos,* emphasized their literary roots within the oral tradition, they asserted the urgency of transforming the previously oral records of Latina literary artifacts into written form. Because those Latinas see themselves as marginalized exiles in danger of losing their historical and cultural records, they recognize the importance of interrupting the cultural hegemony of the U.S. literary establishment. Equally important is *how* Chicana feminist writers change oppressive literary forms (folklore) into something else. In "Woman Hollering Creek" that something else is the transformation of a tale of male dominance and female submission and treachery, the traditional tale of La Llorona, into a story of strong women who, in solidarity with one another, transform the powerless lament into a battle cry of resistance against male dominance.

As New Mestiza theorist in action, Cisneros confronts a major misogynist cultural legend, La Llorona, the Weeping Woman, and transforms her into a source of female power. In this frontera tale, a Mexican woman grows up on popular culture, the written and televised novelas and popular legends like that of La Llorona, and confronts what it takes to remove herself from the power they hold over her. Cisneros has told us that as a child constantly uprooted by family migrations between Mexico City and Chicago, always the new kid in school and in the neighborhood, she sought refuge in books. Clearly influenced by the fairy tales of her childhood, in this story Cisneros transforms the fairy tale of the prince who rescues the princess from the clutches of an evil man into a transfrontera feminist fable in which the prince who "saves" the heroine is a feminist in practice and could even be figured as a Chicana lesbian.[16] The sexual implications of this transformation as well as the reformulation of la familia lay the groundwork for new possibilities for women's sexuality in a culture that completely devalues women who stray from male-defined roles.

In addition to posing crucial questions about female sexuality and gender inequities within Mexican and Chicano culture, Cisneros exhibits her feminism on the border with her equally incisive critique of U.S. economic policies. Mexico's dependence on the United States extends far beyond its huge debt. That dependence is seen as well in its role as the supplier of surplus laborers both in the maquiladora (border factory) system and in its export of exploited laborers to the factories and agricultural fields of the United States. In the few years since Cisneros wrote this story, NAFTA (the North American Free Trade Agreement) has served as one more legally sanctioned economic mode to exploit female labor on the U.S. and Mexican sides of the border.

Since the 1970s, when Mexico imported the latest television technology from the United States, the Mexican masses have been inundated with consumer ideology as well as with morality tales that serve to keep women docile and poor women and men satisfied with their conditions of poverty as "just the way things are."[17] In Cleófilas, the protagonist of "Woman Hollering Creek" and a representative of the Mexican women who cross the border to el norte believing in the myth of the American Dream, we see how hegemony works.

The narrative begins with Cleófilas "safe" within her father's home; and in the opening scene of paternal protection, she anticipates a new life of material comfort and romance with her bridegroom in the United States. Encouraged by the foto- and telenovelas to believe that all spaces across the border are lined with gold, Cleófilas dreams of her crossing: "*Seguín*. She had liked the sound of it. Far away and lovely. Not like *Monclova*. *Coahuila*. Ugly. *Seguín, Tejas*. A nice sterling ring to it. The tinkle of money. She would get to wear outfits like the women on the *tele*, like Lucía Méndez. And have a lovely house, and wouldn't Chela be jealous" (45).

While Cleófilas's historia remains situated within the patriarchal structure of the family, Cisneros begins a subtle subversion of that structure. Cleófilas is totally immersed in a culture that encourages young women to believe that their goal in life is marriage and the children who will naturally and quickly follow. When Cleófilas sits with her son next to the creek of the story's title, she remembers her father's parting words as she prepared to leave Mexico proper with her new husband. Trained to believe that the husband, Juan Pedro, would fulfill all her romantic notions of love and that life in the United States would mean comparatively luxurious material comforts, Cleófilas instead finds herself three years later with an abusive husband, a child, and another on the way. Only now does she remember that her father told her he would always welcome her back "home."

Instead of the comfortable life she was told the United States would offer, she lives in isolation from the community of women she once knew across the border. But this transfrontera historia does not romanticize that Mexican community—the culture the women shared included communal lessons learned at the local movie house and from telenovelas. Ultimately, it is the media that construct a version of Mexican womanhood that informs the vision that for Cleófilas contains the true essence of love:

> But what Cleófilas has been waiting for, has been whispering and sighing and giggling for, has been anticipating since she was old enough to lean against the window displays of gauze and butterflies and lace, is passion. Not the kind on the cover of the *¡Alarma!* magazines, mind you, where the lover is photographed with the bloody fork she used to salvage her good name. But passion in its purest crystalline essence. The kind the books and songs and *telenovelas* describe when one finds, finally, the great love of one's life, and does whatever one can, must do, at whatever the cost. (44)

The mass media, in this case fotonovelas, telenovelas, and revistas femeninas (women's magazines), all shape women's consciousness and their limited knowledge of the world.[18] In Mexico, the fotonovela and the telenovela target the barely literate working poor who usually do not have more than a grammar school education.

Cleófilas and her girlfriends learn their place within the class system from such telenovelas as the immensely popular *Los ricos también lloran*, which Cisneros translates as "And the Rich Also Cry."[19] As Cleófilas testifies, women in Mexico "watch the latest telenovela episode and try to copy the way the women comb their hair, wear their makeup" (44). Favorite telenovela actresses such as Lucía Méndez also peddle products in the commercials; their hairstyles (and often their bleached-blonde hair) and "fashionable" attire are indeed emulated throughout the Mexican Republic:

> *Tú o Nadie.* "You or No One." The title of the current favorite *telenovela*. The beautiful Lucía Méndez having to put up with all kinds of hardships

of the heart, separation and betrayal, and loving, always loving no matter what, because *that* is the most important thing, and did you see
Lucía Méndez in the Bayer aspirin commercials—wasn't she lovely?
Does she dye her hair do you think? Cleófilas is going to go to the
farmacia and buy a hair rinse; her girlfriend Chela will apply it—it's not
that difficult at all. (44)

As Jean Franco states in her essay on popular narratives in Mexico,
"The Incorporation of Women," "Mass culture narrative guides
women through the social labyrinth. . . . There are various plots which
may be differentiated according to what it is that women are being
asked to sacrifice. In the case of romantic fiction, women are asked to
sacrifice their intelligence, whereas in the comic strip novels they often
sacrifice romance" (123).

As consumer of both forms, Cleófilas finds she must sacrifice both
her intelligence and any hope of romance. Immediately after her marriage and ensuing isolation in rural Seguin, Cleófilas must put the lessons provided by the novelas into practice when her husband asserts
his role as head of the family through the power of his fists. Like the
heroine of the novelas, Cleófilas endures Juan Pedro's blows "until the
lip split and bled an orchid of blood, she didn't fight back, she didn't
break into tears, she didn't run away as she imagined she might when
she saw such things in the telenovelas" (47). She responds exactly as
the tele programmed her to do; she accepts her place and her submission to "this man, this father, this rival, this keeper, this lord, this
master, this husband til kingdom come" (49).

While Cleófilas wants to believe the message to which the popular
culture urges her to adhere, her reality with Juan Pedro, the husband
who becomes the sign for the type of abusive men Cisneros relentlessly
exposed in *Mango Street*, demands different alternatives. Alternative
discourses, however, are not readily available to her. Cleófilas disdains
the sexually explicit *¡Alarma!* magazines because they purport to be
based on "real cases." In her case, to ensure pleasure and a sense of
safety, her reading material should not resemble the reality of the men
she knows, men like Juan Pedro's best friend, Maximiliano, "who was
said to have killed his wife in an ice-house brawl when she came at
him with a mop. I had to shoot, he had said—she was armed" (51).

The obscenity that these men represent to Cleófilas appears glorified
in the *¡Alarma! ¡Casos reales!* magazines. These often sexually explicit
fotonovelas gush their class- and sex-role contradictions. An examination of one such story, *¡El infiel!*, reveals that the titular exclamation

points are faithful indications of the alarming and sensational bent of these publications.

The cover page of the story, ostensibly about adultery, exclaims that "Because of sexual passion he lost his family!" *The Unfaithful One!* actually espouses female/maternal sacrifice above all else (Figure 1). But the husband's infidelities merely provide an opportunity to include photos of women in various states of undress and graphic pictures of the adulterous couple in bed, with the husband enjoying the "youthful and vibrant flesh" that his mistress "unhesitatingly offered him" (Figures 2 and 3). The emphasis on the lover's youthful flesh is a comment on the wife's folly at having married a much younger man. When the wife, Rosalia, discovers proof of her husband's adultery, she merely examines herself in the mirror and decides, "Perhaps I *have* become ugly . . . I no longer please him?" She relies on her cultural script as proper wife and figures that as long as he "respects my house," she will tolerate his mistress. Nonetheless, Rosalia confronts the errant husband, Raúl, that night, and the narrative captions underscore his "arrogance and stupidity" because of his "muy macho" attitude.

Rosalia's mother-in-law embodies the voice of tradition, the maternal patriarch, urging her to do as women must and "close [her] eyes" to things she cannot change; after all, "Raúl es hombre" [Raúl is a man]. When Raúl dallies with his mistress while his wife is giving birth to their son, Rodolfo, Rosalia decides that her destiny as a woman—motherhood—will be her strength: "Ya soy mujer y sabré luchar sola por mi hijo [Now I am a woman and I will know how to struggle alone for my son]." (Figure 4). What the reader is encouraged to see as Rosalia's feminism is a reduction to maternal "instinct," which remains bound by traditional patriarchal constraints: her duty is now as a mother to a male child rather than as a wife to her husband.

When Raúl dares bring his mistress to his son's second birthday celebration, Rosalia strikes an uncharacteristically passive Raúl and immediately decides on divorce (Figure 5). Given that Raúl has already been plotted as macho, his failure to retaliate physically speaks volumes about the genre. Raúl has broken the unspoken condition that he "respect" Rosalia's house. Once again the mother-in-law serves as the voice of paternalistic traditions, urging Rosalia to do as she herself did with Raúl's father: "All wives are supposed to be dedicated and long-suffering." The reader is led to understand that it was this very tolerance of her husband's infidelities that made Raúl the "infiel" that he is.

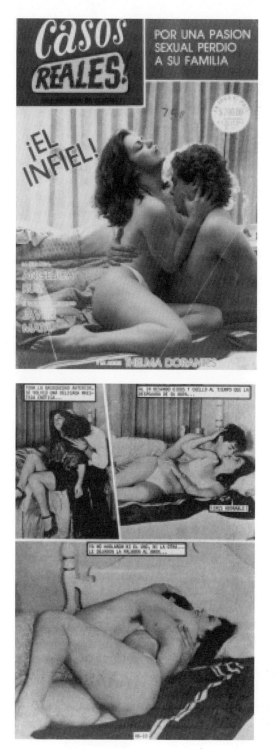

Figure 1. From *¡Casos reales!*, no. 86 (17 May 1988). Courtesy Hermanos Cia. Editorial.

Figure 2. From *¡Casos reales!*, no. 86 (17 May 1988). Courtesy Hermanos Cia. Editorial.

Figure 3. From *¡Casos reales!*, no. 86 (17 May 1988). Courtesy Hermanos Cia. Editorial.

Figure 4. From *¡Casos reales!*, no. 86 (17 May 1988). Courtesy Hermanos Cia. Editorial.

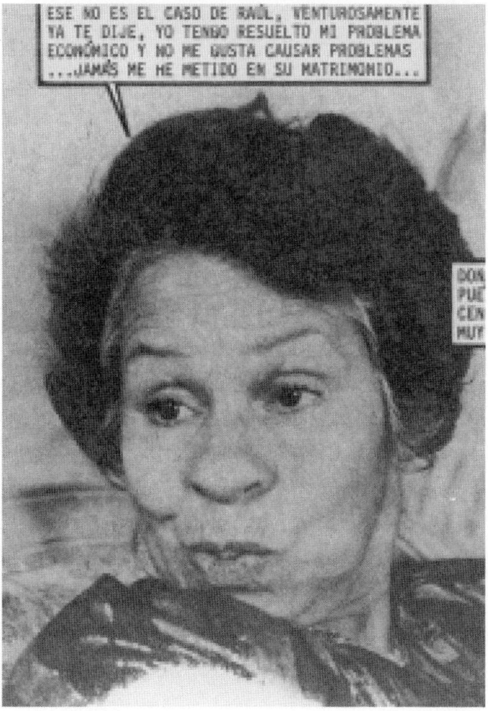

Figure 5. From *¡Casos reales!,* no. 86 (17 May 1988). Courtesy Hermanos Cia. Editorial.

Figure 6. From *¡Casos reales!,* no. 86 (17 May 1988). Courtesy Hermanos Cia. Editorial.

The narrative unambiguously blames the women for their men's de-based character.

From one photo to the next, sixteen years pass. Rosalia is now gray-haired. Rodolfo, a fine example of true manhood, rejects his long-lost grandmother's attempt to bribe him with money and chooses instead to stay with his humble mother. The photos, however, show that theirs is an extremely comfortable middle-class existence. Rosalia claims to consider herself not a "heroine or martyr" but simply a woman who dedicated her life to her son.

A reader searching for the "true essence of love" might be disturbed by the cynical presentation of Raúl as "arrogant and stupid" in his machismo. Also disturbing would be the version of feminism that Ros-alia's character seems to represent. In spite of the clear critique of Raúl's transgressions and the obvious caricature of the mother-in-law as rep-resentative of the old customs that urged women's tolerance of men's "escapades," the fotonovela does nothing to promote women's role in any different configuration (Figure 6). While encouraging women not to tolerate men's sexual infidelities, it merely transfers women's duties to the role of supermother.

Even as Cleófilas witnesses the men around her behaving like Raúl, she refuses to acknowledge the blatant contradictions in the "true sto-ries" of ¡Casos reales! Her refusal to read the text hints at her realization that the plot against her lies in the very institution of marriage and familia. Jean Franco points out that the thematically similar texts, libros semanales, comic strip novels, "focus. . . not so much on women as on the family as an institution" ("Incorporation of Women," 133). Franco continues:

> Both the romance and the libro semanal plot the incorporation of women into society, though the libro semanal may ultimately be more insidious, since it sanctions economic exploitation in the guise of eman-cipation from the violence and oppression of working class males. In any case, what is crucially missing from mass literature is any form of female solidarity; the plots of both types of narratives reinforce the se-rialization of women—the very factor that makes their exploitation, both as reproducers of the labor force and as cheap labor, so viable even in corporate society. (137)

Isolated in Seguin, Texas, Cleófilas faces the violence she glimpsed in the fotonovelas and witnessed in the telenovelas, but she can no longer watch them for solace with her telecompañeras. Her husband cannot even afford to buy them a television set; the "good job" with a beer or tire company is actually a menial job at the local icehouse bar/cantina. Cleófilas next attempts to escape by devouring romances by the popular author Corín Tellado.

In Virginia Erhart's detailed study of these romance novels, "Amor, ideología y enmascaramiento en Corín Tellado," she reveals that Tellado provides her readers detailed descriptions of her upper-class characters' clothing, going to great pains to name the individual designers they patronize. Erhart further points out that love and consumption of luxury items are always linked in the Tellado romances.

Clearly, the media's mission is to transform the largely female audience into consumers, both of material products and, worse, of a conservative ideology: the traditional configuration of the family; women's inherent passivity and fatalism; promises of upward mobility; and, ultimately, sacrifices rewarded either in their children's success (as in the case of *¡El infiel!*) or in the afterlife (as the other religion promises).

The Tellado romances and the telenovelas that Cleófilas consumes encourage her to ignore her own class limitations. Mexican romances, as well as Mexican romance readers, however, prove the exceptions to Janice Radway's conclusions in her classic study *Reading the Romance*. Radway goes to great pains not to impose elitist judgments on the group of Euro-American romance readers she studies, but her conclusions, instructive as they are, elide the fact that her subjects were comparatively wealthy, middle-class, U.S. white women. Radway's romance readers can afford to indulge in pure escape; Tellado's readers are taught to believe in a social fantasy in which anyone can live anywhere in the world and succeed financially. In a dissonant strategy, Radway cites the Chicano scholar José Limón in her assertion that the romance readers' escape is in itself an oppositional strategy against the demands of the patriarchy. She claims that the act of making time to read the romances in spite of the derision by husbands and society at large is an instance of "counter-valuation"—"a process of inversion whereby the original socioeconomic limitations and devaluations of a subordinate group are first addressed by the folkloric performance and then transformed within or by it into something of value to the group" (211–12). Radway admits, however, that the women she studied never transformed anything about their individual middle-class existences. Though I do not place greater value on the Mexican women's circumstances, I do stress the *difference* in their situation as women of color who are at greater risk of economic exploitation and male violence as a result of race and class inequities. Cleófilas's performance as a consumer of the novelas and the Tellado romances never "counter-valu-ates" her subjugation as battered wife.

Fearing the "reactionary and conformist" power of the Tellado nov-els, which predate Harlequin romances by about a decade, Virginia Erhart points out that they preach absolute moral order while obscur-ing class and marital conflict and asserting that marriage and love serve to level socioeconomic differences as they additionally mask the sexual ("Amor, ideología y enmascaramiento," 93).

But for Cleófilas, who reads the Tellado novelas as primers for her future as wife and as self-help manuals that feed her aspirations to upward mobility, the romances are most insidious in their denial of race, class, and cultural differences. Tellado's tomes, as Erhart also ob-serves, erase national boundaries as they encourage readers to assume that their lives and customs in Latin America are universal. Tellado's ahistorical narratives urge the reader to imagine that her world is the only one "possible, a strategy that distances all troubling questions she may have about the order in which she finds herself. It is not about there being other systems—good, bad, or at least possible; what results is that either they are eliminated or she renders the differences so in-significant that they can easily be disdained" (101; my translation).

Cleófilas has an opportunity to marry a man who works in the United States, but she is unclear about whether he works for a beer company or a tire company, but she is confident that he "has a very important position in Seguín" (45). Her limited education does not allow her to question "proper" documentation of their legal status as immigrants to the United States; it does encourage her to imagine a life with unlimited economic possibilities. What she gets instead is a man and a life firmly situated within static gender and class posi-tions:

> She has to remind herself why she loves him when she changes the
> baby's Pampers, or when she mops the bathroom floor, or tries to make
> curtains for the doorways without doors, or whiten the linen. Or won-
> der a little when he kicks the refrigerator and says he hates this shitty
> house and is going out where he won't be bothered with the baby's
> howling and her suspicious questions, and her requests to fix this and
> this and this because if she had any brains in her head she'd realize he's
> been up before the rooster earning his living to pay for the food in her
> belly and the roof over her head and would have to wake up again early
> the next day so why can't you just leave me in peace, woman. (49)

Cleófilas believes she has no alternative but to stay with this man, regardless of the physical and mental abuse she suffers at his hands.

She remains until the day his actions force her to reanalyze her constructed fantasies of what it means to be a woman: "He had thrown a book. Hers. From across the room. A hot welt across the cheek. She could forgive that. But what stung more was the fact it was *her* book, a love story by Corín Tellado, what she loved more now that she lived in the U.S., without a television set, without the telenovelas" (52).

From Fotonovelas to Folktales

The dreams fashioned by the Tellado romances and the telenovelas are literally thrown at Cleófilas by the man who can never live up to her expectations. But what keeps her story from becoming a parody of novelas like *¡El infiel!* is Cisneros's refusal to give us a facile, uncomplicated happy ending. Unlike Rosalia in the fotonovela, Cleófilas is not magically transformed into a self-sacrificing but solid career woman from one page to the next. Her reality is that she is once again pregnant and has nowhere to turn except back to Mexico and "the chores that never ended, six good-for-nothing brothers, and one old man's complaints" (44).

What Cisneros does offer is the possibility of social change through communal female solidarity. Cleófilas's decision to return to Mexico and her father's house does not give us a utopian reading; nor does it do something worse: turn to the Third World and to Third World women for a quick solution to what will inevitably be a long historical process.[20] Yet Cleófilas's story undeniably signals an alternative vision.

Cleófilas circles back to the other oral tradition that informed her consciousness as a woman—the legend of La Llorona. And here is where Cisneros presents an overtly feminist revision of a powerful cultural plot. The cuento plots out how the oral tradition (the Llorona legend) and secondary orality (the cultural productions of the fotonovelas, telenovelas, and romances) join to coerce Cleófilas.

Jean Franco reminds us that the romance and the telenovela rely on formulas that connect them with "orally transmitted tales" ("Incorporation of Women," 126). The foto- and telenovelas are in fact what Walter Ong, in *Orality and Literacy,* called "secondary orality": in "present-day high technology culture, . . . a new orality is sustained by telephone, radio, television, and other electronic devices that depend for their existence and functioning on writing and print" (11).

Cleófilas, like most Mexican and Mexican American women of her class, constructs her idea of women's place in the world through the versions of female behavior provided by men and male-identified women. In addition to the new orality of the media, she must contend with the legend of La Llorona. Now Cleófilas lives up to her name as she becomes a daughter of history.[21] There have been many studies of the Llorona folktale, some of them linking her to the European Medea story; yet no one to my knowledge has discussed this story's overtly feminist implications and its similarity to stories of infanticide in the African American tradition.[22]

In "Mexican Legendry and the Rise of the Mestizo," Américo Paredes calls legends "ego-supporting devices"; they "may appeal to the group or to individuals by affording them pride, dignity, and self-esteem: local or national heroes to identify with, for example. . . . Whether in doing so they validate or challenge the social structure, ease tensions or exacerbate them is beside the point" (98). Paredes correctly points out that "frustration and defeat" feed the ego as well as "victory and conformity" do. He examines Mexican legends in order to construct the uniquely *Mexican* national character of the mestizo; that is, "the distinctive blend of Spaniard and Indian, with contributions by the Negro and other ethnic groups" (98). The legend of La Llorona contains such a story of mestizaje, of miscegenation, which Paredes locates within Hernán Cortés's conquest of Mexico.

An audience more familiar with European narratives than with Aztec or other indigenous tales of the Americas can find analogies, as Paredes does, in Euripides' *Medea* and Puccini's *Madama Butterfly* (103).[23] The legend grafts European traditions about women's vengeance against men onto indigenous pre-Columbian myths:

> The literary legend of La Llorona struck deep roots in Mexican tradition because it was grafted on an Indian legend cycle about the supernatural woman who seduces men when they are out alone on the roads or working in the fields. At times she destroys her lovers after giving herself to them, but often she is helpful as well as passionate and may make a man's fortune or help him raise a fine crop of corn. She is *matlacihua* or Woman of the Nets among the Nahuatl speakers, and other language groups such as the Mexes and the Popolucas know her by other names. As *la segua*, she has been reported as far north as Texas, and she is also known as far south as Panama. (103)

José Limón, in "La Llorona, the Third Legend of Greater Mexico," suggests that La Llorona, after La Malinche and la Virgen de Guadalupe, is the "third, comparatively unacknowledged, major female symbol of Greater Mexican socio-cultural life" (2). Drawing on Marxist and feminist theories, he grounds her story in "concrete historical experience." He agrees with Bacil Kirtley that the legend also grafts her onto "another distinctive Indian legend, that of Cihuacoatl, the Aztec goddess, who, according to Sahagún, appeared in the night crying out for dead children" (10). According to Limón,

> What the Europeans seem to add are the motifs of (1) a woman with children (2) betrayed by an adulterous lover, their father, followed by (3) insane revenge infanticide in which she is typically the killer, concluding with her anguished repentance during which she cries for her children.... The indigenous peoples seem to add (1) an *Indian* woman sometimes in a flowing white dress, (2) crying *in the night*, (3) near a body of water (an important element in Aztec mythology) and (4) meeting people, mostly men who are shocked when they see her. (11)

In Cisneros's story, La Llorona functions as an unspoken, perhaps unspeakable presence for Cleófilas. Trusting that her audience will know the plot of the legend, Cisneros need only have her character be drawn to a creek whose name only hints at the Spanish name Llorona; it has become Woman Hollering. It is not accidental that in this New Mestiza retelling, the woman is no longer weeping but hollering. Cleófilas's betrayal both by her man and by the promises of the mass media sends her to the creek with her infant son. Whether or not she considers drowning the child in revenge for Juan Pedro's violence and infidelities we are not told. For Chicana readers, however, the force of the legend's trajectory to infanticide is too strong to resist.

The variant of the Llorona legend that I grew up with in Brownsville was emphatically aimed at frightening boys and men. In the stories I heard from grandmothers and the many women who crossed the bridge to Brownsville from Matamoros to labor as domestics in Mexican American and Anglo homes, La Llorona's appearances were always near a body of water: a lake, an arroyo, the resacas of Brownsville, or the levee on the banks of the Rio Grande. I found it pleasurable to listen to these Mexican ghost stories and did not feel particularly frightened by them; it was the males, after all, who were the ones threatened by Llorona. She appeared to men who were ready to sexually betray their wives or girlfriends. The moral of the story was always that the men to whom she appeared deserved to be frightened to death because of their disregard for women and the patriarchal rules they had established. After the part where the storyteller (in my memory, always a

woman) informed her audience of the most recent appearance of Llorona, usually to a comadre's friend or distant relative, she would sometimes go into Llorona's history.

That history, I now understand, was the history of the conquest of
Mexico by the Spanish forces. While I understand that, technically,
these two legends are distinct, in the variants I heard as a child, Llorona
and La Malinche were the same figure. La Malinche was the indigenous
woman who was sold into slavery, and, as a slave, was given to Hernán
Cortés. Male historiography has it that she was Cortés's mistress. As
his slave, she used her proficiency at languages and became his translator and eventually bore him a child. As a result, the woman popularly
known as Malinche, Malintzín Tenépal, has been blamed for the Spaniards' conquest of Mexico. To be a malinchista is to be a traitor to
Mexico or to Mexican customs. La Llorona murdered her children
because she was betrayed by a Spanish "gentleman"; La Malinche symbolically murdered her "children," the Indian tribes that Cortés and the
Spanish conquistadores massacred.[24]

The storytellers of my youth insisted on portraying La Llorona sym-
pathetically. She was a young woman, either mestiza or Indian, who
was engañada (fooled) into betraying her race and herself by "marry-
ing" a wealthy Spaniard who would leave her for a woman of his own
race and class. Llorona drowns her children when she learns that he
intends to take them away (to Spain?). Since the storytellers of my
childhood were working-class women, their versions of the story never
stated that the children were being "saved" by their father or that he
was sending them off for proper education; rather, he was taking them
to *work* on one of his ranchos. As I read more on the history of the
conquest, I realized that the story I heard as a child was a version of
the enslavement of the indigenous Mexicans; the infanticide is what I
now recognize as a political act of resistance by mestiza indigenous
women.

If the creek indeed calls to Cleófilas, it is a more contemporary variant of the legend that Cisneros creates from the present historical moment. Drawing on the current impulse of feminist revisions of women's
roles, Cisneros's revision offers the possibility of seeing Llorona as a
powerful woman who *encourages* new alternatives to old discourses.
Instead of a stereotypical view of Mexican women as passively accepting male violence, we get resistance and action through Cleófilas's contact with a society of women.

Limón concludes that by killing her children La Llorona "symbolically destroys the familial basis for patriarchy" ("*La Llorona*," 20). But then she returns to search for those children at the lake where she drowned them. Limón, citing Freud, asserts that water is closely associated with birth and rebirth: "As such, I submit that *la llorona* offers us a fascinating paradox: the symbolic destruction of the nuclear family at one stage but also, the later possible restoration of her maternal bonds from the waters of rebirth which one must conclude will also heal her patriarchally induced insanity. And . . . it points to the interesting image of a restored world of love in which men—at least men as she experienced them—are absent" (20).

Another feminist reading, however, would remind us that water is a common mythological residence of female spirits and a place of power and transformation. Both Cleófilas and Llorona are drawn to water. Instead of using the traditional (male) Freudian equation of water with birth and rebirth (actually birth *of* men *by* men), it seems more appropriate to turn to a female source: the Aztec goddesses associated with water. What we find transforms the water motif into a site where women can find refuge from the forces of hegemony.[25] Llorona's act of infanticide in the traditional legend, then, can be read as an extreme act of resistance in the face of the barbarity of "el desastre" (the disaster), the conquest of Mexico and the ensuing rape and murder of indigenous people. Like the women in the slave narratives compiled by African Americanist scholars and in Toni Morrison's *Beloved,* who kill their children rather than have them live under slavery, an alternative discourse for La Llorona would have her drown her children rather than submit them to the slavery of the conquest.[26] The infanticide is not an act by an "insane" or "insanely jealous" woman; rather, it is a rational, political act of opposition against the Spanish colonizers.

In Cisneros's story, Cleófilas does not murder her son, but her decision to return to Mexico would signal to many Mexicans of her class the murder of her children's futures. What Cisneros presents is an overtly feminist revision of a powerful misogynist folktale. Given the opportunity to meet some women who have the means of helping victims of physical abuse—the Chicanas that she meets through the obstetrical clinic—Cleófilas begins to take control of her historia. Cisneros shows how feminist solidarity, the feminismo popular in which many Chicanas of the U.S. borderlands and Mexicanas in Greater Mexico engage, puts theory into practice and begins to cross both the geopolitical border and class lines.

Cleófilas becomes a *producer* of meaning rather than merely a consumer of dominant ideology—transforming herself from the *object* of dominant discourse to the *agent* of an alternative vision. As Felice, a Chicana whose sexual identity is pointedly ambiguous, drives Cleófilas to the bus that will take her back to Mexico, Cleófilas observes a different picture of how to be a woman:

> When they drove across the arroyo, the driver opened her mouth and let out a yell as loud as any mariachi. Which startled not only Cleófilas, but Juan Pedrito as well.
>
> Should've warned you. Every time I cross that bridge I do that. Because of the name, you know. Woman Hollering. Pues, I holler. She said this in a Spanish pocked with English and laughed. Did you ever notice, Felice continued, how nothing around here is named after a woman. Really. Unless she's the Virgin. I guess you're only famous if you're a virgin. She was laughing again. That's why I like the name of that arroyo. Makes you want to holler like Tarzan, right?
>
> Everything about this woman, this Felice, amazed Cleófilas. The fact that she drove a pickup. A pickup mind you, but when Cleófilas asked if it was her husband's, she had said she didn't have a husband. The pickup was hers. She herself had chosen it. She herself was paying for it.
>
> I used to have a Pontiac Sunbird. But those cars are for viejas. Pussy cars. Now this here is a *real* car.
>
> What kind of talk was that coming from a woman, Cleófilas thought. But then again, Felice was like no woman she'd ever met. Can you imagine. When we crossed the arroyo she just started yelling like a crazy, *she would say later to her father and brothers*. Just like that. Who would've thought? (56; emphasis added)

Cleófilas returns to Mexico, her material condition relatively unaltered. She returns to her father and brothers, to familia, a subject in process, telling stories that might include the activist Chicana feminists at the obstetrical clinic. Reading Felice as a woman who transgresses scripted gender roles also opens up a radical political trajectory for this text. Felice owns a pickup truck, she is not connected to a husband, and she dares to "holler" rather than weep. Her willingness to transport Cleófilas signals a woman "like no woman she'd ever met" (56). Felice embodies the Chicana feminist that Cherríe Moraga envisioned ten years before this story was published. In Moraga's words, "this is what being a Chicana feminist means—making bold and political the love of the women of our race" (*Loving in the War Years,* 139). Cleófilas correctly reads Felice as a "different" kind of woman. As a Chicana feminist reader of the Chicana feminist novela, however, I read Felice's difference either as lesbian or as a heterosexual woman-identified woman who, as in Cisneros's poem "Loose Woman," rejects homophobic, misogynistic Chicano community roles that naturalize heterosexuality:

> They say I'm a *macha*, hell on wheels,
> *viva la vulva*, fire and brimstone,
> man-hating, devastating,
> boogey-woman lesbian.
> Not necessarily,
> but I like the compliment. (112)

In "Woman Hollering Creek," Sandra Cisneros skillfully rewrites la novela. But in this subversive novela, Felice, a politically active Chicana who defies heterosexual and lesbian labels but who flaunts her feminist politics, hints at the possibility that Cleófilas can cross over to her compañeras in Mexico with "hollering" narratives, new legends that have the power to change the subject of the old Llorona laments and other ultimately misogynist plots. As readers of these contemporary Chicana feminist novelas, we, like Cleófilas, can hear the hollering of mujeres de fuerza and begin to reconsider what "Ya soy mujer" signifies.

5

"I Hear the Women's Wails and I Know Them to Be My Own"

From Mujer to Collective Identities in Helena María Viramontes's U.S. Third World

By 1985, more Chicana feminists had smuggled new words into U.S. publishing houses. Among the women's texts published by Arte Público was Helena María Viramontes's first collected cuentos, *The Moths and Other Stories*. These short stories elaborate on the transformation of narrative form and the mobilization of Chicana aesthetics by activist writers in the service of social change. For Viramontes, aesthetics is a *practice* of political *intervention* carried out in literary form.[1] Viramontes, a daughter of the working class, transforms her class instinct into a political position.[2] Her literary discourse springs from her perception of the social and political domains of many fronterista Chicanas. Moreover, Viramontes utilizes a profoundly moving Chicana vernacular in the service of subaltern political aesthetics. Her literary intervention chronicles previously contained experiences of life on the border. These transfrontera (transnational) texts capture the struggles endured by newly arrived Latina/o immigrants inhabiting the crowded tenements of urban barrios and border towns.

The border, in this feminist articulation, cuts through the Anzaldúan open wound I discussed in Chapter 3. The geopolitical border for Viramontes manifests itself in constructed gender barriers within traditional Mexican-origin family units. In the Americas, the border enforces the class system as well as the legal manifestations of race discrimination. If the guarded U.S.–Mexico border es una herida abierta, as in Anzaldúa's figuration, the women whom Viramontes narrativizes hemorrhage the brutality of fathers, husbands, unfaithful lovers, and male-identified women. In this other view of the Chicana borderlands, women as well as men endure the blows from the military might of the local militia, in their incarnations as both INS Border Patrol agents and local police forces.[3]

While Viramontes's cuentos draw on oral traditions, they transform these traditional cautionary tales of women's instability, such as the legend of La Llorona. In border feminist art, the Llorona of Chicana feminists no longer figures as enemy or as victim. Chicana border feminism, feminismo fronteriza, narrativizes the weeping woman's hysterical laments into historically based, residual memories of the disastrous encounter between sixteenth-century indigenous America and Europe's conquerors.[4] Feminist writers on the border forge complex narratives that bring to bear the nuances of the theories of intersectionality.[5] While Viramontes centers much of this collection on women's positions in Chicano or Mexican family structures, with "The Cariboo Cafe" she ultimately moves toward what Gayatri Spivak calls "identitarian collectivities."[6]

Many of her stories in the collection are feminist statements on the status of women within la familia in Chicana/o communities. The narratives transform the concept of familia in the same way that the infusion of Central American refugees fleeing civil wars transforms already politically diverse Mexican-origin communities. What were once predominantly Mexican American barrios are now international Latina/o communities within the borders of the United States.[7] The new immigrants bring with them histories, political affiliations, and cultural practices that form constellations, narratives closely paralleling those of Americans of Mexican origin.

Moreover, Viramontes's stories intervene in Chicano nationalist debates within communities of Chicana/o scholars, academics, and activists. Chicana feminists on the border challenge the perception of a monolithic Chicano identity within the construct of the family unit. *The Moths and Other Stories* narrativizes and complicates the internal debates among women who believe that questioning male dominance means the destruction of "sacred truths," and among feminist Chicanas who insist on addressing gender oppression and exploitation in the community as issues connected to analyses of race and class.

Although the collection of stories contains separate and distinct narratives, taken as a whole it reveals a larger story that examines how Chicanas are cast into what Norma Alarcón identifies as the symbolic contract in which *mujer* becomes a curse.[8] Seven of the eight stories present explicitly Chicana/o characters and situations; Viramontes un-ravels her internationalist vision in "The Cariboo Cafe," a complex story that propels feminism on the border into its transnational trajec-tory by showing the emergence of Los Angeles as a U.S. Third World city. The urban maze in this narrative localizes U.S. policies that sup-port repressive dictatorships in Central America. The actions of U.S.-trained armies bleed through the frontera to stain people in countries like El Salvador, Honduras, and Guatemala, and Mexican regions such as Chiapas.

When Viramontes deconstructs a monolithic Chicano familia, she crosses the border south of Mexico to create a political familia. She infiltrates her study of Chicano and Chicana experiences with the similar yet different stories of the aboriginal Americans as she aligns Chicana feminists with political exiles. Her rearticulation of Chicana identity politics points to a new mode of expression, el testimonio. Viramontes's collection gives urgent testimony using the contraband words of the frontera vernacular. With that action, Helena María Vir-amontes's literary production embodies feminism on the border.

Chicano Nationalism, Familia, and Machismo

As I discussed in Chapter 2, Chicanas active in the Chi-cano movement of the 1960s and 1970s were often at the center of internal contradictions and conflicts. Chicana feminists addressed the sexual inequities inherent in a homophobic and phallocentric nation-alist movement whose emphasis on family unity and the concept of carnalismo (brotherhood) implicitly omitted women from egalitarian positions of power within the liberation movement. Heterosexual and lesbian Chicana feminists in that historical theater were cast as traitors to the mestizo community or demeaned as Anglicized and acculturated by homophobic and misogynist cultural nationalists.[9] The hegemony of the Chicano caciques (chieftains) within the Movement called for Chicanas to produce a counterhegemony that interfered with the phal-logocentric reproduction of domination. Their interventions chronicle Chicana feminists' resistance to a lived hegemony, which Raymond Williams describes as "a process that does not just passively exist as a form of dominance. It has to be renewed, recreated, defended, and modified. It is also continually resisted, limited, altered, challenged by pressures not all its own" (*Marxism and Literature,* 112). This alternative hegemony produced by feminists on the border resists both racism and class exploitation by Anglo-Americans as it resists androcentric Chicano domination on the basis of gender and sexuality.

Viramontes's project in *The Moths and Other Stories* gives historical context and voice to the women that many Chicano writers silence through the appropriation of female historicity. Further, as the narratives challenge uncritical views of "the" traditional Chicano family, they offer an altered version of *familia* that makes more sense in a world where governments and politicians continue to exert power over women's bodies while they proudly proclaim their adherence to family values. Advocates of a monolithic, static tradition exploit and destroy members of families who do not conform to a reactionary political agenda or whose class positions or ethnicity and race automatically disqualify them from inclusion in a brotherhood of Anglo America.

Since the early 1970s, Chicano and Chicana social scientists have been producing revisionist studies that disprove the debilitating stereotypes of Chicano family pathology, machismo, and the Chicana passivity of la mujer sufrida, the longsuffering mother/wife—all of which were promoted in earlier studies conducted by Anglo-American and Mexican (national) social scientists.[10] Maxine Baca Zinn's essay "Political Familism: Toward Sex Role Equality in Chicano Families" serves as an intriguing Chicana intervention in those studies of "the" Chicano family structure. In this modified nationalist theory, the Chicano family structure acts as a tool for resistance against the dominant group. This position rejects other views that credit the gradual transformation of rigid family customs in the Chicano community to the positive forces of acculturation to American life. Baca Zinn alleges that if the traditional family enacts transformations, they are one result of Chicanas' new participation in the liberatory politics of the Chicano Movement. Infused with the optimism allowed by her historical moment of 1975, Baca Zinn offers an analysis based on what contemporary social scientists identify as the "internal colonialism" model.[11] She asks that studies move from the assimilation model and turn to

> a perspective which includes the concepts of oppression, opposition and change. The internal colonialism framework best incorporates these notions. This framework, based on similarities between classic colonialism and oppression of racial groups in the U.S. posits that the subordination of Chicanos is the result of oppression by a dominant Anglo minority. It also posits inevitable opposition by those groups subject to racial subordination. In this resistance and opposition to colonial status we

find conditions specifically relevant to changing familial patterns occur-
ring among Chicanos. (15)

History, however, shows what Baca Zinn could not foresee in the
mid-1970s. When she speculated that Chicanas' work within the nationalist Movimiento would inevitably alter the way women are perceived within the Chicano community, she assumed that the power of
the Movement would extend to the majority of Mexican American or
Chicano families in the United States. Her analysis does not address
the multitude of women who for various reasons had no access to the
nationalist group's proposals. For countless isolated Chicanas, in both
the rural and urban terrains of the borderlands, economic limitations,
undereducation, and entrenchment within a masculinist family structure impeded participation in organizations that were considered radical and dangerous. With the good faith that many activist mujeres of
the Movimiento exhibited, Baca Zinn trusted that "La familia de la
Raza" and "carnalismo" would unite all Chicanos in a new type of
family. Her miscalculation lies in the tendency to rely on a constructed,
monolithic Chicano familia, and in the inability, at that historical moment, to conceptualize a female *a* in *Chican*A. She claims that "orga-
nizational commitment to total family involvement in the Chicano
Movement results in new patterns of behavior as women take part in
Movement activities," but she offers no specific examples of recon-
structed, egalitarian families.

Baca Zinn comprehends, however, that activist women can begin to
think of a distinct "women's consciousness" (19). Moreover, she realizes that many Chicanas "find themselves in the ambiguous position of
consciously striving to alter traditional subordinate roles while at the
same time having to defend Chicano cultural conditions" (21). At the
conclusion of this pathbreaking essay, Baca Zinn valiantly attempts to
defend the concept of machismo with the standard apologia of Movimiento rhetoric. Her response reacts to the dominant social science
literature that blamed Chicanos' low socioeconomic position in the
United States on a cult of machismo that reflected Mexican males'
inherent traits of "irresponsibility, inferiority, and ineptitude" (22).
Machismo, in this construction, is men's overcompensation for psychological feelings of "inadequacy and worthlessness" (22). Rather than
rely on stereotype, she proposes that the ideology of machismo be
liberated, reclaimed, and redefined by Chicanos themselves:

> Such an investigation would undoubtedly yield some indication of the
> positive dimensions of machismo. This approach may enable us to ask

questions that would lead to an understanding of male dominance and aggression of the oppressed as a *calculated* response to hostility, exclusion, and racial domination in a colonized society. It is possible that aggressive behavior of Chicano males has been both an affirmation of Mexican cultural identity and an expression of their conscious rejection of the dominant society's definition of Mexicans as passive, lazy, and indifferent. (23)

Baca Zinn concludes her study with individual objections by Chicanas dissatisfied with their subordination within the Movimiento. The final paragraphs clash with the earlier defense. In one final attempt to unify women's growing discontent within a masculinist liberation movement, she turns to the Movimiento theoretician Armando Rendón. In his *Chicano Manifesto* (1971), he attempts to transform static notions of manhood into politically useful moves toward shifting categories of Chicanohood. For Rendón, machismo "is in fact an underlying drive of the gathering identification of Mexican Americans which goes beyond a recognition of common troubles. The Chicano revolt is a manifestation of Mexican Americans exerting their manhood and womanhood against the Anglo society. Macho, in other words, can no longer relate merely to manhood, but must relate to nationhood as well" (24). Rendón may have offered viable alternatives to antiquated traditions, but not until Cherríe Moraga's "Queer Aztlán" (in *The Last Generation,* 145–74) did we have a clear articulation of an inclusive nation where feminists, lesbian and heterosexual, together with gay and heterosexual men, can transform Chicano nationalism into what is actually Chicana feminism in its most transformative possibility.[12]

While contemporary feministas fronterizas offer moments of resistance within the domestic space, Alfredo Mirandé and Evangelina Enríquez, in *La Chicana: The Mexican American Woman* (1979), insufficiently probe the nationalist ideology that romanticizes and devalues women's work. As unreconstructed Chicano nationalists, they turn to Aztec origins for legitimization of androcentric customs: "The [Aztec] mother's exhortation focused on personal dress, behavior and demeanor. Cleanliness of body, clothing, and mind was urged, as were an honest face and bearing. These two virtues paid public homage to her revered ancestors and helped her hold a man. The virginal purity of a freshly scrubbed face and clean, simple clothing were preferred to the painted faces, attire, and behavior of loose women" (21). Mirandé and Enríquez innocently accept the words of conquest chroniclers. While the sources themselves have much to offer contemporary researchers, Mirandé and Enríquez err when their self-described feminist analysis does not question Fray Bernardino de Sahagún's sixteenth-century assumptions about women. Further, the authors use such terms as "virginal purity" and "loose women" without noting the implications of such arbitrary signifiers.[13]

The contemporary Chicano historian George Sánchez offers one of the most comprehensive reviews of the early proclamations that construct a pathological, monolithic family that does not yield to the forces of change and adaptation to life in the United States. Sánchez asserts that what Mexican (national) and Anglo American studies and the Chicano revisionists of the 1970s held in common "was a unidimensional view of the Mexican family, a caricature suspended in time and impervious to the social forces acting upon it" (131).[14] In his review of the literature on machismo, he acknowledges that "the debate concerning to what extent machismo permeated male-female dynamics in the Mexican family has yet to be settled" (32).

Like the work of the feminist historians Vicki Ruiz, Antonia Castañeda, and Deena González, Sánchez's history reflects contemporary Chicana/o transformation of a traditional field. Throughout his study, Sánchez blends oral history and information gathered from such literary sources as Ernesto Galarza's semiautobiographical *Barrio Boy*. In turning to oral history and other historias, what I recognize as forms of testimonio, Sánchez fleshes out a constantly shifting, resisting, and multivalent study of a community. He integrates information about both women and men in Mexican and Mexican American Los Angeles. The works of contemporary Chicana/o feminist scholars, like those of border literary artists, encompass different traditions as they create emergent, liberatory women's spaces.

Tú Eres Mujer: Tyranny of the Family

As more Chicanas/os gain access to the new literary production of feministas fronterizas, we observe how the narratives in *The Moths and Other Stories* signal the point at which activist Chicana feminists take control of our historicity and subject positions. Viramontes's stories are not a quest for origins; what the historias offer are alternatives. In these cuentos, she seeks to transform and rework the concept of the Chicano family, not to destroy it. The stories offer us an emergent vision of family—they disrupt the static notion of a mono-lithic familia as refuge from outside racism and class exploitation. Vir-amontes's productions *relocate* Chicano families from secretive, barri-caded sites of male rule to contested terrains where girls and women perform valued rituals that do not necessarily adhere to androcentric familial traditions or to more (norte)Americanized, assimilative behav-iors. Viramontes's stories remind feminist readers of the urgency of telling family secrets to transform unquestioned "traditions" into dif-ferent ways of being that permit both Chicanas and Chicanos to exist as gendered and racialized subjects in U.S. Latin(a) América.

The title story in the collection, "The Moths," illustrates border fem-inism's rebellion against the sacrifice of women for the sake of family unity, the nationalist allegory of the safe site against capitalist and An-glo domination. In the simply elegant story of a fourteen-year-old Chi-cana and her status in the nuclear family, Viramontes offers a viable alternative to the patriarchal family as she explicitly challenges the ab-solute rule of the father. The counterhegemonic strategy Viramontes offers Chicanas is the formation of woman-to-woman bonds estab-lished in a separate female sphere. Unlike Enríquez and Mirandé's sep-arate spheres, however, Viramontes's female spaces are not limited to practices sanctioned by male rule.

"The Moths" centers on the gender and political ties between the unnamed narrator and her abuela (grandmother). The Abuelita's house serves as sanctuary for the young woman in her escape from her father's brutality. Engaging in a relentless critique of cultural traditions that trade on the economy of female labor and female adherence to the reproduction of male privilege, Viramontes refuses mute and blind pi-ety before a romanticized male privilege promoted by a male liberation movimiento.

The narrator resists imposing a socially constructed definition of "woman." Instead, she opens the narrative with a series of oppositions to what the culture sanctions as "female," as "tradition," and as "re-spect." When the dying grandmother requests the girl's "help," we learn that the old woman is asking her granddaughter to face her im-pending death from cancer. Battered by the familia's demands on her, as well as the manner in which they have diminished and demeaned her, the narrator cannot imagine why her grandmother would ask for her help: "Not that I was her favorite granddaughter or anything spe-cial. I wasn't even pretty or nice like my older sisters and I just couldn't do the girl things they could do. My hands were too big to handle the fineries of crocheting or embroidery and I always pricked my fingers or knotted my colored threads time and time again while my sisters laughed and called me bull hands with their cute waterlike voices" (23). With this series of negations, the young woman accomplishes something more than mourn her difference from her feminine sisters. The list of characteristics that guides many Chicanas into their culture's version of the cult of true womanhood—the cult of domesticity—emerges as a list that she consciously and subconsciously resists. She is not "pretty" or "nice" and cannot create traditional women's artistry with needles and thread. Her creative impulse blooms as an alternative mode of artistic production, grounded in neglected indigenous traditions and linked to the earth itself.

Limited by "too big" bull hands, she does not realize that by claiming the bull, she can save herself from incorporation into the economy of trade in women. Rather than excel at culturally sanctioned "girl things," the narrator practices her indigenous artistry with hammer and nails as she helps her abuela plant a garden of the vegetables and herbs that provide barrio subproletariats a measure of independence from the marketplace.

When the story's young protagonist remembers the kindness of her grandmother, the primary nurturer and spiritual healer who sees her "through several whippings" (23), Viramontes refuses silent complicity with the women who sustain the patriarchal family structure.[15] The sisters' silence participates in the father's physical abuse: "He strategically directed his anger at Amá for her lousy ways of bringing up daughters, being disrespectful and unbelieving, and my older sisters would pull me aside and tell me if I didn't get to mass right this minute, they were all going to kick the holy shit out of me. Why am I so selfish? Can't you see what it's doing to Amá, you idiot?" (25)

While the father demands that his daughters attend church, religion for the young girl who prays for her grandmother's recovery is just an empty building: "I went in [to the chapel] just the same to search for candles. I sat down on one of the pews because there were none. After I cleaned my fingernails, I looked up at the high ceiling. I had forgotten the vastness of these places, the coolness of the marble pillars and the frozen statues with blank eyes. I was alone. I knew why I had never returned" (25).

God is indeed dead for the unincorporated Chicanas of Viramontes's world; at best he is but an absentee landlord who allows his agents to deceive people into passivity. When the narrator sits in the cold church and cleans her fingernails, what might be seen as a vulgar action actually signifies an alternative religious tradition for the young woman. The earth under her fingernails comes from Abuela's garden, and with this oppositional spiritual act she signals that indigenous resistance is incompatible with the Catholic Church. But if Western religion cannot work for the young woman, she finds solace in the relationship with her abuela and the indigenous traditions surrounding her.

Abuela's house is a space that, in Spivak's terms has "no established agency of traffic with the culture of imperialism" ("Woman in Difference," 78). As the narrator lists the ways her abuela has saved her from her family's bullying, she allows us to question the myth of Chicano family unity and address the politics of the family. Being with her abuela, working with her in the herb-filled garden, makes her feel "in a strange sort of way, safe and guarded and not alone. Like God was supposed to make you feel" (24). The grandmother's indigenous knowledge heals her granddaughter with a power once reserved for a male deity. The father's Western religious traditions bring to mind Raymond Williams's caveat that "tradition is in practice the most evident expression of the dominant and hegemonic pressures and limits. It is always more than an inert historicized segment; indeed it is the most powerful means of incorporation" (*Marxism and Literature*, 115). Moreover, Viramontes, through the young woman of this story, focuses on traditional Chicano definitions of femininity to question the very "process of social and cultural definition and identification" (Williams, *Marxism and Literature*, 115).

The young woman's rejection of tradition is also tied to Abuelita's inevitable death from cancer. She associates the sun, typically a male symbol, with the grandmother. The abuela defies conventions; even in her final illness she lives independently and not with the family. Quietly, Abuelita makes the girl her apprentice, teaching her the value of what she *can* do well. The grandmother's ties to an indigenous culture no longer valued in an urban setting are represented by images of the women planting herbs, flowers, and vegetables. What the Abuelita passes on to the girl is the appreciation of a heritage in which the earth itself is a source of spirituality as well as a counterhegemonic reclamation of a discarded indigenous culture. The alternative culture the girl receives from her Abuelita further transforms "bull hands" into healing hands as the girl massages her dying grandmother with marijuana and alcohol (24).

Viramontes is not content to present a reductionist critique of how women are used as agents of the patriarchy and therefore responsible as reproducers of their own oppression. "The Moths" must also be read as a complex story of female solidarity. Helping her grandmother in the passage to death, the girl spends hours with the old woman whose lessons she does not understand until the moment of the Abuela's death.

Viramontes also challenges genteel literary traditions when she refuses to omit the brutal, lived experience of a barrio subproletarian's death. Life in the greater Chicana/o borderlands is much more than metaphor for subalterns in the Viramontean Los Angeles barrio: "The room smelled of Pine Sol and vomit and Abuelita had defecated the remains of her cancerous stomach. She had turned to the window and tried to speak, but her mouth remained open and speechless. I heard you, Abuelita, I said, stroking her cheek, I heard you" (27). Speechlessness does not prevent the granddaughter from decoding the Abuela's message. What the girl hears are the lessons her Abuela taught her through her example. The grandmother's legacy includes the wealth of alternative meanings in female images: the molcajete, the traditional Mexican mortar and pestle that she uses to grind the chiles, the hammer and nails that she uses to plant the garden. To Chicanas the image of the molcajete evokes not only a rough stone grinding away at women's spirits, but a rough stone pulverizing traditions that destroy women's lives.

The young woman further empowers herself as she ritually cleanses her grandmother's body:

> With the sacredness of a priest preparing his vestments, I unfolded the towels one by one on my shoulders. I removed the sheets and blankets from her bed and peeled off her thick flannel nightgown. I toweled her puzzled face, stretching out the wrinkles, removing the coils of her neck, toweled her shoulders and breasts. Then I changed the water. I returned to towel the creases of her stretch-marked stomach, her sporadic vaginal hairs, and her sagging thighs. I removed the lint from between her toes and noticed a mapped birthmark on the fold of her buttock. The scars on her back which were as thin as the life lines on the palms of her hands made me realize how little I really knew of Abuelita. (27)

The scars on the Abuela's back tell another story whose lacunae speak volumes of women's untold lives. Reminiscent of the great-grandmother's forgotten history in Sandra Cisneros's *The House on Mango Street* and Sethe's scarred back in Toni Morrison's *Beloved*, the Abuela's scars speak to contemporary readers who are learning the sign systems needed to decipher these stories. Reading the hieroglyphics of her back—the wrinkles, the scars, the mapped birthmark—we attempt to decipher her life. We wonder if her husband beat the abuela, and if so, if this is the reason for the narrator's mother's fear of her own husband. Is this why the abuela tried to save her nieta, why she offered sanctuary for this granddaughter with bull hands? The old woman's body maps new cartographies for the young Chicana narrator.

Of further significance is how Viramontes juxtaposes the harsh realities of the Abuelita's material existence with a magical scene that can easily be linked to the Latin(a) American literary trope, lo real maravilloso, magical realism. "The Moths" is grounded, however, in the Chicana writer's location within the Third World of the other America. In the powerful final passage, the granddaughter carries her dead Abuelita to a ritual bath: "I stepped into the bathtub one leg first, then the other. I bent my knees slowly to descend into the water slowly so I wouldn't scald her skin. There, there Abuelita, I said, cradling her, smoothing her as we descended, I heard you. Her hair fell back and spread across the water like eagle's wings. The water in the tub overflowed and poured onto the tile of the floor" (28). Here Viramontes cultivates the traditions of the Américas when she adapts magical realism in a manner that deconstructs the stereotyped vision of superstitious, mystical Latinos. When a Chicana activist writer such as Viramontes employs this literary device, she does so in ways that undercut dominant ideologies and make palpable the material conditions of border subjects that magical desires cannot erase:

> Then the moths came. Small, gray ones that came from her soul and out through her mouth fluttering to light, circling the single dull light bulb of the bathroom. Dying is lonely and I wanted to go to where the moths were, stay with her and plant chayotes whose vines would crawl up her fingers and into the clouds; I wanted to rest my head on her chest with her stroking my hair, telling me about the moths that lay within the soul and slowly eat the spirit up; I wanted to return to the waters of the womb with her so that we would never be alone again. (28)

The moths emerging from the grandmother's mouth may indeed be magical—more to the point, however, these moths are also agents of reality for women in the traditional patriarchal Chicano family. Unlike the magical butterflies deployed by Gabriel García Márquez in *One Hundred Years of Solitude* or the rose petals imagined by Laura Esquivel in *Like Water for Chocolate,* Viramontes's gray moths circling a dull light bulb evoke working-class subjects in U.S. barrios.[16] Moths emerge from the Abuela's mouth only after having eaten away at the tapestry of what her life could have been.

The moths, however, play a dual role. Even after her death, the abuela warns her granddaughter of the dangers of submitting passively to incorporation; she urges her granddaughter to recognize the need to rip apart patriarchal versions of the real, of what constitutes necessity for women. While moths may have eaten the grandmother's youth, her ability to retain a measure of independence in her old age and final illness allows the abuela to communicate alternate possibilities to her granddaughter.

The use Viramontes makes of an American Third World literary convention—lo real maravilloso—emerges for the Chicana as a combination of the spiritual and magical—lo maravilloso—and the concrete—lo real. When she releases mystical folk images as harbingers of feminist messages, Viramontes further subverts dominant versions of reality. Clearly, Viramontes offers hope for a new vision of family in this grandmother-to-granddaughter story.

In addition to grieving for her Abuelita, the young woman also mourns her absent mother: "Amá, where are you?" (28). While Viramontes clearly advocates the possibility of women's spheres separate from patriarchal impositions, a feminist hermeneutics explains the estrangement between mother and daughter. The mother is resigned to her life as an object, submissive to her husband's domination. In contrast, the daughter seeks an alternative existence, which is made possible through the Abuelita's example. The alienation between daughter and mother, at this point in the story, seems unalterable. The mother is too incorporated within strategies of domination to connect with her daughter. In the larger analysis, what Viramontes insists we acknowledge is the displacement of women's power in the traditional, patriarchal nuclear family.

Because Chicano nationalist rhetoric has so insistently invoked the mother as the center of Chicano culture, it takes Chicana feminist writers to tease out and present alternatives to women's unequal position in that family structure. The young woman receives the Abuela's warning and, in a moth-filled room, she mourns the loss of her ally and laments over the realization of how Chicano patriarchal ideology devours the cloth of women's spirits. The story ends without offering a quick solution; it leaves us instead with the image of a feminist counter-Pietà, the granddaughter holding the body of her dead Abuelita. And it is essentially the subversive force of this new consciousness, this new imagery, that permits us a glimpse of alternative possibilities for Chicanas.

Continuing the metaphor of fragile family bonds, in "The Broken Web" Viramontes presents three women entangled in a spider's web of sexual infidelities, illegitimacy, and family secrets. The lies collide in an explosive scene when the injustice of men's ownership of women's bodies and women's sexuality erupts in violence. Using stream of consciousness and multiple narrators to tell this complex tale, Viramontes shows her mastery of narrative technique as she untangles the web of a young girl's nightmare.

Even more important than her experimentation with narrative structure, however, is Viramontes's experimentation with topics deemed appropriate for Chicano literary works. Viramontes's political decision gives voice to three women linked not so much through their filial relationship as through their affiliation as oppressed and exploited border women in a transglobal patriarchal society.

Martha's story serves as the framing device, as we enter the narrative with her confession of a nightmare to a voyeuristic parish priest who hopes for a narrative of sexual indiscretion. When Martha confides that she is "still having that bad dream," he responds from the privilege of the confessional: "Are you dreaming unnatural acts?" (49). He clarifies his interests: "Is it anything sexual?" (50). What he hears is Martha's vivid memory of the night her mother shot Tomás, the man Martha had assumed was her father. The bullet that kills Tomás, the man who binds three women—Martha, her unnamed mother, and Tomás's lover in Mexico, Olivia—in a web of male betrayal, also shatters a statue of Jesus. As she recounts her nightmare/memory of that night, Martha reports to the parish priest: "I'm asleep; I see a speck on the screen. A far away speck coming closer and bigger and bigger and closer and soon the speck shapes into a statue. Our Lord with His hands outstretched. I feel comforted, even if he is only a statue in the living room. I don't hear voices. Good. I'm in the living room" (50). What she doesn't tell the priest, however, is what she does remember of that night: *"He's on the couch. Please my God, he's full of blood. Wake up, Martha, quick, pleaseohmygod....* Someone broke a statue of Jesus—the one with His hands outstretched, and now he's bleeding on the couch. I heard the crash and the bones shatter like sparks from wall to wall, but I want to be left alone"(51). With this double death blow, Viramontes irrevocably breaks Chicano literary traditions as well as the stereotype of Chicanas deferring to Father and Son. Martha's younger sister, Yreina, provides her narrative in italicized words. Martha does not want to see and keeps her eyes shut to the domestic horrors. What she cannot fend off, however, are Yreina's screams: *"Wake up, Martha, jesusmío, Mama shot..."* (51). The first section of the fractured narrative ends with the ellipsis.

Never far from the heart of this story are the material conditions that these U.S. Mexicanas endure. Perhaps for the first time in Chicano literature, an outcast of Chicana/o culture, la cantinera (the barmaid), appears as subject. On the other side of the U.S. border, in Tijuana, Olivia knows that her days at the bar are numbered because her labor depends on her youth, which is quickly fading: "Already her youth was peeling off her face like the paint on the saloon walls" (52). To employ Gayatri Spivak's formulations, the displaced space for subaltern Chicanas and Mexicans is the female body.[17]

In this second section of the story, with no transition except a new paragraph, we suddenly come to Martha's mother's story. As Olivia anticipates her lover's visit, we shift to Tomás's wife, who has accompanied him to the border. She enjoys the motel room Tomás leaves her in on the U.S. side of the border. For this laboring woman, "it was like a vacation long deserved, to stay at a place where she didn't have to make beds or clean toilets, or wash off graphic depictions of sexual acts penciled on the walls." We learn that "only in complete solitude did she feel like a woman." She luxuriates in gazing at "the full view of herself" in the motel mirror (52). But her brief time caring for her body comes to an end when her material conditions interrupt her reverie: "Too soon would the grape harvest return; the Fresno sun was almost mockingly waiting to bleed the sweat from all five of them" (53). She mourns for her children, who labor alongside her in the fields. Again without transition, the omniscient narrator links her with Olivia, whom the wife/mother has met at Tomás's favorite Tijuana bar. Rather than suspect her of sexual betrayal with Tomás, the wife/mother links her dependency on him with Olivia's condition: "She wondered if Tomás left her, would she become like her?" (53).

Continuing her insistence on turning tradition on its ear, Viramontes encourages the reader to note who spins the web. We find not the traditional women viewed as dangerous black widows but men whose own insecurities and exploitation within an unjust class system push them to punish women, whose sexuality they attempt to control. This second section of the story alternates between the wife's story and Olivia's story. Soon we realize that in patriarchy, both of these women are economically and structurally in the same position vis-à-vis men. Olivia depends on the bar's male customers to "love" her; Tomás's wife depends on this man who married her. For both women, however, the economic and social dependence is more imagined than real.

Martha's mother's anonymity robs her of her subjectivity. Tomás supplements the family wage by working as a coyote, helping undocumented workers from Mexico enter the United States. Clearly, Viramontes's "fictional" world is not the comfortable, bourgeois world of dominant society. The workers whom Tomás recruits are not the blue- or white-collar workers who "steal jobs" from legitimate Americans.

In the fourth section of "The Broken Web" Tomás's voice further complicates the analysis of male violence and aggression. The narrative insists that we hear his rage; we learn that Martha's mother was pregnant with Martha, another man's child, when they married. He sees his own sexual infidelity with Olivia as his prerogative, since his wife was not "pure" herself. In a drunken outburst he rages: "I should have spied on you that night you let him rip the virginity out of you, the blood and slime of your innocence trailing down the sides of his mouth. You tramp. You righteous bitch. Don't I have the right to be unfaithful? Weren't you? Vete mucho a chingar a tu madre, más cabrona que la chingada ..." (55). When he calls her la chingada (the fucked one), we are confronted with a resounding echo of the larger story of Mexican and Chicana women's identity within traditional narratives.[18] Section four returns to where the story began, just before the wife/mother pulls the trigger. The raging, battering Tomás salts his tirade by doubting the paternity of all three children. The difference here, however, is that this woman refuses to endure her fate passively. She pulls the trigger in the middle of his tirade: "Perra, don't rage to me about that barmaid! Answer me, vieja cabrona, ans..." (55–56). Completely cognizant of the cultural imperatives she has lived out, Tomás's wife, widow, and executioner finds no solution to her entrapment: "She had tried to defy the rules by sleeping with another man; but that only left her worse off. And she could not leave him because she no longer owned herself. He owned her, her children owned her, and she needed them all to live. And she was tired of needing" (56).

The Chicano nationalist liberation movement of the 1970s emphasized the need to reclaim Brown subjectivity in the internal colony of Aztlán, but for Brown women nationalism did not trickle down to reclamation of their bodies. The code of family loyalty begins with the assumption that men can claim possession of female sexuality. Tomás's wife resists the rules and hence appears to violate the sanctity of the family unit.[19]

The historia's fifth section introduces still another voice, which brings the disjointed narrative into focus yet casts the mother into the realm of folklore. An aunt tells Martha the truth about her real father, but telling her wreaks a final revenge against the mother. We are left to fill in the rest—in this Chicana borderland, there can be no closure. Politically engaged feminist writing insists that we recognize that for many Chicanas, women must enforce the patriarchal ideology. Martha is told by her maternal aunt that her mother is condemned to lament her fate as a woman. In the final chilling scene, the reader witnesses Martha being reincorporated by the aunt into serving what her mother defied: "Do you hear the crickets? Our mother warned us against killing crickets because they are the souls of condemned people. Do you hear their wailing, Martita? They conduct the mass of the dead only at night. You will say a rosary with me tonight, won't you?" (58). Martha's aunt chillingly articulates the imperatives of patriarchal familias and the Catholic Church. The recoding power of dominant ideology, as Spivak points out in another context, shows how "collectivities in bondage" are not viable solutions for the mujeres in Viramontes's short stories. Spivak's analysis of Mahasweta Devi's fiction discusses similar families. Devi's formulations travel to Viramontes's U.S. Third World in Spivak's discussion of "cartographies of bonded space": "The family is the first step towards collectivity. Mahasweta moves us to a space where the family, the machine for the socialization of the female body through affective coding, has itself been broken and deflected" ("Woman in Difference," 82).

Further building Viramontes's chronicle of the Chicana/o family, "Growing" takes us to the moment of puberty, which for the Chicana signals more than the end of childhood. The story is told from the point of view of Naomi, a girl poised at that critical moment between childhood and adolescence. Deceptive in its simplicity, "Growing" presents the girl at the border of womanhood, yet yearning to join in a game of baseball with the children, whose play she can no longer enjoy because of that impending transition. It is indeed a woman's story, commenting on the strictures placed on the Chicana female as she approaches puberty, a time when her sexually maturing body is claimed by the father's word "MUJER."

The narrative becomes more complex, however, when we begin to understand how Viramontes subtly presents Naomi's historical context alongside her cultural and sexual overdeterminations. Not only does Naomi have to struggle with a body in transition from childhood to adolescence, she also has to struggle with the cultural transition that her family must undergo in a new country. She feels that her parents are unduly strict with her because they come from Mexico. They do not understand, Naomi believes, that "the United States is different. Here girls don't need chaperones. Parents trust their daughters. As usual Amá turned to the kitchen sink or the ice box, shrugged her shoulders, and said: 'You have to ask your father' " (31).

To add to Naomi's problems, her father has brought with him his patriarchal privileges. Viramontes, however, does not allow us to assume that his privilege as patriarch is purely a Latino prerogative. When he thunders, "TÚ ERES MUJER" (You are a woman) in his effort to control his daughter, the author links his voice with that of the deity, to all men whose male rules transcend borders, classes, and cultures.

"Snapshots," another recuerdo in Viramontes's trunk, rips apart the by-now rotten rebozo that hides the fallacy of Chicana/o family unity. Here Viramontes comments on the fact that domestic labor is unpaid and therefore not valued as "real" work. Olga is a postmenopausal woman who struggles to reconcile the women she was raised to be— wife, mother, ama de casa (literally the wife of the house)—with the woman she now is, divorced, alone with the static photographs of her life. What her grown daughter and ex-husband do not recognize, however, is that Olga's depression over the divorce is actually an inexpressible rage over the wasted years spent perfecting a career without material value in late capitalism. The story, then, is a scathing critique of the politics of housework, of unpaid domestic labor. Olga emerges as the alienated laborer whose usefulness has expired. Once the machine of the institution of marriage, she is now obsolete, and has acquired the consciousness to ask: "How can people believe that I've fought against motes of dust for years or dirt attracting floors or perfected bleached white sheets when a few hours later the motes, the dirt, the stains return to remind me of the uselessness of it all? I missed the sound of swans slicing the lake water or the fluttering wings of wild geese flying south for a warm winter or the heart beat I could have heard if I had just held Marge a little closer" (93).

Olga's sexuality died long before the divorce. The Vaseline jar on the night table signifies the premature death of her passion. Her husband sees the emptiness in her eyes and eventually realizes that the marriage is dead as well. The snapshots she vacantly gazes at in her moment of deep regret reflect, as did the moths in the earlier Viramontes story, the death of women's souls. The meaningless snapshots in her trunk signal Olga's unvoiced understanding of what Chicana/o family ideology, with its emphasis on women's asexuality, portends for mujeres who absorb its lessons.

Such socialist feminist texts as Patricia Zavella's *Women's Work and Chicano Families* address some of these issues. This socialist feminist hermeneutics demands that we not ignore the harsh realities of what la familia means to us.[20] To end this discussion of Viramontes's "mujer" stories, I turn again to Spivak's assertion that activist authors do not often present subaltern women as emancipatory figures with solutions. For subproletarian women of the Third World—both the resisting women and the incorporated women, in the "real" world as in the imagined world of fictions—there is often "no opportunity for collective resistance" ("Woman in Difference," 93). As Chicanas come to a structural understanding of family, we see the urgency of reconstituting the meaning of familia—from filiation to affiliation.

No More Laments

I believe Salvadorans in the United States have been sentenced without trial. When you think about it, it is not very different from the way our people are treated in El Salvador.

Gloria Bonilla, "Talking: Testimonio"

With Cherríe Moraga's transnationalist manifesto in the foreword to *This Bridge Called My Back*, Chicanas signaled an expansion of the issues they considered on the agenda for radical women of color. I locate Chicana feminism on the border in these statements of political solidarity. Echoing Moraga's commitment to speak to political issues that Chicanas, themselves daughters of campesinas, perceive as legitimate topics of literary discourse, Helena María Viramontes in "The Cariboo Cafe" makes the explicit connection between Chicanas and refugees from Central America.

This story, written in early 1984, identifies Viramontes as an organic intellectual who, alongside other Chicana community activists, witnessed the transformation of once purely Chicana/o barrios into Third World enclaves of newly arrived Mexican, Salvadoran, Honduran, and Guatemalan refugees.[21] In spite of limited economic resources, which tend to pit the more recent immigrant groups against longer-established yet equally impoverished Chicana/o populations, these Chicana intellectuals refuse to ignore the connection between the populations (e)merging in U.S. cities along the border. Since the U.S. government turns a deaf ear to human rights abuses by governments it supports, political refugees from those countries flee for their lives across the border only to find themselves, once in the United States, at the source of their oppression, or to use José Martí's phrase in *Nuestra América*, "in the belly of the beast."

"The Cariboo Cafe" presents the Chicana feminist's oppositional stance against the political power of the U.S. government and its collaborators south of the border. Viramontes presents the oppression and exploitation of the reserve army of laborers that the United States creates and then designates as the "illegal" immigrants—the Other. Further, in this story Viramontes shows us that we *can* combine feminism with race and class consciousness, even if we recognize the fallacies of an all-encompassing sisterhood. In this Chicana political discourse, Viramontes commits herself to a transnational solidarity with the working-class political refugee seeking asylum from right-wing death squads in countries like El Salvador.

In addition to her overt political concerns, however, in "The Cariboo Cafe" Viramontes's narrative structure makes an implicit connection with the literary traditions of such Latin American political writers as Gabriel García Márquez and Isabel Allende. Like the complex form of "The Broken Web," the fractured narrative of this story hurls the reader into a complicated relationship with the text. This narrative strategy, itself a part of the Chicana's exploration of genre, breathes fire—and the fire is as political as it is radical. The reader enters the text as an alien to this refugee culture; Viramontes crafts a fractured narrative to reflect the disorientation that the immigrant workers feel when they are subjected to life in a country that controls their labor but does not value their existence as human beings.

The narrative structure also hurls the reader into a world as disorienting as that of the story's characters: two lost Mexican children, a Salvadoran refugee whose mental state reflects the trauma of losing her five-year-old son to the labyrinth of desaparecidos in El Salvador, and, as an ironic representative of the dominant Anglo-American culture, a working-class man who runs the cafe.[22] The city of Los Angeles is not a safe haven for these people—the angels in Viramontes's metropolis have passed through the portals of hell and burn in the flames fed by a Satan who presents himself as a kindly tío. The reader, particularly the reader unfamiliar with life in the border regions of that other America, has to work to decipher the signs in the same way the characters do. Viramontes, through the artistry of her cuento, shows us how a Chicana oppositional art form can also become an arena that reflects politics.

"They arrived in the secrecy of night, as displaced people often do, stopping over for a week, a month, eventually staying a lifetime" (61). So Viramontes begins her "testimonio-like" text, to apply John Beverley's description of a type of writing that, as he states, has "existed for a long time at the margin of literature, representing in particular those subjects—the child, the 'native,' the woman, the insane, the criminal, the proletarian—excluded from authorized representation when it was a question of speaking and writing for themselves" (*Against Literature,* 13). "They" are the "illegal aliens," the racist label by which the U.S. government designates an exploited subculture it has created. The media's use of the label "illegal" to unname the people upon whose backs the wealth of the United States has been built demands that we examine what exactly we mean by designating a mass of people illegal. As James Cockcroft asks: "If so many employers and all consumers depend so heavily on these people, then why is it that they are viewed as a 'problem' or as 'illegals'? Human beings can *do* illegal things, but can a human being actually *be* illegal? Moreover, since when under capitalism is it an illegal act to sell one's labor power for a low wage to an employer engaged in a socially approved business?" (*Outlaws in the Promised Land,* 64).

In "The Cariboo Cafe," Viramontes emulates the arpilleras of Chile whose scraps of cloth construct the stories of disappeared children. Using powerful words and imagery as her cloth and thread, she stitches together three narrative scraps to produce a tapestry telling the unspeakable horrors that are the history of the undocumented worker and political refugee in the United States.[23] Here Viramontes displays the concerns that distinguish feminism on the border from other types of Chicana feminism: she makes that final leap from filiation to affiliation, from ties to men and women of her own blood to political ties with peoples across national borders who enter the United States in search of political liberation.

Viramontes gives the story of the murder of an undocumented Salvadoran refugee political significance in a heteroglossic version of life at the border, at the periphery of North American society. The Cariboo Cafe, which the Chicana critic Roberta Fernández recognizes as a metaphor for Los Angeles (" 'Cariboo Cafe,' " 71), is the center around which Viramontes constructs her revision of history. The cafe, a sleazy diner on the wrong side of the tracks, attracts the outcasts of late capitalism. Burned-out drug addicts, prostitutes, and undocumented workers frequent the place. The petty bourgeois man who runs it becomes the mouthpiece of Anglo America. While his speech places him in the working class, he spouts the ideology of the dominant class. To outsiders like the undocumented workers, his unexamined platitudes—"family gotta be together" (73)—are charged with an ideology that Viramontes resists and counters in her historia.

Viramontes transforms this cynical short-order cook in a grease-stained apron into a grotesque Uncle Sam, a living contradiction of core and periphery. The great irony here is that this man is almost as much a victim of the capitalist system as are the undocumented workers. If the new immigrants are exploited by capital as they labor in the Los Angeles garment sweatshops, this Anglo-American has been similarly victimized by the economic urges of a U.S. government that led the country into a war in Southeast Asia. We learn that the man's only son, JoJo, is dead; it still haunts him that he will never know "what part of Vietnam JoJo is all crumbled up in" (73).

The owner of what the workers call the "zero-zero place" is able to voice the dominant ideology not because of class privilege but because of his privilege as a White man. Here is where Viramontes exposes how the hegemonic forces of race, class, and gender both intersect and collide. When she gives equal weight to the voices of the young daughter of undocumented workers and a Salvadoran political refugee, Viramontes gives voice to the counterhegemonic.

The first testimony we hear in this polyphonic text is that of a child, Sonya; we see the urban landscape through her eyes. Both of her parents work so that the family may one day have a "toilet [of] one's own" (61). For the feminist reader, this turn of phrase resonates with Virginia Woolf's desire for financial independence for the woman writer, but it also reminds us of the vast difference between the concerns of bourgeois feminists and border feminists.

Like so many children whose parents' wages cannot support the luxury of extended-hour child care, the five- or six-year-old Sonya is a child whose duties as a female include caring for her younger brother, Macky. Viramontes provides the reader with enough cultural cues (the children's recognition of a poster of the Mexican star Vicente Fernán-dez, their yearning for flour tortillas) for us to identify Sonya and Macky as children of Mexican migrant workers.

When the children lose the key to their apartment and get lost trying to find their way to safety, they remember the premise they were taught for survival in hostile territory: never trust the police. As their father has told them, the "polie" is "La Migra [the INS] in disguise and thus should always be avoided" (61). The omniscient third-person narrator in this section allows us to witness the hostile territory the children call home. Sonya observes one of the countless homeless people who exist alongside them: "She watched people piling in and spilling out of the buses, watched an old man asleep on the bus bench across the street. He resembled a crumbled ball of paper, huddled up in the security of a tattered coat. She became aware of their mutual loneliness and she rested her knees blackened by the soot of the playground asphalt" (61–62). Sonya seems to understand the fragility of her family's own precarious status in this society where home can disappear as quickly as it takes a child to lose the key to her empty apartment. Sonya and Macky's kinship with the old man becomes more pronounced as the evening progresses and the children feel the pains of their desolation alongside the pangs of hunger: "The old man eventually awoke, yawned like a lion's roar, unfolded his limbs and staggered to the alley where he urinated between two trash bins. (She wanted to peek, but it was Macky who turned to look.) He zipped up, drank from a paper bag and she watched him until he disappeared around the corner.... Macky became bored. He picked through the trash barrel..." (62). As her little brother weeps from hunger, Sonya decides that they should return to the woman who watches Macky during the day. Unfortunately, Sonya is herself a child, and "things never looked the same when backwards and she searched for familiar scenes" (62).

Lost in the metropolis, the children see "a room with a yellow glow, like a beacon light at the end of a dark sea," which Sonya thinks will be a sanctuary from the alleys and dead ends of the urban barrio. Ironically, the beacon is the "zero, zero place" (64). The reader searching for a linear narrative will have to search several pages before arriving at the next episode in the children's journey.

In the "double zero cafe," we hear the story of the children's fate in flashback. The cafe owner tells his version as if he were on trial. Indeed,

Viramontes *is* putting U.S. immigration policies and ideology on trial. The man constantly presents himself as honest, yet in the same breath he admits to lacing his hamburgers with something that is "not pure beef." He thinks he can redeem himself when he proclaims that at least "it ain't dogmeat" (64). Then he remembers the basic contradiction of the "American" ideal: "It never pays to be honest." He continues his version of how it came to pass that a Salvadoran refugee was killed in his cafe. When he first saw "that woman," he immediately labeled her as Other: "Anyway, I'm standing behind the counter staring at this short woman. Already I know that she's bad news because she looks street to me. Round face, burnt toast color, black hair that hangs like straight ropes. Weirdo, I've had enough to last me a lifetime. She's wearing a shawl and a dirty slip is hanging out. Shit if I had to dish out a free meal" (65–66). Through his voice we hear Anglo America's rationale when people of color are barred from integration into U.S. society. Because immigrants of different skin color belie the melting pot myth, it is harder for them to be accepted in the same way that European immigrants have been accepted in the history of U.S. colonization. When the woman speaks Spanish to the children who are with her, he says, "Right off I know she's illegal, which explains why she looks like a weirdo" (66). Here Viramontes unmasks how the dominant marginalize on the basis of color and language. The indigenous woman's Brownness signifies alterity to the cafe owner, whose own ethnicity is left vague.

The cafe owner comments on the people who patronize his diner and allows us a glimpse of the working conditions of the men and women who labor in the sweatshops of the Los Angeles garment district. His customers, whom he labels "the illegals," "come in real queen-like, too, sitting in the best booth by the window, and order cokes. That's all. Cokes. Hey, but I'm a nice guy, so what if they mess up my table, bring their own lunches and only order small cokes, leaving a dime as a tip?" (65). The cook's observation of the lives around his cafe includes the regular INS raids, which, as the anthropologist María Patricia Fernández-Kelly has pointed out in her study of the factory system in the border areas, are often instigated by factory bosses just before payday. Since there exists a vast surplus of laborers, the entrepreneurs need not worry about replacing their deported workers (*For We Are Sold*, 80).

Even after the cafe owner himself experiences police harassment after the death by drug overdose of one of his patrons in the cafe's bathroom, he is once again forced into a contradiction as he contributes to the capture of three workers hiding from INS agents in that same bathroom. Again, Viramontes insists that we recognize the kinship between the drug fatalities and the abused undocumented workers: "After I swore I wouldn't give the fuckin' pigs the time of day, the green vans roll up across the street. While I'm stirring the chile con carne I see all these illegals running out of the factory to hide, like roaches when the lightswitch goes on.... Three of them run into the Cariboo. They look at me as if I'm gonna stop them, but when I go on stirring the chile, they run to the bathroom" (67). He points to the bathroom when the INS agents enter his cafe. Even he is shocked by the way the agents abuse the women they handcuff and put "their hands up and down their thighs" (68). At that moment the Salvadoreña enters the cafe with two children.

Only when we get the third voice does Viramontes allow us to realize what has happened to the lost children of the first section. They have been taken by a Salvadoreña who mistakes Macky for her missing son. A modern-day Llorona, this woman has fled her country after her own child has been disappeared and presumably murdered by the right-wing, U.S.-backed Salvadoran government. The child is one of the countless desaparecidos in those countries whose dictators the U.S. government keeps in power.

This third and final section of Viramontes's narrative opens with third-person omniscient narration by the Salvadoran woman. Cast into her tortured mind, the reader is permitted to experience the uncertainty and confusion this terrorized woman feels. For the first several sentences, we are uncertain who the speaker is and where exactly she has taken us. Eventually we understand that she is referring to Macky in her opening comments: "He's got lice. Probably from living in the detainers" (68). But in the same moment, we also understand that the refugee thinks she has found her own son, Geraldo, and the "detainers" in her mind actually exist in El Salvador.

The Salvadoreña gives her testimonio and, indeed, becomes the modern-day wailing woman of Chicana/o folklore, who in this version represents all women who are victimized by conquering races and classes. She represents the mothers of the disappeared who wander the jails, the torture chambers, women who plead with the torturers and jailers trained by U.S. military agents for information about their missing loved ones. In her capacity as a writer, Viramontes leads the reader to an underworld where the women search for their children: "The darkness becomes a serpent's tongue, swallowing us whole. It is the night of La Llorona. The women come up from the depths of sorrow to search for their children. I join them, frantic, desperate, and our eyes become scrutinizers, our bodies opiated with the scent of their smiles. Descending from door to door, the wind whips our faces. I hear the wailing of the women and know it to be my own. Geraldo is nowhere to be found" (68–69).

In his essay "On Language as Such and on the Language of Man," Walter Benjamin argued that the lament "is the most undifferentiated, impotent expression of language; it contains scarcely more than the sensuous breath" (329). Viramontes uses the lament motif in this historia not only to expose the socially sanctioned, passive roles for women within the patriarchy, but to show the powerlessness of the victims of repressive governments; thus the lament contains much more than Benjamin would have it do.

The narrative strategy that Viramontes has crafted for this cuento reflects the disorientation the Salvadoran experiences in her migration to Los Angeles. Believing as she does that she is still in El Salvador and that Macky is her lost son, she cannot understand why the cafe owner would call her act of maternal love a kidnapping. As Viramontes makes the explicit connection between the Salvadoreña, the exploited garment workers, and the Mexican children, we begin to see her radical transformation of familia and motherhood.

Through the woman's testimony, the reader witnesses the destruction of home and of safety for the women and children of El Salvador. Struggling to comprehend how a five-year-old child running an errand for his mother could be detained by a military police force, the woman gives us the details of how repressive governments command the population's docility:

> These four walls are no longer my house, the earth beneath it, no longer my home. Weeds have replaced all good crops. The irrigation ditches are clotted with bodies. No matter where we turn, there are rumors facing us and we try to live as best we can, under the rule of men who rape women, then rip the fetuses from their bellies. Is this our home? Is this our country? I ask Maria. Don't these men have mothers, lovers, babies, sisters? Don't they see what they are doing? Later, Maria says, these men are babes farted out from the Devil's ass. We check to make sure no one has heard her say this. (71)

Her home, child, and country stripped from her, she migrates to the United States and works to repay her nephew's generosity in

crossing her over imposed borders to the U.S. Third World. Viramontes draws the three narratives together as the Salvadoreña rescues
Macky from being run over as he crosses a busy intersection with
Sonya: "My heart pounds in my head like a sledge hammer against the
asphalt. What if it isn't Geraldo? What if he is still in the detainer
waiting for me? A million questions, one answer: Yes. Geraldo, yes. I
want to touch his hand first, have it disappear in my own because it
is so small. His eyes look at me in total bewilderment. I grab him
because the earth is crumbling beneath us and I must save him. We
both fall to the ground" (72). As she grabs Macky, this mother of a
disappeared child erases the borders that separate her country of origin
and East Los Angeles.

She "rescues" Macky, convinced that he is Geraldo. She bathes him,
feeds him, loves him—she becomes his mother. But Viramontes will
not allow the reader to be lulled by a romanticized scene of maternal
nurturing. The discomfort we feel is our realization that in these scenes
Viramontes has forced us to question what exactly "mother" means.
Under what circumstances can we sympathize with a woman who "rescues" a lost child and transforms him into her own son? How, as
feminists, do we reconcile the woman's inability to see the boy's sister,
Sonya?

In her courageous stand against the police who will certainly take
Geraldo from her, the Salvadoreña invokes memories of the countless
women in Guatemala, El Salvador, Chile, and Argentina, to name just
a few countries, who join together with other women and march on
their plazas, at the presidential palaces, demanding that their children's
disappearances be acknowledged and explained. The women tear down
walls that prevent us from recognizing that in this era of wars, women
unite against the brutality of military regimes and transform the meaning and the political significance of "mother."

For the Salvadoran woman, as for the Mexican children, the police
here are no different from the police in the country she has fled. They
will take her "son" away from her. Her confrontation with the police
in the United States appears to her a continuation of her struggles with
the police who detained and murdered Geraldo. She resists arrest and
throws boiling coffee at the man pointing "the steel erection" of a gun
at her forehead. With the Salvadoreña's final act of resistance, Viramontes explodes the boundaries of home, of safety, and of family but
leaves the question of Sonya unanswered.

"Neighbors," another oppositional narrative in *The Moths and Other*

Stories, presents yet another complex view of life in contemporary Los Angeles. The U.S. Third World city represented in this narrative, as in "The Cariboo Cafe," reflects the geopolitical space of a Chicana and Chicano Los Angeles that exists as a police state for U.S. Mexicans as well as for undocumented Central American immigrant workers. Scenes of a seventy-three-year-old woman, Aura, whose body no longer obeys her strong mind's commands, mingle with Viramontes's always sociologically aware analyses of the urban landscape. She transports the reader to a world where the neighborhood's young men cannot find jobs, a world whose postmodern pretensions do not include them. In cities like L.A., urban renewal plans envision skyscrapers and freeways that destroy the barrio and replace it with enclaves of the unemployed army of surplus labor. While it has become fashionable to represent the young men of the Chicano neighborhoods as cholos, or gang members—homeboys, to use a self-identifier—the multivalent irony remains that these "homeboys" exist as deterritorialized subjects of an "America" that refuses to acknowledge Chicano and Chicana identity as indigenous to the geographic area.

In "Neighbors," Aura's deteriorating body figures as the metaphor of the violated neighborhood. Racked by pain, she feels "miserable and cornered," and begins "cursing her body, herself for such weakness" (107). The longtime native of the neighborhood suffers a physical pain that makes her "begin to hate." With the constant howl of police sirens in the background, Aura, the barrio embodied, internalizes the hatred that dominant society breeds. She harbors resentment and grows suspicious of anyone new to the neighborhood. When another old woman appears on her porch looking for Fierro, the man who has lived in the house behind Aura's house for thirty years, Aura's suspicion of any outsider induces the visitor to produce proof of her right to visit Fierro: "[The visitor] began rummaging through her bags like one looking for proof of one's birth at a border crossing" (103). Though this visitor is never named in the story, she figures as a central force in the narrative. Wearing a badly mended dress, unwashed, and "with a distinct scent accompanying her," the apparently homeless woman signifies, if not Death, La Muerte herself, then certainly the harbinger of death. She wears a lopsided cotton wig, so we might read her as La Pelona, another cultural marker of an impending death.

Viramontes presents Aura as the fractured aura of the Chicano neighborhood that internalizes the racism of the dominant media—the press as well as such Hollywood films as *Falling Down*, which can imagine Chicano youth only as cholos, as violent homeboys. The old woman wakes up mentally alert, but her deteriorating body throbbing with arthritis drives her to a state of hatred. As we enter the soul of Aura, we observe her self-loathing:

> She began to hate. She hated her body, the ticking of the hen-shaped clock which hung above the stove or the way the dogs howled at the police sirens. She hated the way her fingers distorted her hand so that she could not even grasp a glass of water. But most of all she hated the laughter and the loud music which came from the boys who stood around the candied-apple red Impala with the tape deck on full blast. They laughed and drank and threw beer cans in her yard while she burned with fever. The pain made her so desperate with intolerance, that she struggled to her porch steps, tears moistening her eyes, and pleaded with the boys. "Por favor . . . Don't you have homes?" The boys, Toastie and Ruben, remind her: "We *are* home!" (108).

With this ironic reply, the Chicanos assert their claim to their land. The young men fight each other to defend their turf, the territory to which the hegemonic group confines them. Bound by these other borderlines, these young men remain locked into a terrain that additionally imprisons them in fixed positions as the subproletariat. Viramontes's insistence on that word *home* recognizes the displacement of the border dweller; *home* signifies the state of homelessness for the Auras as well as for the lost, undereducated young men of the Chicano urban barrios in the United States.

In this political narrative about aging, about violence, about fear, the children of the barrio "gather. . . in small groups to lose themselves in the abyss of defeat, to find temporary solace among each other" (102). When Aura betrays that site of solace by informing to the police about a minor infringement upon her need for silence and solitude, Viramontes brings home to the reader the police state under which many Chicano communities live. The military police are not only in some far-off Latin American country, but in our U.S. neighborhoods:

> Her feeling of revenge had overcome her pain momentarily, but when the police arrived, she fully realized her mistake. The five cars zeroed in on their target, halting like tanks in a cartoon. The police jumped out in military formation, ready for combat. The neighbors began emerging from behind their doors and fences to watch the red lights flashing against the policemen's batons. When the boys were lined up, spread-eagled for the search, Toastie made a run for it, leaping over Aura's wrought iron fence and falling hard on a rosebush. His face scratched

and bleeding, he ran towards her door, and for a moment Aura was sure he wanted to kill her. It was not until he lunged for the door that she was able to see the desperation and confusion, the fear in his eyes, and he screamed at the top of his lungs while pounding on her door, the vowels of the one word melting into a howl, he screamed to her, "Pleeeeeeeease." He pounded on the door please. She pressed her hands against her ears until his howl was abruptly silenced by a dull thud. When the two policemen dragged him down the porch steps, she could hear the creak of their thick leather belts rubbing against their bullets. She began to cry. (108–9)

Like "The Cariboo Cafe," "Neighbors" ends with the image of a gun. While Viramontes's feminist texts refuse closure, in "Cariboo" one cannot imagine the policeman not shooting the refugee woman. In "Neighbors," however, Aura's fatal error occurs when she calls the police to the barrio in an attempt to ensure her safety. Viramontes forces us to rethink simple dichotomies: In the Chicana/o homeland, who is the enemy, who is our ally? Are the young men of the neighborhood Aura's enemies? Are the police her allies? Can we read Aura's loaded gun, intended for Chicano youth, Toastie and Ruben, as a sign of resistance? Against whom do the Auras of these communities resist? Against whom do they rage? Have the Auras of Chicana/o neighborhoods been so incorporated by the dominant group that they internalize their racism and blame the disenfranchised, the undereducated, the underemployed young men of the barrio for all their problems?

If indeed Aura does shoot the gun at the visitor whom I earlier identified as La Pelona, Aura denies for herself and for her neighbors the possibility of a peaceful death. La Pelona's visit to the neighborhood enacts an ancient ritual that eases the old man Fierro to a natural death at the end of a long, if not peaceful, life. For a reader armed with a New Mestiza consciousness, with a recovered mestiza history that restores the memory of the dual nature of Coatlicue as a deity of both life and death, Viramontes's neomyth, as I discussed in Chapter 3, is even more tragic. With Aura's loaded gun, violence from within the Chicana/Chicano neighborhood entraps it as much as violence from the dominating group and its police enforcers. Clearly, Aura's loaded gun in a contemporary Chicana/o neighborhood is not the same weapon that Américo Paredes evoked in his oppositional text *With His Pistol in His Hand*.[24]

In her forthcoming "Paris Rats in L.A.: A Novel in Short Stories," Viramontes takes us back to this metropolitan barrio to reclaim it along with its women and men. Instead of the media oversimplifications of barrio as gang-violence war zone, she presents barrio as township, barrio as home, and its young men and women in gangs. Admittedly the gang ethic is violent, but this political narrative gives us the reasons (or *a* reason) for the violence. She offers us insights into how our children, our young women and men, are tracked to lives on the margins, on the borders, of the United States.

In the title story, "Paris Rats in L.A.," Viramontes introduces her ten-year-old narrator, Ofelia, also known as Champ, and her brother, Gregorio. In Gregorio, Viramontes lifts the mask of hostility that young Chicanos wear in their wars against one another and against the outside world. As poet of the urban barrio, Viramontes's young narrator brings her beloved brother to life:

> His pendelton shirt hangs on him, but it's ironed real smooth though he's been out all night, and buttoned to the neck and wrists even when it's so hot. He always looks mad and jest real mean, though I think he ain't, but everybody kinda moves away like they're ascared of the big scar that streets down from his cheek to his neck cuz he ain't ascared of no knife, no gun, no nuthin'; and nobody says anything when he smokes a Camel on the bus even when you're not supposed to. He's got spiders for eyes and so's everybody, Fox and Horse and stuff, call him Spider, but I can't on account he says to me: "My name is Gregorio, remember that Champ, remember." And to me, he's the most handsomest man in the world. (1–2)[25]

Viramontes gives a name, a face, and ultimately humanity to people whom the dominant group prefers to keep anonymous, sinister, and therefore easier either to kill on the street or to disappear into the labyrinth of the U.S. prison system. Spider is the male subject constructed by the hegemonic group; Gregorio is that subject uncovered. He gains identity with his sister's demolition of false stereotypes within which young Chicanos like him have been rendered invisible.

Since only two of the stories in this collection have been published, "Miss Clairol" and "Tears on My Pillow," I will limit the rest of my analysis to the latter. Here Ofelia negotiates the gendered spaces of the barrio. She is left alone in her Terrace Flats project apartment while her mother, Arlene, an urban proletarian, labors at a garment sweatshop and returns dead tired, the noise of industrial sewing machines ringing in her ears hours after she has left the factory.

Ofelia names her anxiety as a burning. The child's stomach burns as she observes her community: wife beating and killing, neglected children, exhausted women and men whose labors fuel the consumption of luxuries by the upper classes in cities like Los Angeles. One cannot ignore the incidents that the image of a burning Los Angeles evokes: the fires of the Rodney King uprising as well as the other fires in the hills over Malibu sent by that mysterious weather phenomenon, El Niño, fueled by the Santa Ana winds or, as some whisper, perhaps urban guerrillas.

In the same way that the stories "Paris Rats in L.A." and "Spider's Face" give countenance, substance, voice, and identity to the barrio Chicanos, this story gives the female gendered subject, the Chicana Ofelia, visibility and a multilayered identity. From the opening narrative of the ten-year-old child's variant of the Llorona folktale, what emerges is a Chicana "native's" perspective on the historical moment from which we can start theorizing the political in Viramontes's text.

In the interview "The Problem of Cultural Self-Representation," Gayatri Spivak suggests that we ask the literary texts we examine as cultural critics "in what way, in what contexts, under what kinds of race and class situations, gender is used as what sort of signifier to cover over what kinds of things" (52). In the Chicano context, the legend of La Llorona typically functions as a masculinist tale that illustrates women's innate depravity and treachery. But one of Viramontes's accomplishments in this very short story of only five pages is the uncovering of male privilege within the Chicano cultural context. Rendered in the vernacular, young Ofelia's version of La Llorona begins the story:

> Mama María learned me about La Llorona. La Llorona is the one who doing all the crying I been hearing all this time with no one to tell me who it was til Mama María. She told me La Lauren's [Llorona's] this mama, see, who killed her kids. Something like that. How does it goes? Something like there's this girl and some soldiers take her husband away and she goes to the jail to look for him, asses why these soldiers took him. And she gots I don't member how many kids all crying cause their daddy's gone, you know. And the soldier being mean and stupid and the devil inside him . . ., he points a gun to her head and says, "I gonna kill you." But she looks at him and says, "Do me the favor." That's like something Arlene would say, you know. But the girl, she don't know when to stop. "You kill everything so go ahead and kill me," she tells the soldier, "but first kill my kids cause I don't want 'em hungry and sick and lone without no 'ama or 'apa or TV." So the devil says "Okay," and shoots all the kids, bang, bang, bang. But you know what? He don't kill her. Cold shot, huh? She goes coocoo and escapes from the

nut house.....And to this day, the girl all dressed up in black like Mama María cause she killed her kids and she walks up and down City Terrace with no feet, crying and crying and looking for her kids. For reallies, late in the dark night only. (110)

When we trace the legend of La Llorona, we find that this tale actually chronicles the historical moment of violence against the indigenous female subject in the Americas. The popular tradition of La Llorona for many Chicanas/os, however, covers up this original moment of colonial contact with the aboriginal women in the sixteenth century.[26]

As Miguel León-Portilla asserts, a source for the legend emerges in Aztec mythology. Ten years before the conquest there were visions and sightings—omens—according to Fray Bernardino de Sahagún's *Historia general de las cosas de Nueva España*. Sahagún notes that "people heard a weeping woman night after night. She passed by in the middle of the night, wailing and crying out in a loud voice, 'My children, we must flee far away from this city!' At other times she cried, 'My children, where shall I take you?'" (quoted in *Broken Spears*, 6).

According to Diego Muñoz Camargo in *Historia de Tlaxcala*, "the people heard in the night the voice of a weeping woman, who sobbed and sighed and drowned herself in her tears. This woman cried: 'O my sons, we are lost...!' Or she cried: 'O my sons, where can I hide you...?'" (quoted in León-Portilla, *Broken Spears*, 9–10).

If these versions, allegedly narrated by native informants to Spanish chroniclers, authorize the Llorona legend as having to do with conquest, with imperialism, with the violence inflicted on the indigenous Americans, then Viramontes maps out how a contemporary Chicanita bears witness to the conquest of her own world in the East Los Angeles barrio. Ofelia transforms the story told by her grandmother, Mama María, when the child's lived experience in the City Terrace government housing project spills over into her Llorona narrative. The child's variant testifies to the moment of violence against the male and female mestizo and mestiza subjects in the U.S. borderlands. Hers is a variant that uncovers her cultural, class, and gender positions.

The tears on Ofelia's pillow mark her construction by patriarchal culture as a weeping (hysterical?) woman, una llorona. But in contemporary Chicana feminist discourse, Ofelia's tears cry out for her powerful cultural and ancestral link to those of the indigenous earth goddess Cihuacoatl, "who wept and called out in the night" (León-Portilla, *Broken Spears*, 12). Rather than being drowned by an insane mother, this Ofelia, who recalls Shakespeare's drowned woman but offers a radical transformation, drowns herself only in figurative tears as she witnesses the brutality and violence in her neighborhood. Rather than the European figure of the insane, rejected, victimized Ophelia, the Chicana representation of the female subject lives to tell the tale. Again, drawing on Spivak's textual strategies in the interview *The Post-Colonial Critic* (71), I propose that if sanctioned infanticide is the regulative psychobiography of the indigenous or mestiza woman in the Americas, then Ofelia's powerful revision of the cultural script portends the possible transformations that occur when Chicanas produce alternative cultural self-representations.

Ofelia begins her Llorona narrative with the familiar version that blames the woman for the murder of the children. But her memory of the cuento clashes against the realities of her life. Surrounded by other refugee families in the Terrace Flats government housing projects, families possibly from Latin American countries where *desaparecidos* is a noun referring to men and women who resist the hegemonic group, Ofelia retells the story as a tale of desaparecidos. The husband is not the Spanish conquistador who seduces the India, the indigenous woman, and attempts to take his children back to work the land in Spain; this husband is imprisoned. Like so many Guatemaltecos and Salvadoreños in their countries, and Chicanos in U.S. prisons for various unjust reasons, the father in Ofelia's version is blameless.

La Llorona confronts the imperialist soldier, and in spite of her resistance and confrontation (or because of it?), he murders her children. The soldier kills her children to establish his supremacy and to ensure her submission. Her defeat is translated by the child Ofelia as going "coocoo." Then there is a break in the narrative that mimics the slippage in the historical memory of a people who disremember the violence of the conquest. It was not a traitorous Malintzín Tenépal or a hysterical Llorona bent on insane revenge who kills her hijos, who commits infanticide, but the occupying soldados intent on complete conquest and the submission of the indigenous peoples. Only after Ofelia establishes a different version, gives a different point of view, does the child narrator slip back to the more familiar androcentric, hegemonic tale that blames the woman for the infanticide, that blames the conquered for the conquest. The popular narrative intrudes with an ending that Ofelia does not recognize from her own experience.

But there is much more to this narrative. Viramontes demolishes the popular narrative of La Llorona when the City Terrace women's identities emerge as single parents, all with different ways and with different levels of success in raising children, not drowning them. Ofelia swears that she has heard La Llorona in her neighborhood. Indeed, as Ofelia's mother, Arlene, knows, what Ofelia hears is not legend but the real cries of the neighbor woman, Lil Mary G., who endures beatings by her man and who is eventually murdered by him. City Terrace is no Aztlán, the mythical homeland of the Aztec natives and the utopian dreamland of the Chicano nationalists of the 1960s and 1970s. For Lil Mary G. and her daughter Veronica, for Arlene, Ofelia, and Gregorio, Aztlán does not exist.[27]

Ultimately, Viramontes captures in "Tears on My Pillow" the political problematic of the gendered subject in the Chicana and Chicano cultural arena. The Chicana narrator uncovers the missing memory of the imperialist moment of violence against the indigenous women in the sixteenth century. But she also confronts the clash within her own world in City Terrace, in the Chicano "homeland." Women are blamed and beaten by their kinsmen and exploited by postmodern capitalism. While Viramontes offers an alternative version of the moment of contact with the European conquerors, the soldiers of Ofelia's Llorona narrative, in this story she cannot offer a moment of liberatory self-realization.

"Tears on My Pillow" ends with Ofelia watching her mother's preparations for a night out at a local club, the Palladium, a release from Arlene's mind-numbing workweek at the factory. Ofelia thinks that Veronica's loss of her mother must be the worst thing that can happen to anyone. She innocently links Lil Mary G.'s death with Arlene's repeated absences through the necessities of her position as exploited labor and through her after-hours benign neglect: "They just disappear, leaving you alone all ascared with your burns and La Llorona hungry for you" (115).

Ofelia burns with the anxiety of reincorporation by that master narrative, the tale of La Llorona. Irresolution, or the refusal of closure in Viramontes's political text, signals a complex project currently being undertaken by Chicana feminist writers, critics, and cultural workers. Together they are working to undercut old stereotypes and open up new possibilities for empowerment by forging a self-representation of Chicanas by Chicanas, women who insist on a self-identifier that marks their political subjectivity as feminist as well as their working-class identification.

"Refugees of a World on Fire"

Geopolitical Feminisms

I'm still keeping secret what I think no-one should know. Not even anthropologists or intellectuals, no matter how many books they have, can find out all our secrets.

Rigoberta Menchú

As the Chicana feminist writers whose works I discuss forge bridges with campesinas south of the U.S. border, they disrupt accepted genres as well as traditional topics and subjects of literary representation. Chicana feminism on the border is a literary practice articulated in nonsanctioned sites of theory: in the prefaces to anthologies, in the interstices of autobiographies, and in the cultural artifacts themselves, the cuentos. This epilogue is not intended as a "conclusion" to my discussion of Chicana feminism on the border—it merely begins a different trajectory that I believe Chicana feminist writers/theorists will follow. What I now want to explore is the "new genre" of testimonio and how it allows a previously unheard-of self-representation by subaltern women as it further establishes an important link with the Chicana border feminists.

Publications by Jean Franco, John Beverley, George Yúdice, Barbara Harlow, Doris Sommer, and the contributors to René Jara and Hernán Vidal's *Testimonio y literatura* provide us with substantial research into the genre. Few have addressed the importance of testimonio in gender issues. Testimonio allows such women as Domitila Barrios de Chungara, Rigoberta Menchú, and Elvia Alvarado to theorize the supposed triviality of domestic power relations. In fact, Doris Sommer, in " 'Not Just a Personal Story,' " assumes that Menchú's and Barrios de Chungara's idealization of father figures indicates that in such texts "women acquire a degree of freedom or militancy by privileging male models over female, even though they can get beyond an apprenticeship" (129). Domitila Barrios de Chungara, in her testimonio *Si me permiten hablar . . .* (1977), published in English as *Let Me Speak!* (1978), does idealize her father and often seems to "privilege male models over female." Her ability to analyze women's positions as unpaid laborers, however, shows how her feminism cannot be contained by First World definitions:

> In spite of everything we do, there's still the idea that women don't work, because they don't contribute economically to the home, that only the husband works because he gets a wage. We've often come across that difficulty.
> One day I got the idea of making a chart. We put as an example the price of washing clothes . . . then the cook's wage, the baby-sitter's, the servant's. We figured out everything that we miners' wives do every day. Adding it all up, the wage needed to pay us for what we do in the home, compared to the wages of a cook, a washerwoman, a baby-sitter, a servant, was much higher than what the men earned in the mine for a month. So that way we made our compañeros understand that we really work, and even more than they do in a certain sense. . . . So, even though the state doesn't recognize what we do in the home, the country benefits from it, because we don't receive a single penny for this work. (35)

Domitila Barrios de Chungara's understanding of feminism, like that of the Chicanas whose works I have discussed as feminismo popular, recognizes that women of her class in Latin America are exploited by the economic system as well as by patriarchy. She speaks of how "necessity" has authorized the change in her life from the gender-bound traditions with which she was raised to comply to a life as a labor activist who helped organize the housewives' committee in her Bolivian mining town, Siglo XX. She does, however, acknowledge a chasm between First and Third World feminisms: "Our position is not like the feminists' position. We think our liberation consists primarily in our country being freed forever from the yoke of imperialism and we want a worker like us to be in power and that the laws, education, everything, be controlled by this person. Then, yes, we'll have better conditions for reaching a complete liberation, including a liberation as women" (41). Her statement, however, is problematized by her occasion for speaking. As a participant at the United Nations–sponsored International Year of the Woman Conference held in Mexico City in 1975, Barrios witnessed the co-opting of "feminism" by governments that use women and women's issues to promote their own political agendas. Barrios observed Imelda Marcos, Princess Ashraf Pahlavi, and Jehan Sadat among the official Third World representatives. We begin to reformulate the First World / Third World dichotomy when we no longer choose to see these representatives as Third World feminists but recognize them as agents of their respective governments: agents of patriarchy, capitalism, and imperialism. Suddenly the dichotomy between the ruling class and the working class, between those in power and the disenfranchised, is exposed.

When Barrios disassociates herself from "feminism," she means a hegemonic feminism as defined by women and men of the dominant class. In the paragraph immediately following the one cited above, Barrios speaks as a working-class socialist-feminist, affiliating herself with border feminists such as Anzaldúa, Cisneros, and Viramontes, to name just three. Unlike feminists whose political activities must be tempered by consideration of their positions in academic institutions, these women consider themselves community activists first and, in the case of Moraga and Anzaldúa, academics second.

Barrios, for her part, speaks as the union organizer of the Bolivian tin miners' wives. "For us," she asserts,

> the important thing is the participation of the compañero and the compañera together. . . . If women continue only to worry about the house and remain ignorant of the other parts of our reality, we'll never have citizens who'll be able to lead our country. Because education begins from the cradle. And if we think of the central role played by women as the mothers who have to forge future citizens, then, if they aren't prepared they'll only forge mediocre citizens who are easily manipulated by the capitalist, by the boss. (41)

While she echoes the rhetorical strategy of the nineteenth-century U.S. feminist Margaret Fuller, who also argued that women should be given equal education in order to teach their children, Barrios considers her responsibility to her children's education a cultural imperative.

If Barrios's point of reference is that of a heterosexual woman who does not question women's roles as mothers, we must remember her historical context as a working-class woman in Bolivia, the poorest country in South America. History forces her to accept her position as primary nurturer, as the one who will teach the children about the struggle. History also forces her to act in untraditional ways that ultimately place her in the middle of social and political involvement and, eventually, in the hands of the Bolivian torturers.

In view of the historical and economic realities of Barrios's position as a Bolivian woman, her own discourse echoes Cherríe Moraga's internationalist agenda: "We know there's a long struggle ahead, but that's what we're all about. And we aren't alone. How many peoples are in the same struggle! And, why not say it? Every people needs the solidarity of others, like us, because our fight is big. So we have to practice proletarian internationalism that many people have sung about, and many countries have followed. Many other countries suffer persecutions, outrages, murders, massacres, like Bolivia" (42).

Like Barrios de Chungara, Rigoberta Menchú, in her testimonio *Me llamo Rigoberta Menchú y así me nació la conciencia* (1983), published in English as *I, Rigoberta Menchú: An Indian Woman in Guatemala* (1984), articulates a feminist consciousness that cannot be separated from its connection to race and class. Women who are engaged in a revolutionary struggle against the government of Guatemala cannot imagine liberation as women separately from liberation for the Quiché and the other Indian peoples of Guatemala.

Reminiscent of Gloria Anzaldúa's *Borderlands*, Menchú's testimonio presents a history of her people, dispossessed of their ancestral lands by Europeans: "My village has a long history—a long and painful history" (4). But for Menchú, the "enemy" is the majority population of Guatemala—the people called ladinos, mostly but not necessarily mestizos—who do not live as Indians. Menchú notes that her "consciousness was born" when, as a child, she watched her mother labor as a cook during the family's seasonal migration to the coffee plantations (34). Her recognition of what wage labor means to Guatemalan Indians—exploitation by the land "owners"—eventually develops into a class analysis when she recognizes that there are exploited ladinos as well as rich, exploiting ladinos: "I started wondering: 'Could it be that not all *ladinos* are bad?' I used to think they were all bad. But *they* [the Mam and Achi Indians she met] said that they lived with poor *ladinos,* and they were exploited as well. That's when I began recognizing exploitation" (119). Unfortunately, Menchú perceives that even the poor ladinos in Guatemala have learned the privileges of their non-indígena mode of life when one ladino child says in front of her, "Yes, we're poor but we're not Indians" (119).

Once she becomes active in the revolution, she works alongside other ladinos. She learns that there are some who are her compañeros in the struggle and that "being an Indian was an added dimension because I suffered discrimination as well as suffering exploitation" (166).

A former catechist for her Catholic church, Rigoberta Menchú soon comes to believe that the church and Christianity "are weapons they use to take away what is ours" (171). She further insists that she must keep her Indian identity and details of the Indian customs "secret" in the resistance struggle: "It was the community who taught me to respect all the things which must remain secret as long as we exist, and which future generations will keep secret. That is our objective anyway. When we began to organize ourselves, we started using all the things we'd kept hidden. Our traps—nobody knew about them because they'd been kept secret" (170).

Much later, after witnessing the torture and murders of her father, mother, and younger brother, she further develops her conscientization, her political consciousness—what I interpret as her feminist theory and practice: "My mother used to say that through her life, through her living testimony, she tried to tell women that they too had to participate, so that when the repression comes and with it a lot of suffering, it's not only the men who suffer" (196). Menchú's mother, whose name she chooses to keep "secret," lived her feminism—lived, as Menchú acknowledges, a feminism born of revolutionary struggle. Unlike most academic Western feminisms, this Quiché woman's feminism creates no dichotomy between theory and praxis: "Women must join the struggle in their own way. My mother's words told them that any evolution, any change, in which women had not participated, would not be a change, and there would be no victory. She was as clear about this as if she were a woman with all sorts of theories and a lot of practice" (196).

As Menchú records what her mother taught her, she regrets that she did not learn as much as she could have from her mother, who, in addition to her duties as the village midwife, practiced medicine using local leaves and plants.

Rigoberta Menchú's testimonio was originally spoken to the Venezuelan intellectual Elisabeth Burgos-Debray, and in the colonizer's language, Spanish. Menchú "theorizes" about the necessity of learning the oppressor's language. When the Quiché Indians speak the master's tongue, they can defend themselves against his tricks. When her father was imprisoned, the Menchú family paid a translator to communicate with the Spanish-speaking people in control of the legal system. The Menchús soon realized that the translator had been bought off by the government agents interested in keeping Vicente Menchú imprisoned.

What Rigoberta Menchú does not recognize, however, is that her testimonio, which witnesses to her people's lives, is in fact a theoretical statement; "You have to remember that my mother couldn't read or write and did not know any theories either" (216). As Menchú recounts her mother's life, we see how theory is transformed from "high" theory into the praxis of these women's lives:

> When [my mother] talked to me, before I had any specific work for the CUC [Peasant Unity Committee]. . . she said: "My child, we must organize. It's your duty to put into practice what you know. The days of paternalism, of saying 'poor girl, she doesn't know anything,' are over." My mother made no distinction between the men's struggle and the women's struggle. She said: "I don't want to make you stop feeling a woman, but your participation in the struggle must be equal to that of your brothers. But you mustn't join as just another number, you must carry out important tasks, analyze your position as a woman and demand a share." (219)

And finally, in Rigoberta Menchú's decision to break with the traditions of marriage and mothering we hear another version of revolutionary feminist theory: "I analyzed my ideas about not getting married with some of my compañeros. I realized that what I said wasn't crazy, that it wasn't some personal mad idea, but that our whole situation makes women think very hard before getting married, because who will look after the children, who will feed them?" (223). She understands as well that hers is a decision that only a minority of her compañeras advocate and that only few can realize. Many other women in the revolution marry, have children, and still engage in the struggle.

In *Crossing Borders,* published in 1998, Menchú chronicles her continued commitment to the revolution. Now married and a mother, Menchú understands that in the face of the notoriety that accompanied her 1992 Nobel Peace Prize award, her story and her integrity as a spokesperson will be challenged.[1] She resides in Guatemala City but she is a citizen of the world. Her diplomatic work extends to the struggle of indigenous people throughout the globe. While she no longer lives in the impoverished village she represented in her first testimonio, she claims a larger tribal community:

> I will never forget that I have a commitment to my humble home, to my own poor people, women with callused hands and shy uncertain smiles, a people with a profound sense of dignity. My debt to this people is not easily repaid. My commitment to them is not just from the past, it is in the present and the future. I know that millions of people would like to speak the words I speak, but they do not have the chance. They know their own reality, and I know the things I have related. I stand as a witness and, if I do not speak out, I would be party to great injustices. (1)

In *Crossing Borders*, Menchú discusses the transfrontera feminist philosophy that her mother practiced as a woman and as an indígena. Menchú acknowledges her mother as a "symbol of women and of indigenous peoples. She personifies two kinds of discrimination. Women and indigenous peoples have both been mistreated" (87). While disclaiming the status of philosopher, Menchú offers a vision of feminism as a political philosophy that centers on social justice for women and men. She critiques other liberation movements that were blind to the specific problems of women and indigenous people: "The liberation movements took a different approach, but they had no real understanding of the struggles of women and indigenous peoples either. They understood that privation and property were unjust, and they knew that they had to fight for social equality. No one can deny that this profound social awareness marked a big breakthrough towards democratisation. Yet it did not affect the position of women and indigenous people" (88).

Menchú emerges as a student of political ideologies she practiced as a leader of the indigenous Guatemalans. Her non-indigenous political allies offered inadequate political perspectives because they failed to consider indigenous values. She notes: "I tried to get hold of some of the important documents of the liberation movements in order to understand them better. Their theoretical manifestos are really limited. I imagine it's been the same in practice. If they don't grasp the theory properly, they won't grasp the practicalities either" (88). Clearly understanding the nuances of internalized racism and the existence of patriarchal women, she explains that the mere presence of indigenous people—or, in the case of gender issues, the presence of women—will not necessarily ensure their race or gender awareness.

The Sexuality of Latinas, edited by the Chicanas Norma Alarcón, Ana

Castillo, and Cherríe Moraga, includes an excerpt from Elvia Alvarado's testimonio *Don't Be Afraid, Gringo*. The complete work had been published in book form two years earlier, in 1987. As its subtitle, *A Honduran Woman Speaks from the Heart,* indicates, the testimonio is the genre emerging from the Third World that permits the literate, though not necessarily literary, campesina to address the reading world in a language and on topics not sanctioned by the literary institution. When U.S. Latinas include excerpts from Alvarado's testimony in their anthology on women's sexuality, we witness the extent to which Chicana feminism on the border transgresses geopolitical boundaries.

Unlike Barrios de Chungara and Menchú, Alvarado refuses to present an idealized version of the men in her life. Her own father, an alcoholic campesino, physically abused Alvarado's mother so violently that she left him when Alvarado was seven years old. Alvarado recounts that her mother "worked like a mule" to care for the children. Six years later, her mother left the children to live with a man who refused to support children not biologically his. With the restraint of a seasoned veteran of the Honduran prison system, Alvarado reports, "I never really had much of a childhood at all. By the time I was 13, I was already on my own. My mother went to live with a man in town. He didn't want to take care of her children, so she left us behind in the village. I wouldn't say she abandoned us; it's just one of those things that happens in life. She kept coming around to see how we were. To this day my mother always comes by my house to see how we're doing" (Alarcón et al., *Sexuality of Latinas,* 47). As we see in such texts as Viramontes's "Cariboo Cafe"; Claribel Alegría's collection of testimonios about the life and death of El Salvador's Comandante Eugenia, *They Won't Take Me Alive* (1987); and the anthology edited by Alicia Partnoy, *You Can't Drown the Fire* (1988), "mothering" and "motherhood" are complicated and transformed by women in the midst of revolutionary struggles.

Elvia Alvarado plots her transition from individual woman who joined a "mothers' club" sponsored by the Catholic Church to politically aware feminist who joins the struggle for land reform in her country of Honduras. She maps the transformation of church-sponsored mothers' clubs into consciousness-raising groups in which campesinas change the personal, the daily, the domestic, the so-called trivial, into the political. These consciousness-raising groups, however, diverge from their Western liberal feminist counterparts, where, as Sheila Rowbotham says, "To respond 'I feel better' about this or that was more important than a discussion of the strategic impact of action" (33). For Elvia Alvarado and her compañeras, the club meetings "became the high point of my week, because it was a chance to get together with other women and talk about the problems we had in common—like how to keep our children fed and our husbands sober. We learned that we had rights just like men did. We learned that we had to stop being so passive and start sticking up for our rights" (*Don't Be Afraid, Gringo*, 11).[2]

After a year of participation in the club, Alvarado attends a church-sponsored "course for social workers," in which she looks at "the reality of Honduran campesinas—what we did in our homes, what problems we had" (13). Initially worried about what to say to the "intellectuals" who ran the workshop, Elvia Alvarado demystifies the figure of the intellectual/político by asserting that the domestic problems the campesinas face are in fact the basis of political concerns. The women share their experiences as women and mothers, as well as community problems such as "the lack of good drinking water, no health clinic, no transportation, things like that. And we talked about how we could solve some of these problems" (13). The consciousness-raising group becomes a step in her overall conscientization wherein gender, racial, class, and agrarian reform issues are interconnected. For Alvarado, the project that initially began as a church-sanctioned means to discuss local domestic issues takes on a political language and purpose; she now intends "to take what I learned and share it with others" (13).

This politically charged language provides her with further impetus to proclaim her right to her sexuality; in so doing, Alvarado presents a scathing critique of leftist men whose politics do not extend to women's rights: "Many of the men who are involved in the struggle still want their wives to stay at home. They don't want their women to be active. So I've got a tall order to fill—to find a man who's not only sensitive to the campesino struggle but to the women's struggle as well!" (16). She understands that in her work throughout the Honduran countryside, a woman traveling without a male escort can be perceived as a sexual threat to other women. Alvarado notes that she has "learned to control" her desires, unlike many of the "male leaders," who leave their wives at home and "go with other women" in the city. In her opinion, these leaders are guilty of violating the campesinos' principles (90). "Another thing about the male leaders is that they often don't want their own wives to participate. They talk a good line about 'the role of women,' but when it comes to their women—well, that's a different story. I've never even seen the wives of some of the leaders, they're so well hidden. So I tell them, 'Hey, you big talkers, why don't you unlock your wives and let them out of the cage? Bring them around sometime so we can make sure they really exist' " (90).

Moreover, Alvarado's growing political consciousness extends to a critique of the Catholic Church, which drops the mothers' club as soon as the women begin to transform themselves: "We think they were afraid how far we'd gone.... The church forged a path for us, but they wanted us to follow behind. And when we started to walk ahead of them, when we started to open new paths ourselves, they tried to stop us.... They wanted us to give food out to malnourished mothers and children, but they didn't want us to question why we were malnourished to begin with. They wanted us to grow vegetables on the tiny plots around our houses, but they didn't want us to question why we didn't have enough land to feed ourselves" (16). The women's gatherings allowed political growth and sophistication: "Once we started getting together and talking to each other, we started asking these questions" (16). Women's issues remained central to Elvia Alvarado's activism even after the group changed its name in 1977 from Mothers' Club to Honduran Federation of Campesina Women (FEHMUC).

As I discussed in Chapter 2, the U.S. Latinas of the *Cuentos* anthology resisted the pressures of their histories of exile, struggle, and opposition through writing about what was once recounted through the oral tradition. Likewise, Elvia Alvarado resists her initial inclination not to serve as "raw material" for the interrogator, Medea Benjamin, and concludes that she must literally risk her life to tell the "gringa" intellectual her story. What she produces, however, is more than a cultural artifact: her text urges the reader to action. Just four days after being released from prison, where she was tortured for her work in the CNTC, the National Congress of Rural Workers, Alvarado meets Benjamin, her eventual editor, and fears that she is from the U.S. military base in Palmerola: "But then I decided that I couldn't pass up a chance to tell the world our story. Because our struggle is not a secret one, it's an open one. The more people who know our story the better. Even if you are a gringa, I thought, once you understand why we're fighting, if you have any sense of humanity, you'll have to be on our side" (xiii).

Indeed, it is its usefulness as a goad to action, to political praxis, that Alvarado envisions as the real value of her book. Further disrupting the traditional purpose of a literary text, she and her editor include a "Pledge of Support" at the end of the book. The reader is encouraged to send the pledge to the president of Honduras, urging him to "protect [her and others like her] who are working for justice" and to ensure their freedom of speech and assembly in Honduras (173). Alvarado problematizes the relationship between herself as an activist and the intellectuals who traditionally consume books for other purposes: "I hate to offend you, but we won't get anywhere by just writing and reading books. I know that books are important, and I hope this book will be important for the people who read it. But we can't just read it and say, 'Those poor campesinos. What a miserable life they have.'. . . But the important thing is not what you think of me; the important thing is for you to do something" (146).

As Doris Sommer understands, "the testimonial 'I' does not invite us to identify with it. We are too different, and there is no pretense here of universal or essential human experience" (" 'Not Just a Personal Story,' " 108). In addition, the "authors" of the testimonios do not worry about themselves as writers; their authority rests on their lives of action.

The parallels between the testimonios of Barrios de Chungara, Menchú, and Alvarado and the literary texts produced by the Chicana feminists on the border are in their purpose for writing—their challenge to the reader to *act*. At the Inter-American Book Fair held in San Antonio in October 1989, Sandra Cisneros read from her work in progress; she also passed out a flyer urging her audience to donate books to some of the United States' political prisoners, the refugees at the INS detention center in Laredo, Texas.

Also at the book fair was Demetria Martínez, the Chicana poet, reporter, and novelist from Albuquerque, New Mexico, whose own political commitment as writer and activist led to her arrest.[3] Her crime was her involvement with the sanctuary movement. She was indicted in December 1987 for helping two Salvadoreñas enter the United States. At the trial, the government's attorney used her poem "Nativity: For the Two Salvadoran Women, 1986–1987" as evidence against her. Here is an excerpt from the incriminating evidence:

Sisters I am no saint. Just a woman
who happens to be a reporter,
a reporter who happens
to be a woman,
squat in a forest, peeing
on pine needles,

watching you vomit morning sickness,
a sickness as infinite as the war in El Salvador,
a sickness my pen and notebook will not ease,
tell me, ¿Por qué están aquí?,
how did you cross over?
In my country we sing of a baby in a manger,
finance death squads,
how to write of this shame,
of the children you chose to save? (132–33)

Before Helena María Viramontes wrote "The Cariboo Cafe," she noted in her journal, "How can we sit here peacefully when we know that our tax dollars are supporting death squads in Central America? . . . Our silence is our submission."[4] The publication of contemporary Chicana political texts and the Latin American testimonios shatters the silence of acquiescence. As literary and cultural workers voice secrets that need to be told, we engage in resistance strategies as we report and analyze the struggles and their complexities. And when U.S. feministas develop a New Mestiza consciousness, we can begin to imagine encounters with women south of the U.S. border and formulate politically nuanced global mestiza coalitions.

Notes

Chapter 1. Reading Tejana, Reading Chicana

1. In a consciously political act, what Gloria Anzaldúa calls "linguistic terrorism," I will not italicize Spanish words or phrases unless they are italicized in direct quotations. I invite readers not fluent in Spanish to experience a sense of life on the border as we switch from English to Spanish. Sometimes we translate, at other times we assume the nonnative speaker will understand from the context. Many Chicanas/os speak only English. Reading Chicana texts puts several demands on the reader, including the expectation that the reader will be knowledgeable in multiple Chicana and Chicano linguistic, cultural, and historical contexts. While most contemporary Chicana writers and critics have been formally educated in the United States and are fluent in English and Spanish, many of the writers code-switch between the two languages in a conscious act of identity politics. The trajectory of this study moves from the personal, a lived experience, to more explicit global concerns of Chicana cultural workers. My political practice as a transfrontera border feminista informs my linguistic acts of "identitarian collectivities." Once I have given the non-Spanish-literate reader a sense of "alien" disorientation in the text, I move toward more inclusionary tactics and offer translations in Chapters 3 through 5.

2. See, for example, Sara Suleri's "Women Skin Deep."

3. My testimonio about living in South Texas in the 1960s and 1970s, a time before we had access to the term *Chicana* or to oppositional ideologies, is a work in progress, tentatively titled "Memorias Fronterizas: Memoirs of a Chicana Feminist."

4. Rodolfo Acuña's *Occupied America* offers a counterhistory of the Alamo. In addition to an overview of the political and economic impulses behind the Texas war, he presents an alternative version of the men who fought at the Texas shrine (8–9).

5. See Ramón Saldívar's *Chicano Narrative*, 5. In "The Folk Base of Chicano Narrative: Américo Paredes's *With His Pistol in His Hand* and the *Corrido* Tradition," Saldívar discusses the corrido as an early form of cultural resistance as well as a historical armed resistance by the Chicano population against Anglo-American domination.

6. In addition to Castañeda's essay, see Ramón Gutiérrez, *When Jesus Came, the Corn Mothers Went Away*, and the dissertation by Omar Valerio-Jiménez, "Tejanos in Nineteenth-Century South Texas."

7. See Angie Chabram-Dernersesian's excellent essay "I Throw Punches for My Race, But I Don't Want to Be a Man" for an analysis of the narrow patriarchal vision offered by the Movement.

8. Ruiz offers the following translation: "They'd hit us on the head, but good, or they'd paddle us with what they called the board of education for speaking Spanish. I didn't understand what they were telling me, not one iota. That's why I'm so committed to the bilingual program, heart and soul, because I suffered so horribly. I wasn't the only one, there were thousands of people who suffered in Arizona, Colorado, New Mexico, Texas, California; they degraded us horribly but we asserted ourselves."

9. In "Institutional Responsibility in the Provision of Educational Experiences to the Hispanic American Female Student," Mari Luci Jaramillo urges us not to internalize the failure of the educational system. She discusses the educational experiences of women of Mexican descent in the United States and argues that educators' emphasis should not focus on "dropout rates" or on "low performance levels." What we must examine, rather, are the "low *retention* rates and the inadequate instructional *socialization* practices" (26). See also Adelaida del Castillo and María Torres, "The Interdependency of Educational Institutions and Cultural Norms," in which they support Jaramillo's contention with an extensive review of ethnocentric social science literature that blames cultural traits (such as inherent passivity, fatalism, and even masochism) for Mexican Americans' inability to succeed in the U.S. educational system.

10. I attribute this well-known aphorism to Professor Paredes, from whom I heard it first in a graduate seminar on Mexican popular culture at the University of Texas at Austin in the fall of 1988.

11. The first two essays by Chicana scholars that presented a radical revision of La Malinche are "Malintzín Tenépal," published by Adelaida del Castillo in 1977; and Norma Alarcón's brilliant study of La Malinche in "Chicana Feminist Literature." Other important essays on La Malinche as subject in Chicana literary production include "The Concept of Cultural Identity in Chicana Poetry," by Elizabeth Ordóñez, and "Yo Soy La Malinche," by Mary Louise Pratt.

12. Angie Chabram-Dernersesian's "And Yes. . .the Earth Did Part," offers a detailed analysis of other texts by early-1970s Chicana poets. That literature signaled, in her words, "the ideological formations that led to the splitting of Chicana/o subjectivity . . . in which Chicanas consciously disassociated themselves from male hegemonic constructions of group identity" (39). In this chapter, I single out Angela de Hoyos's poetry to trace my own introduction in

the 1970s to the Movement literature. I do not intend to canonize de Hoyos's poetry or imply that it, though exemplary, was the only important literary work of the time.

Chapter 2. Chicana Feminisms

1. See Alma M. García's anthology, *Chicana Feminist Thought,* for several essays that refute or complicate that well-known statement, especially "La Feminista," by Anna NietoGomez, and "Chicanas and *El Movimiento,*" by Adaljiza Sosa Riddell.

2. For an example of how Moraga's theory enriches our readings of Chicana texts, see Chapter 4.

3. Muñoz points out that recent texts by New Left scholars omit contributions by Chicanos, African Americans, and other people of color, promoting the illusion that "the history of the 1960s was a history centered on white radical middle-class youth" (*Youth, Identity, Power,* 3).

4. See Yvonne Yarbro-Bejarano, "Expanding the Categories of Race and Sexuality in Lesbian and Gay Studies," for an analysis of how to engage in this type of Chicana feminism that destabilizes heterosexual privilege.

5. In "The Theoretical Subject(s) of *This Bridge Called My Back* and Anglo-American Feminism," Norma Alarcón critiques MacKinnon's tactics: "With gender as the central concept in feminist thinking, epistemology is flattened out in such a way that we lose sight of the complex and multiple ways of which the subject and object of possible experience are constituted" (361).

6. My use of the term *politics* is influenced by my reading of Gramsci's *Prison Notebooks* as well as Eric Hobsbawm's "Gramsci and Marxist Political Theory."

7. Bourne's inability to read the Combahee statement is yet another example of the exclusionary practice of European and Euro-American feminists with regard to the feminisms practiced by U.S. women of color. I again refer the reader to Norma Alarcón's "The Theoretical Subject(s) of *This Bridge Called My Back* and Anglo-American Feminism." On identity politics as a strategic practice, see Laura Elisa Pérez, "Opposition and the Education of Chicanos/as."

8. See the Epilogue for a preliminary discussion of the testimonio as a literary and political form and how feminism on the border makes the connection with activist Latinas and indigenous women across geopolitical boundaries.

9. In Moraga's subsequent text, *The Last Generation*, she continues her political feminist theorizing, updating the list she began in *Bridge*. My work in progress, "Between My Art and Activism," again relies on Moraga's formulations as she transforms Chicano nationalism and Aztlán into this political border feminism.

10. See Fernández Retamar's essay "Calibán." José Saldívar, in both "Calibán and Resistance" and *The Dialectics of Our America*, applies Fernández Re-

tamar's theory to texts by Richard Rodriguez, Ernesto Galarza, and Cherríe Moraga. Eliana Ortega, however, argues in "Poetic Discourse of the Puerto Rican Woman in the United States" that Calibán "signifies only a half liberation" for Latin American women "because as long as the mother figure (Sycorax) remains forgotten, as long as women continue to be silenced, there can be no liberation for an entire people" (125).

11. Random House issued the Cisneros work in 1994, but I cite the 1988 edition, published by Arte Público Press.

Chapter 3. Mestiza Consciousness and Politics

1. With the publication of Anzaldúa's text, a cottage industry in border writing began. Many specialists in Chicana and Chicano studies would remind contemporary readers that at least since the 1950s, with Américo Paredes's work as an anthropologist and folklorist, the U.S.–Mexico border has been studied in its historical and geographical specificity. For Chicano studies scholars, the political location between the United States and Mexico is the crucial locus for borderlands studies. More recently, the border has been colonized and appropriated as mere metaphor. For a brilliant discussion and critique of these absorption strategies see Yvonne Yarbro-Bejarano's essay "Gloria Anzaldúa's *Borderlands / La Frontera*," 8–10.

2. See Chela Sandoval's important essay "U.S. Third World Feminism."

3. *Fronterista* is a word I coin to merge *frontera* (border) and *feminista* (feminist). My thanks to Clara Lomas for pointing out that my Chicana dialect may not be understood by standard Spanish readers.

4. In her essay "Chingón Politics Die Hard," Elizabeth Martínez discusses how the continued sexism in Chicano activist circles is ingrained in the misogynist, patriarchal concept of Aztlán. Martínez speaks to contemporary Chicana feminist concerns that the nationalism of the Movimiento is "reactionary on issues of race and class relations. . . . Not surprisingly, the concept of Aztlán has always been set forth in ferociously macho imagery. The average Chicano today hardly takes Aztlán seriously as a goal, but he might secretly imagine himself garbed in an Aztec warrior outfit gazing on the naked breasts of some red-lipped princess. If you note the whiff of sexual possession there, it's no accident. Merely as a symbol, the concept of Aztlán encourages the association of machismo with domination" (47).

5. See Yarbro-Bejarano's discussion of the charges of essentialism in Anzaldúa's work in "Gloria Anzaldúa's *Borderlands*," 12–13.

6. See "Teoría y creación en la prosa de Gloria Anzaldúa" by María Socorro Tabuenca Córdoba for a discussion of "La Prieta."

7. In her essay "La Prieta" in Moraga and Anzaldúa, *This Bridge Called My Back,* Anzaldúa discusses the onset of her precocious menarche as a three-month-old infant. I thank Felix Hull, M.D., for the medical information on early-onset menarche.

Chapter 4. Mujeres en Lucha / Mujeres de Fuerza

1. As this book goes to press, over 49,000 copies of Cisneros's *Woman Hollering Creek and Other Stories* had been sold, in both hardcover and paperback. My thanks to Theresa Delgadillo for this figure.

2. For a classic Chicana statement on the notion of Chicana triple oppression see Denise Segura, "Chicanas and Triple Oppression in the Labor Force." She emphasizes "*class* as opposed to culture [as] the arena in which triple oppression is organized and expressed" (61).

3. The term *conscientization* is a translation of the Portuguese *concientização*, elaborated by Paulo Freire. In *Pedagogy of the Oppressed*, Freire explores the politics of literacy in the Third World, specifically Brazil and Chile, and discusses how teaching the masses how to "read" the world and develop a critical consciousness is as important as teaching them how to read a written text. See also Anzaldúa's theory of New Mestiza consciousness in *Borderlands* for a similar oppositional strategy.

4. "Greater Mexico," according to Américo Paredes and other borderlands critics, extends farther than the arbitrary borders that the United States maps out. Wherever there is a cluster of Mexican Americans or people of Mexican origin in the United States, we can claim the area as Mexican territory, culturally if not legally.

5. Rodríguez and Gutiérrez were among the first critics to present readings of *The House on Mango Street*. For discussions of genre and Chicana/o literature, see Héctor Calderón's important essay "Rudolfo Anaya's *Bless Me Ultima*." Calderón categorizes Tomás Rivera's . . . *Y no se lo tragó la tierra* as a novel "following the realistic, exemplary tradition of Cervantes allowing for the reader's sense of discernment in the performative situation" (26). See also Erlinda González-Berry and Tey Diana Rebolledo's "Growing Up Chicano," Julin Olivares's "Sandra Cisneros' *The House on Mango Street* and the Poetics of Space," and Ellen McCracken's "Sandra Cisneros' *The House on Mango Street*." In "The Deterritorialization of Esperanza Cordero," Alejandro Morales reads the text as a pessimistic exercise in "isolation and exile" (227). He perceives Esperanza as a "character without a history" (230), because he does not recognize the alternative history of subaltern women.

6. I owe much of my formulation about Third World literatures and theory to Barbara Harlow, whose graduate seminar on Third World literature at the University of Texas in 1988 opened up a new context for my early thoughts on Chicana literature and theory. Harlow's *Resistance Literature* served as a model for my rethinking of Chicana literature in a global context.

7. See Rey Chow, "Rereading Mandarin Ducks and Butterflies."

8. See Manuel Peña, *The Texas-Mexican Conjunto*. Additionally, while many Chicanists find Michael Fischer's essay "Ethnicity and the Post-Modern Arts of Memory" useful, his inattention to historical specificity leaves him vulnerable to charges of culture collecting. José David Saldívar, in "The Limits of Cultural Studies," critiques Fischer and other cultural studies scholars whose projects universalize "minority" experiences.

9. Acuña's discussion of the bracero program in *Occupied America* remains one of the most insightful and comprehensive sources. He notes that when Mexico lifted the blacklist against Texas, it affected Chicano migration to the Chicago area (263). In her 1928 dissertation, "Conditions Surrounding Mexicans in Chicago," Anita Edgar Jones chronicles the presence of Mexicans in the Midwest. Chicago's steel mills and railroad industries drew Chicano job seekers to the area. Jones cites census records from the 1850s to document the presence of Mexicans in Chicago.

10. See bell hooks's *Ain't I a Woman* for a critique of nineteenth-century feminism and an analysis of how the movement was led by white women who could not restrain their own racism and class prejudices. In her discussion of Gilman's radical politics, Josephine Donovan, in *Feminist Theory*, failed to mention Gilman's class and race prejudices. Servants, according to Gilman in *The Home*, are "strangers by birth, by race, by education.... They invade the *privacy* of middle-class women; they possess 'uncultivated minds'... Is this the kind of mind to which we offer the close and constant inspection of our family life?" (42–43).

11. In a conversation with Cisneros, I learned that the original manuscript showed a multiracial, multiethnic neighborhood, more closely reflecting one of the borderlands barrios that the Cisneros family occupied in its migrations between Chicago and Mexico City. Her revisions reflect the pressures of attempting to market the book as depicting a specifically Chicana/o, Latina/o barrio. Also, see Acuña, *Occupied America*, 408, for documentation of the relationship between Chicanos and Puerto Ricans in the Midwest. For Chicana and Puerto Rican feminists who bond through their political identification as women of color in the United States, see Alma Gómez et al., *Cuentos*, and Asunción Horno-Delgado et al., *Breaking Boundaries*.

12. See Frigga Haug, *Female Sexualization*, especially 174–75.

13. My thanks to José David Saldívar for pointing out "Sire" as the story's shorthand for "desire" and for the long discussions on the "aesthetics of the border."

14. I analyze "Remember the Alamo" in "Between My Art and Activism," my manuscript in progress. Cisneros's insistence on including Chicanas/os and Latinas/os in the list of AIDS fatalities interrupts the representation of AIDS as a white gay male's province. For an excellent reading of "Never Marry a Mexican," see Katherine Rios's " 'And you know what I have to say isn't always pleasant.' " See also "A Geography of Scars," Mary Pat Brady's important exploration of spatiality and the construction of Chicana subjectivity. In " 'A Silence between Us Like a Language,' " Harryette Mullen explores the nuances of language and Chicana class transgression in Cisneros's "Bien Pretty" and "Never Marry a Mexican."

15. Interview with Cisneros, Austin, Texas, July 1988. Cisneros began "Woman Hollering Creek," the first of her "Texas stories," in the spring and summer of 1987, when she lived in Austin. She taught at California State University at Chico that fall and revised the story in January 1988 in California. As of this writing, Cisneros has returned to San Antonio, Texas, where she is working on a novel, "Caramelo."

16. See Cisneros, "From a Writer's Notebook."

17. See Raúl Trejo Delarbre, *Televisa: El quinto poder*. Particularly relevant is the "Cronología" by Fernando Mejía Barquera, 19–39, which documents the contradictory impulses of the Mexican television industry: at times it has been fiercely nationalistic, yet its programming is undeniably what he calls "pro-Yankee."

18. See Carola García Calderón, *Revistas femeninas,* for a discussion of such women's journals as the Latin American version of *Cosmopolitan,* which are available in the United States. See also Cornelia Butler Flora and Jan L. Flora, "The Fotonovela as a Tool for Class and Cultural Domination."

19. The telenovela *Los ricos también lloran* was presented on Univisión in 1989–90. Unlike U.S. soap operas, the Latin American soaps do not continue their story lines for years; each sequence lasts only a few months. Some novelas that have set viewing records are updated with new actors and showcase the latest fashions, cars, and other consumer items.

20. My thanks to Barbara Harlow, whose words and teachings I echo here and throughout my work.

21. I am indebted to my colleague Katherine King, who pointed out that Cleófilas indeed means "daughter of history."

22. At the annual meetings of the Modern Language Association in 1989, Hortense Spillers's presentation "Eva Peace, So Early in the Morning," on infanticide in Toni Morrison's *Sula* and *Beloved,* influenced my reading of Cisneros's text. Spillers's readings of Morrison's texts corroborated the connection between this African American tradition and the Chicana oral traditions of La Malinche and La Llorona. I also thank Jane Marcus for her early discussions with me of these similarities.

23. Among the essays that place the legend of La Llorona in a European context are "La Llorona and Related Themes" by Bacil Kirtley. My own memory of the legend differs from the variants cited by Kirtley. See his essay for the "typical" [male] version. See Thomas Janvier's text for his assertion that La Llorona is an entirely indigenous Mexican creation because of her strong resemblance to two Aztec goddesses. Marta Weigle, in *Spiders and Spinsters,* contextualizes La Llorona within a female tradition of strong goddess figures both in Europe and among Amerindians. Gloria Anzaldúa in *Borderlands* and Cherríe Moraga in *The Last Generation* also have extensive discussions of La Llorona. Chapter 5 in this book elaborates Chicana feminist revisions of La Llorona in an urban, transnational context.

24. For other essays on Malintzín Tenépal, see my citations in Chapter 2.

25. My formulations here rely almost totally on tutorial sessions with the noted folklorist Beverly Stoeltje early in my graduate career. Professor Stoeltje generously shared her extensive bibliography on La Llorona as well as a copy of José Limón's "Folk Performance of 'Chicano.' " My own work on Chicana writers would not have continued without her support.

26. Fray Diego Durán, in *"The Book of the Gods and Rites" and "The Ancient Calendar"* (1576–79) and *The History of the Indies of New Spain* (1580?–81), among the earliest histories of the conquest, documents the enslavement of the Indians. In the introduction to the first work, the editor and

the translator cite Durán's eyewitness account of the evidence of slavery in Mexico (12).

Chapter 5. "I Hear the Women's Wails and I Know Them to Be My Own"

1. This is a paraphrase of Althusser's statement on the role of philosophy: "Philosophy is a *practice* of political *intervention* carried out in a theoretical form" ("Ideology and the State," 107).

2. See ibid., 12.

3. George Sánchez, in *Becoming Mexican American*, explains that the creation of the Border Patrol in 1924 "was crucial in defining the Mexican as 'the other,' the 'alien,' in the [Southwest]." One of Sánchez's sources reports that in the late 1920s, "some of the early immigration inspectors were members of the Ku Klux Klan, which was a leading organization in the El Paso region at the time" (58–59). A more recent example of how local police and sheriff departments enforce U.S. policy is the beating of a female undocumented worker in Riverside County, California, on April 1, 1996. The *Los Angeles Times* reported the incident in a series of articles on April 2 (A1, A20), 3 (A8, A12), and 4 (A18). What makes that incident unusual is that a news camera captured it.

4. See Raymond Williams's extensive discussion of dominant, residual, and emergent practices in *Marxism and Literature*. He defines a residual practice as one that was

formed in the past, but is still active in the cultural process, not only and often not at all as an element of the past, but as an effective element of the present. Thus certain experiences, meanings, and values which cannot be expressed or substantially verified in terms of the dominant culture, are nevertheless lived and practiced on the basis of the residue—cultural as well as social—of some previous social and cultural institution or formation. It is crucial to distinguish this aspect of the residual, which may have an alternative or even oppositional relation to the dominant culture, from that active manifestation of the residual. . .which has been wholly or largely incorporated into the dominant culture. (122)

In my discussion of "The Moths," women turn to residual indigenous practices to survive patriarchal traditions that Chicanos have chosen to perpetuate in an attempt to resist domination in the United States.

5. In "Demarginalizing the Intersection of Race and Sex," Kimberle Crenshaw offers an excellent definition of intersectionality.

I am suggesting that Black women can experience discrimination in ways that are both similar to and different from those experienced by white women and Black men. Black women sometimes experience discrimination in ways similar to white women's experiences; sometimes they share very similar experiences with Black men. Yet they often experience double-discrimination—the combined effects of practices which discriminate on the basis of race, and on the basis of sex. And sometimes, they experience discrimination as Black women—not the sum of race and sex discrimination, but as Black women. (63–64)

My reliance on theories of intersectionality articulated by African American feminists merely echoes the Chicana feminism that Cherríe Moraga developed in the late 1970s. (See Chapter 2.)

6. In "Marginality in the Teaching Machine," Gayatri Chakravorty Spivak elaborates a theory about "the relationship between academic and 'revolutionary' practices in the interest of social change." She cautions the contemporary "radical academic" not to "[establish] 'marginality' as a subject-position in literary and cultural critique. The reader must accustom herself to starting from a particular situation and then to the ground shifting under her feet" (53). This is familiar terrain for Alma Gómez and her colleagues, the Latina editors who wrote Latina feminist theory in the introduction to *Cuentos*. I refer you to my discussion in Chapter 2.

7. In "Sin Fronteras," Devra Weber asserts that many parts of the U.S. Southwest have been "re-Mexicanized." As she states: "Shifts in immigration have reinfused the community with Mexicans and different regions of Mexican culture. The barrio of East Los Angeles, for example, which was Chicano or Mexican American ten years ago, is now clearly more Mexican" (16). More recently, Chicana/o barrios in Greater Los Angeles have become not only more Mexican but more Central American.

8. Norma Alarcón, in "Making 'Familia' from Scratch," deploys Julia Kristeva's term *symbolic contract* in her analysis of Chicana fiction. She notes that for Kristeva the symbolic contract "refers to the Patriarchal Law and/or linguistic domain. In [Kristeva's] work the subject, who is almost always male, is conjectured as one who finds 'his identity in the symbolic, [and] *separates* from his fusion with the mother' " (158, citing Kristeva, "Revolution in Poetic Language").

9. Feminist Chicanas in the late 1960s and 1970s had to confront both Chicano nationalists and the emergent Women's Movement simultaneously. See Patricia Zavella, "The Problematic Relationship of Feminism and Chicana Studies." As she reminds us, at that time, "when white feminists were recognizing the tyranny of the traditional family, Chicana activists were celebrating the unity of the traditional Chicano family." Zavella urges us to remember that there were other significant differences between White and Chicana feminists: "at a time white feminists were demanding reproductive rights, including the right to abortions, Chicana activists were fighting forced sterilizations and defending the right to bear children" (27). Zavella's assertions further complicate my discussion about family and women's rights within the family.

10. For a complete review of these essays, see Richard Griswold del Castillo, *La Familia*, particularly chap. 1. Also see Octavio Romano's classic essay on traditional social scientists' biases, "The Anthropology and Sociology of the Mexican-Americans." Of further interest is William Madsen, *The Mexican Americans of South Texas*, in which Madsen adapts the infamous Moynihan report on African Americans to the Chicana/o situation.

11. Baca Zinn cites the following texts for discussions on the internal colony model: Tomás Almaguer, "Toward the Study of Chicano Colonialism," *Aztlán* 2, no. 1 (Spring 1971); Rodolfo Acuña, *Occupied America;* Joan W. Moore, "Colonialism: The Case of the Mexican American," *Social Problems* 17, no. 4

(Spring 1970); Mario Barrera, Carlos Muñoz, and Charles Ornelas, "The Barrio as an Internal Colony," in *People and Politics in an Urban Society*, ed. Harlan Hahn, vol. 6 of *Urban Affairs Annual Reviews* (1972).

12. In my work in progress, "Between My Art and Activism," I elaborate on how Moraga's manifesto in *The Last Generation* begins a transformation of exclusionary Movimiento practices into a nationalism that is in reality a brilliant rearticulation of Chicana activist feminism. For a complete analysis of Rendón's manifesto, see Angie Chabram-Dernersesian's "I Throw Punches for My Race, but I Don't Want to Be a Man," (83–85).

13. For a contemporary revision of the epithet "loose woman," see Sandra Cisneros's poetry collection *Loose Woman*. In the title poem she proclaims: "I break laws, / upset the natural order, / anguish the Pope and make fathers cry. / I am beyond the jaw of law. / I'm *la desperada*, most-wanted public enemy. / . . . I strike terror among the men" (114). See my "Feminism on the Border" for a detailed critique of Mirandé and Enríquez, *La Chicana*, and Mirandé's *Chicano Experience*.

14. I differentiate between Mexican national, an upper-class, educated citizen of Mexico, and Mexican American and Chicano.

15. Kalpana Bardhan states that patriarchal women express "female conservatism," which "is often explained in terms of 'false consciousness' (or cognitive dissonance, an euphemism for underdeveloped psyche). . . . However, female conservatism develops logically out of women's strategies of influence and survival within patrilocal, patriarchal structures. They are . . . the product of resourceful behavior under extremely disadvantageous circumstances" (quoted in Spivak, "Women in Difference," 89).

16. It is interesting to note that earlier in this story, when the narrator eats a final meal that her abuela has prepared, "a fine Sunday breeze entered the kitchen and a rose petal calmly feathered down to the table" (26).

17. In "Woman in Difference," Spivak's proposals about women's spaces in the decolonized nation are quite appropriate for Chicana and Mexicana positions in post–nationalist liberation Aztlán. "It must be admitted that there is always a space in the new nation that cannot share in the energy of this reversal [the interests of the new nation after liberation]. This space had no established agency of traffic with the culture of imperialism. Paradoxically, this space is also outside of organized labor, below the attempted reversals of capital logic" (78). The space in Viramontes's narrative of Chicana and Mexicana subproletariat is women's space.

18. See my discussions on how Mexican women and Chicanas are figured as Malinches and Lloronas in Chapters 2 and 4 and at the end of this chapter.

19. My reading here is clearly indebted to Spivak's influential essay "Women in Difference," 81–82.

20. See also Alarcón, "Making 'Familia' from Scratch."

21. In an unpublished interview Viramonte noted that a newscast about the Salvadoran death squads spurred her to write "The Cariboo Cafe." While the woman in this historia could have come from any of several Latin American countries, Viramontes's words inspire me to locate her in El Salvador.

22. Because of its eloquence and comprehensiveness, I will use Marjorie Agosín's definition of *desaparecidos:*

The term *disappearances* was used for the first time to describe a specific governmental practice which was applied on a wide scale in Guatemala after 1966, in Chile toward the end of 1973 and in Argentina beginning in March, 1976. *To disappear* means to be snatched off a street corner, or dragged from one's bed, or taken from a movie theater or a café either by police, soldiers, or men in civilian clothes, and from that moment on, to disappear from the face of the earth, leaving not a single trace. It means that all knowledge of the *disappeared* is totally lost. Absolutely nothing is to be known about them. What was their fate? What are they enduring? If they are dead, where are their bones? (*Scraps of Life*, 3–4)

23. Once again, I rely on Agosín's influential *Scraps of Life* for my use of the arpillera imagery. Chilean women wove their testimonios against Pinochet's dictatorship into their tapestries.

24. For a different reading of "Neighbors," see Pavletich and Backus, "With His Pistol in *Her* Hand."

25. As of this writing, "Paris Rats in L.A." remains unpublished. I cite the page numbers in the author's manuscript.

26. I indicate additional sources on La Llorona in Chapter 4.

27. For further discussion of the Chicano nationalist notion of Aztlán, see the anthology edited by Rudolfo A. Anaya and Francisco Lomeli, *Aztlán: Essays on the Chicano Homeland.*

Epilogue: "Refugees of a World on Fire"

1. See Stoll, *Rigoberta Menchú,* for an example of how the right attempts to discredit her historia.

2. All subsequent quotations are from this text.

3. See Martínez's novel *Mother Tongue* for yet another example of Chicana feminism on the border.

4. My thanks to Helena María Viramontes for sharing the journal with me as well as allowing me to read early drafts of her works in progress. In *Under the Feet of Jesus*, Viramontes offers a different study of the Chicana Third World, this time in the rural camps of agricultural migrant workers.

References

Acuña, Rodolfo. *Occupied America: A History of Chicanos.* 2d ed. New York: Harper & Row, 1981.

Agosín, Marjorie. *Scraps of Life: Chilean Arpilleras / Chilean Women and the Pinochet Dictatorship.* Trans. Cola Franzen. Trenton, N.J.: Red Sea Press, 1987.

Alarcón, Norma. "Anzaldúa's *Frontera:* Inscribing Gynetics." In *Displacement, Diaspora, and Geographies of Identity,* ed. Smadar Lavie and Ted Swedenburg, 35–58. Durham: Duke University Press, 1996.

———. "Chicana Feminism: In the Tracks of 'the' Native Woman." *Cultural Studies* 4, no. 3 (1990): 248–55.

———. "Chicana Feminist Literature: A Re-vision through Malintzín: Putting the Flesh Back on the Object." In *This Bridge Called My Back: Writings by Radical Women of Color,* ed. Cherríe Moraga and Gloria Anzaldúa, 2d ed., 182–90. New York: Kitchen Table–Women of Color Press, 1983.

———. "Chicana Writers and Critics in a Social Context: Towards a Contemporary Bibliography." In *The Sexuality of Latinas,* ed. Norma Alarcón, Ana Castillo, and Cherríe Moraga. *Third Woman* 4 (1989): 169–78 (special issue).

———. "Conjugating Subjects: The Heteroglossia of Essence and Resistance." In *An Other Tongue: Nation and Ethnicity in the Linguistic Borderlands,* ed. Alfred Arteaga, 125–38. Durham: Duke University Press, 1994.

———. "Making 'Familia' from Scratch: Split Subjectivities in the Work of Helèna María Viramontes and Cherríe Moraga." In *Chicana Creativity and Criticism: Charting New Frontiers in American Literature,* ed. María Herrera-Sobek and Helena María Viramontes. *Americas Review* 15, nos. 3–4 (Fall–Winter 1987): 147–59 (special issue).

———. "The Theoretical Subject(s) of *This Bridge Called My Back* and Anglo-American Feminism." In *Making Face, Making Soul / Haciendo Caras: Cre-*

ative and Critical Perspectives by Women of Color, ed. Gloria Anzaldúa, 356–69. San Francisco: Aunt Lute Foundation Books, 1990.

———. "Tradutora, Traditora: A Paradigmatic Figure of Chicana Feminism." *Cultural Critique* 13 (Fall 1989): 57–87.

———, ed. *Chicana Critical Issues.* Berkeley: Third Woman Press, 1993.

Alarcón, Norma, Ana Castillo, and Cherríe Moraga, eds. *The Sexuality of Latinas. Third Woman* 4 (1989) (special issue).

Alegría, Claribel. *They Won't Take Me Alive: Salvadorean Women in Struggle for National Liberation.* Trans. Amanda Hopkinson. London: Women's Press, 1987.

Althusser, Louis. "Ideology and the State." In *Lenin and Philosophy and Other Essays.* Trans. Ben Bruster. New York: Monthly Review Press, 1971, 127–86.

Alvarado, Elvia. *Don't Be Afraid, Gringo: A Honduran Woman Speaks from the Heart.* Ed. Medea Benjamin. San Francisco: Institute for Food and Development Policy, 1987.

Anaya, Rudolfo A., and Francisco Lomeli. *Aztlán: Essays on the Chicano Homeland.* Albuquerque: University of New Mexico Press, 1989.

Anzaldúa, Gloria. *Borderlands / La Frontera: The New Mestiza.* San Francisco: Spinsters/Aunt Lute, 1987.

Anzaldúa, Gloria, and Cherríe Moraga, eds. *This Bridge Called My Back: Writings by Radical Women of Color.* 2d ed. New York: Kitchen Table–Women of Color Press, 1983.

Apodaca, María Linda. "A Double-Edge Sword: Hispanas and Liberal Feminism." *Crítica* 1, no. 3 (1986): 96–114.

Baca Zinn, Maxine. "Chicanas: Power and Control in the Domestic Sphere." *De Colores* 2, no. 3 (1975): 19–31.

———. "Political Familism: Toward Sex Role Equality in Chicano Families." *Aztlán* 6, no. 1 (1975): 13–25.

Bakhtin, Mikhail. "Discourse in the Novel." In *The Dialogic Imagination: Four Essays by M. M. Bakhtin*, ed. Michael Holquist, 259–442. Austin: University of Texas Press, 1981.

Barrios de Chungara, Domitila, with Moema Viezzer. *Let Me Speak! Testimony of Domitila, a Woman of the Bolivian Mines.* Trans. Victoria Ortiz. New York: Monthly Review Press, 1978.

Baym, Nina. *Women's Fiction: A Guide to Novels by and about Women in America, 1820–1870.* Ithaca: Cornell University Press, 1978.

Bejar, Ruth. *Translated Woman: Crossing the Border with Esperanza's Story.* Boston: Beacon Press, 1993.

Benjamin, Walter. "On Language as Such and on the Language of Man." In *Reflections: Essays, Aphorisms, Autobiographical Writings*, ed. Peter Demetz, 314–32. New York: Harcourt Brace Jovanovich, 1978.

Beverley, John. *Against Literature.* Minneapolis: University of Minnesota Press, 1993.

———. "The Margin at the Center: On *Testimonio* (Testimonial Narrative)." *Modern Fiction Studies* 35, no. 1 (Spring 1989): 11–27.

Beverley, John, and Marc Zimmerman. *Literature and Politics in the Central American Revolutions*. Austin: University of Texas Press, 1990.

Bonilla, Gloria. "Talking: Testimonio." In *You Can't Drown the Fire: Latin American Women Writing in Exile,* ed. Alicia Partnoy, 34–37. Pittsburgh: Cleis Press, 1988.

Bourne, Jenny. "Homelands of the Mind: Jewish Feminism and Identity Politics." *Race and Class* 29 (1987): 1–24.

Brady, Mary Pat. "A Geography of Scars: Desire, Mobility, and Memories of Violence in Sandra Cisneros's *Woman Hollering Creek and Other Stories*." In "Extinct Lands, Scarred Bodies: Chicana Literature and the Reinvention of Space." Ph.D. dissertation, University of California, Los Angeles, 1996, 125–97.

Calderón, Hector. "Rudolfo Anaya's *Bless Me Ultima*: A Chicano Romance of the Southwest." *Crítica* 1, no. 3 (1986): 21–47.

———. "To Read Chicano Narrative: Commentary and Metacommentary." *Mester* 2, no. 2 (1982): 3–14.

Calderón García, Carola. *Revistas femeninas: La mujer como objeto de consumo*. Mexico City: El Caballito, 1980.

Carby, Hazel V. " 'On the Threshold of Woman's Era': Lynching, Empire, and Sexuality in Black Feminist Theory." *Critical Inquiry* 12 (1985): 262–77.

———. *Reconstructing Womanhood: The Emergence of the Afro-American Woman Novelist*. New York: Oxford University Press, 1987.

Castañeda, Antonia. "Presidarias y pobladoras: Spanish-Mexican Women in Frontier Monterey, California, 1770–1821." Ph.D. dissertation, Stanford University, 1990.

———. "Sexual Violence in the Politics and Policies of Conquest." In *Building with Our Hands: New Directions in Chicana Studies*, ed. Adela de la Torre and Beatríz M. Pesquera, 15–33. Berkeley: University of California Press, 1993.

Castillo, Ana. "1975." In *Women Are Not Roses*. Houston: Arte Público Press, 1984.

Cervantes, Lorna Dee. "Refugee Ship." In *Emplumada*. Pittsburgh: University of Pittsburgh Press, 1981.

Chabram-Dernersesian, Angie. "And Yes. . . the Earth Did Part: On the Splitting of Chicana/o Subjectivity." In *Building with Our Hands: New Directions in Chicana Studies*, ed. Adela de la Torre and Beatríz M. Pesquera, 34–56. Berkeley: University of California Press, 1993.

———. "I Throw Punches for My Race, But I Don't Want to Be a Man: Writing Us—Chica-nos (Girl, Us) / Chicanas—into the Movement Script." In *Cultural Studies*, ed. Lawrence Grossberg, Cary Nelson, and Paula A. Treichler, 81–95. New York: Routledge, 1992.

Chávez, Denise. *The Face of an Angel*. New York: Farrar, Straus & Giroux, 1994.

———. *The Last of the Menu Girls*. Houston: Arte Público Press, 1986.

———. "Novena Narrativas y Ofrendas Nuevo-Mexicanas." In *Chicana Crea-

tivity and Criticism: Charting New Frontiers in American Literature, ed. María Herrera-Sobek and Helena María Viramontes. *Americas Review* 15, nos. 3–4 (1987): 85–100 (special issue).

Cheung, King-Kok. Introduction. In *Seventeen Syllables and Other Stories*, by Hisaye Yamamoto, xi–xxv. New York: Kitchen Table–Women of Color Press, 1988.

Chow, Rey. "Rereading Mandarin Ducks and Butterflies: A Response to the 'Postmodern' Condition." *Cultural Critique* 5 (Winter 1986–87): 69–93.

Cisneros, Sandra. "Cactus Flowers: In Search of Tejana Feminist Poetry." *Third Woman* 1–2 (1986): 73–80.

———. "From a Writer's Notebook: Ghosts and Voices: Writing from Obsession." *Americas Review* 15 (1987): 69–73.

———. *The House on Mango Street*. 2d rev. ed. Houston: Arte Público Press, 1988.

———. *Loose Woman*. New York: Random House, 1994.

———. "Woman Hollering Creek." In *Woman Hollering Creek and Other Stories*. New York: Random House, 1991.

Cockcroft, James D. *Outlaws in the Promised Land: Mexican Immigrant Workers and America's Future*. New York: Grove Press, 1986.

Cotera, Martha. *The Chicana Feminist*. Austin: Information Systems Publications, 1977.

———. *Diosa y hembra*. Austin: Information Systems Publications, 1976.

Crenshaw, Kimberle. "Demarginalizing the Intersection of Race and Sex: A Black Feminist Critique of Antidiscrimination Doctrine, Feminist Theory, and Antiracist Politics." In *Feminism in the Law: Theory, Practice, and Criticism. University of Chicago Legal Forum*, 1989, 139–67.

de Hoyos, Angela. *Arise! Chicano, and Other Poems*. San Antonio: M & A Editions, 1975.

———. *Chicano Poems for the Barrio*. San Antonio: M & A Editions, 1975.

de la Torre, Adela, and Beatríz M. Pesquera, eds. *Building with Our Hands: New Directions in Chicana Studies*. Berkeley: University of California Press, 1993.

del Castillo, Adelaida R. "Malintzín Tenépal: A Preliminary Look into a New Perspective." In *Essays on la Mujer*, ed. Rosaura Sánchez and Rosa Martínez Cruz, 124–49. Los Angeles: Chicano Studies Research Center Publications, University of California, 1977.

———. "Mexican Women in Organization." In *Mexican Women in the United States.: Struggles Past and Present*, ed. Magdalena Mora and Adelaida R. del Castillo. Los Angeles: Chicano Studies Research Center Publications, University of California, 1980, 7–16.

del Castillo, Adelaida R., and María Torres. "The Interdependency of Educational Institutions and Cultural Norms: The Hispana Experience." In *The Broken Web: The Educational Experience of Hispanic American Women*, ed. Teresa McKenna and Flora Ida Ortiz. Claremont, Calif.: Tomás Rivera Center; Berkeley: Floricanto Press, 1988, 39–60.

del Castillo, Richard Griswold. "Commentary." In *Western Women: Their*

Land, Their Lives, ed. Lillian Schlissel, Vicki L. Ruiz, and Janice Monk. Albuquerque: University of New Mexico Press, 1988, 43–46.

———. *La Familia: Chicano Families in the Urban Southwest, 1848 to the Present.* Notre Dame: University of Notre Dame Press, 1984.

De León, Arnoldo. *The Tejano Community, 1836–1900.* Albuquerque: University of New Mexico Press, 1982.

———. *They Called Them Greasers: Anglo Attitudes towards Mexicans in Texas, 1821–1900.* Austin: University of Texas Press, 1983.

Dobie, J. Frank. *The Flavor of Texas.* Dallas: Dealey & Lowe, 1936.

Donovan, Josephine. *Feminist Theory: The Intellectual Traditions of American Feminism.* New York: Ungar Press, 1985.

Du Bois, W. E. B. *The Souls of Black Folk.* 1903. Library Classics of the United States. New York: Viking, 1986.

Durán, Fray Diego. *"The Book of the Gods and Rites" and "The Ancient Calendar."* Ed. and trans. Fernando Horcasitas and Doris Heyden. Norman: University of Oklahoma Press, 1971.

———. *The History of the Indies of New Spain.* Trans. Doris Heyden. Norman: University of Oklahoma Press, 1994.

Eisenstein, Zillah R. "Developing a Theory of Capitalist Patriarchy and Socialist Feminism." In *Capitalist Patriarchy and the Case for Socialist Feminism,* ed. Zillah R. Eisenstein. New York: Monthly Review Press, 1979, 5–40.

Erhart, Virginia. "Amor, ideología y enmascaramiento en Corín Tellado." *Casa de las Americas* 13, no. 77 (March–April 1973): 93–111.

Espinosa Damián, Gisela. "Feminism and Social Struggle in Mexico." In *Third World—Second Sex II,.* ed. Miranda Davies, 31–41. London: Zed Books, 1987.

Fanon, Frantz. *The Wretched of the Earth.* 1961. New York: Grove Press, 1968.

Felski, Rita. *Beyond Feminist Aesthetics: Feminist Literature and Social Change.* Cambridge: Harvard University Press, 1989.

Fernández, Roberta. " 'The Cariboo Cafe': Helena María Viramontes' Discourse with Her Social and Cultural Contexts." In *Women's Studies* 17, nos. 1–2 (1989): 71–85.

Fernández-Kelly, María Patricia. *For We Are Sold, I and My People: Women and Industry in Mexico's Frontier.* Albany: State University of New York Press, 1983.

Fernández Retamar, Roberto. "Calibán: Notes towards a Discussion of Culture on Our America." *Massachusetts Review* 15, nos. 1–2 (1974): 7–72.

Fischer, Michael M. J. "Ethnicity and the Post-Modern Arts of Memory." In *Writing Culture: The Poetics and Politics of Ethnography,* ed. James Clifford and George E. Marcus, 194–233. Berkeley: University of California Press, 1986.

Flora, Cornelia Butler, and Jan L. Flora. "The Fotonovela as a Tool for Class and Cultural Domination." *Latin American Perspectives* 5, no. 1 (Winter 1978): 134–50.

Flores-Hughes, Grace. "Why the Term 'Hispanic'?" *Hispanic: Business, Career, Politics and Culture* 9, no. 9 (September 1996): 64.

Franco, Jean. "The Incorporation of Women: A Comparison of North American and Mexican Popular Culture." In *Studies in Entertainment: Critical Approaches to Mass Culture*, ed. Tania Modleski, 119–38. Bloomington: Indiana University Press, 1986.

———. "Si me permiten hablar: La lucha por el poder interpretativo." *Casa de las Americas* 171 (November–December 1988): 88–94.

Freire, Paulo. *Pedagogy of the Oppressed*. Trans. Myra Bergman Ramos. New York: Continuum, 1989.

Fuller, Margaret. *Woman in the Nineteenth Century*. 1845. New York: Norton, 1971.

Galaraza, Ernesto. *Barrio Boy*. Notre Dame: University of Notre Dame Press, 1971.

Galeano, Eduardo. "In Defense of the Word: Leaving Buenos Aires, June 1976." In *The Graywolf Annual Five: Multi-Cultural Literacy*, ed. Rick Simonson and Scott Walker, 113–25. St. Paul: Graywolf Press, 1988.

García, Alma M., ed. *Chicana Feminist Thought: The Basic Historical Writings*. New York: Routledge, 1997.

García, Mario T. "The Chicana in American History: The Mexican Women of El Paso, 1880–1920—A Case Study." *Pacific Historical Review* 49, no. 2 (1980): 315–37.

García-Bahne, Betty. "La Chicana and the Chicano Family." In *Essays on la Mujer*, ed. Rosaura Sánchez and Rosa Martínez Cruz, 30–47. Los Angeles: Chicano Studies Research Center Publications, University of California, 1977.

Gilman, Charlotte Perkins. *The Home: Its Work and Influence*. 1903. Urbana: University of Illinois Press, 1972.

———. *Women and Economics: A Study in the Economic Relation between Men and Women as a Factor in Social Evolution*. 1898. New York: Harper & Row, 1966.

Gómez, Alma, Cherríe Moraga, and Mariana Romo-Carmona, eds. *Cuentos: Stories by Latinas*. New York: Kitchen Table–Women of Color Press, 1983.

González-Berry, Erlinda, and Tey Diana Rebolledo. "Growing Up Chicano: Tomás Rivera and Sandra Cisneros." In *International Studies in Honor of Tomás Rivera*, ed. Julián Olivares. *Revista Chicano-Riqueña* 13, nos. 3–4 (1985): 109–19.

Gramsci, Antonio. *Selections from the Prison Notebooks*. Ed. and trans. Quintin Hoare and Geoffrey Nowell Smith. New York: International Publishers, 1971.

Gutiérrez, Ramón A. *When Jesus Came, the Corn Mothers Went Away: Marriage, Sexuality, and Power in New Mexico, 1500–1846*. Stanford: Stanford University Press, 1991.

Gutiérrez-Revuelta, Pedro. "Género e ideología en el libro de Sandra Cisneros: *The House on Mango Street*." *Crítica* 1 (Fall 1986): 48–59.

Harlow, Barbara. *Resistance Literature*. New York: Methuen, 1987.

———. "Testimonio and Survival: Roque Dalton's *Miguel Marmol.*" In *The Real Thing: Testimonial Discourse and Latin America*, ed. Georg M. Guzelberger, 70–83. Durham: Duke University Press, 1996.

Haug, Frigga. *Female Sexualization: A Collective Work of Memory.* London: Verso, 1987.

Heyden, Doris, and Luis Francisco Villaseñor. *The Great Temple and the Aztec Gods.* Mexico City: Minutiae Mexicana, 1984.

Hobsbawm, Eric J. "Gramsci and Marxist Political Theory." In *Approaches to Gramsci*, ed. Anne Showstack Sassoon, 20–36. London: Writers and Readers Publishing Cooperative Society, 1982.

hooks, bell. *Ain't I a Woman: Black Women and Feminism.* Boston: South End Press, 1981.

Horno-Delgado, Asunción, Eliana Ortega, Nina M. Scott, and Nancy Saprota Sternbach, eds. *Breaking Boundaries: Latina Writings and Critical Readings.* Amherst: University of Massachusetts Press, 1989.

Jameson, Fredric. *The Political Unconscious: Narrative as a Socially Symbolic Act.* Ithaca: Cornell University Press, 1981.

Janvier, Thomas A. *Legends of the City of Mexico.* New York, 1910.

Jara, René, and Hernán Vidal, eds. *Testimonio y literatura.* Edina, Minn.: Society for the Study of Contemporary Hispanic and Lusophone Revolutionary Literatures, 1986.

Jaramillo, Mari Luci. "Institutional Responsibility in the Provision of Educational Experiences to the Hispanic American Female Student." In *The Broken Web: The Educational Experience of Hispanic American Women*, ed. Teresa McKenna and Flora Ida Ortiz, 25–35. Claremont, Calif.: Tomás Rivera Center; Berkeley: Floricanto Press, 1988.

Jones, Anita Edgar. "Conditions Surrounding Mexicans in Chicago." Ph.D. dissertation, University of Chicago, 1928.

Jones, Robert C., and Louis R. Wilson. *The Mexican in Chicago.* Chicago: Chicago Congregational Union, 1931.

Kim, Elaine H. *Asian American Literature: An Introduction to the Writings and Their Social Context.* Philadelphia: Temple University Press, 1982.

Kingston, Maxine Hong. *The Woman Warrior: Memoirs of a Girlhood among Ghosts.* New York: Vintage Books, 1977.

Kirtley, Bacil F. "La Llorona and Related Themes." *Western Folklore* 19 (1960): 155–68.

Kolodny, Annette. *The Land before Her: Fantasy and Experience of the American Frontiers, 1630–1860.* Chapel Hill: University of North Carolina Press, 1984.

Kristeva, Julia. "Revolution in Poetic Language." In *The Kristeva Reader,* ed. Toril Moi, 90–136. New York: Columbia University Press, 1986.

———. "Women's Time." In *Feminist Theory: A Critique of Ideology,* ed. Nannerl O. Keohane, Michelle Z. Rosaldo, and Barbara C. Gelpi, 31–53. Chicago: University of Chicago Press, 1981.

Leal, Luis, Fernando de Necochea, Francisco Lomelí, and Roberto G. Trujillo, eds. *A Decade of Chicano Literature (1970–1979): Critical Essays and Bibliography.* Santa Barbara: La Causa, 1982.

León-Portilla, Miguel. *The Broken Spears: The Aztec Account of the Conquest of Mexico*. Boston: Beacon Press, 1962.

Limón, José. "The Folk Performance of '*Chicano*' and the Cultural Limits of Political Ideology." In "*And Other Neighborly Names": Social Process and Cultural Image in Texas Folklore,* ed. Richard Dorson, 216–26. Bloomington: Indiana University Press, 1981.

———. "La Llorona, the Third Legend of Greater Mexico: Cultural Symbols, Women, and the Political Unconscious." Paper presented in the Renato Rosaldo Lecture Series, University of Arizona, June 26, 1985.

———. "El primer congreso mexicanista de 1911: A Precursor to Contemporary Chicanismo." *Aztlán* 5, nos. 1–2 (1974): 85–106.

Lipsitz, George. "Cruising around the Historical Bloc—Postmodernism and Popular Music in East Los Angeles." *Cultural Critique* 5 (Winter 1987): 157–77.

———. *Time Passages: Collective Memory and American Popular Culture*. Minneapolis: University of Minnesota Press, 1990.

Lomas, Clara. "The Border, the Mexican Revolution, and Women Writers." Work in progress.

López, Sonia. "The Role of the Chicana within the Student Movement." In *Essays on la Mujer*, ed. Rosaura Sánchez and Rosa Martínez Cruz, 16–29. Los Angeles: Chicano Studies Research Center Publications, University of California, 1977.

Lorde, Audre. "The Master's Tools Will Never Dismantle the Master's House." In *This Bridge Called My Back: Writings by Radical Women of Color*, ed. Cherríe Moraga and Gloria Anzaldúa, 2d ed., 98–101. New York: Kitchen Table–Women of Color Press, 1983.

Lubiano, Wahneema. "Constructing and Re-constructing Afro-American Texts: The Critic as Ambassador and Referee." *American Literary History* 1 (Summer 1989): 432–47.

———. "The Harlem Renaissance and the Roots of Afro-American Literary Modernism." In "Messing with the Machine: Four Afro-American Novels and the Nexus of Vernacular, Historical Constraint, and Narrative Strategy," 44–87. Ph.D. dissertation, Stanford University, 1987.

Luna Lawhn, Juanita. "*El Regidor* and *La Prensa:* Impediments to Women's Self- Definition." In *The Sexuality of Latinas*, ed. Norma Alarcón et al. *Third Woman* 4 (1989): 134–42 (special issue).

MacKinnon, Catharine A. "Feminism, Marxism, Method, and the State: An Agenda for Theory." In *Feminist Theory: A Critique of Ideology,* ed. Nannerl O. Keohane, Michelle Z. Rosaldo, and Barbara C. Gelpi, 1–30. Chicago: University of Chicago Press, 1981.

Madsen, William. *Mexican-Americans of South Texas*. 2d ed. New York: Holt, Rinehart & Winston, 1973.

Marcus, Jane. *Art and Anger: Reading Like a Woman*. Columbus: Ohio State University Press, 1988.

Marks, Elaine, and Isabelle de Courtivron, eds. *New French Feminisms: An Anthology*. New York: Schocken Books, 1981.

Marin, Lynda. "Speaking Out Together: Testimonials of Latin American Women." *Latin American Perspectives* 18 (Summer 1991): 51–68.

Martínez, Demetria. *MotherTongue*. Tempe, Ariz.: Bilingual Press / Editorial Bilingüe, 1994.

———. "Nativity: For Two Salvadoran Women, 1986–1987." In *Three Times a Woman: Chicana Poetry,* by Alicia Gaspar de Alba, María Gerrera-Sobek, and Demetria Martínez, 132–33. Tempe: Bilingual Review Press, 1989.

Martínez, Elizabeth. "Chingón Politics Die Hard." *Z Magazine,* April 1990, 46–50.

Mazón, Mauricio. *The Zoot Suit Riots: The Psychology of Symbolic Annihilation.* Austin: University of Texas Press, 1984.

McCracken, Ellen. "Sandra Cisneros' *The House on Mango Street:* Community-Oriented Introspection and the Demystification of Patriarchal Violence." In *Breaking Boundaries: Latina Writings and Critical Readings,* ed. Asunción Horno-Delgado et al., 62–71. Amherst: University of Massachussetts Press, 1989.

McKenna, Teresa, and Flora Ida Ortiz. *The Broken Web: The Educational Experience of Hispanic American Women.* Claremont, Calif.: Tomás Rivera Center; Berkeley: Floricanto Press, 1988.

McLemore, Dale S., and Ricardo Romo. "The Origins and Development of the Mexican American People." In *The Mexican American Experience: An Interdisciplinary Anthology,* ed. Rodolfo O. de la Garza et al., 3–32. Austin: University of Texas Press, 1985.

Meese, Elizabeth A. "(Dis)Locations: Reading the Theory of a Third World Woman in *I, Rigoberta Menchú*." In *(Ex)Tensions: Re-figuring Feminist Criticism,* 97–128. Urbana: University of Illinois Press, 1990.

Menchú, Rigoberta. *I, Rigoberta Menchú: An Indian Woman in Guatemala.* Ed. Elisabeth Burgos-Debray. Trans. Ann Wright. London: Verso, 1984.

Mignolo, Walter D. *The Darker Side of the Renaissance: Literacy, Territoriality, and Colonization.* Ann Arbor: University of Michigan Press, 1995.

Mirandé, Alfredo, and Evangelina Enríquez. *La Chicana: The Mexican American Woman.* Chicago: University of Chicago Press, 1977.

———. *The Chicano Experience: An Alternative Perspective.* Notre Dame: University of Notre Dame Press, 1985.

Modleski, Tania. *Loving with a Vengeance: Mass-Produced Fantasies for Women.* 1982. London: Routledge, 1985.

Moi, Toril. *Sexual/Texual Politics: Feminist Literary Theory.* London: Methuen, 1985.

Montejano, David. *Anglos and Mexicans in the Making of Texas, 1836–1986.* Austin: University of Texas Press, 1987.

Mora, Pat. "Legal Alien." In *Chants,* 52. Houston: Arte Público Press, 1984.

Moraga, Cherríe. "Algo secretamente amado." Review of *Borderlands / Frontera: The New Mestiza,* by Gloria Anzaldúa. In *The Sexuality of Latinas,* ed. Norma Alarcón et al. *Third Woman* 4 (1989): 151–56 (special issue).

———. *The Last Generation: Prose and Poetry.* Boston: South End Press, 1993.

———. *Loving in the War Years: Lo que nunca pasó por sus labios*. Boston: South End Press, 1983.

Moraga, Cherríe, and Gloria Anzaldúa, eds. *This Bridge Called My Back: Writings by Radical Women of Color*. 2d ed. New York: Kitchen Table–Women of Color Press, 1983.

Morales, Alejandro. *The Brick People*. Houston: Arte Público Press, 1988.

———. "The Deterritorialization of Esperanza Cordero: A Paraesthetic Inquiry." In *Gender, Self, and Society: Proceedings of the IV International Conference on the Hispanic Cultures of the United States*, ed. Renate von Bardeleben, 227–35. Frankfurt am Main and New York: Peter Lang, 1993.

Morgan, Lewis Henry. *Ancient Society; or, Researches in the Lines of Human Progress from Savagery through Barbarism to Civilization*. 1877. Chicago: Charles H. Kerr, 1907.

Morrison, Toni. *Beloved*. New York: Knopf, 1987.

———. *The Bluest Eye*. 1970. New York: Washington Square Press, 1972.

———. "Unspeakable Things Unspoken: The Afro-American Presence in American Literature." *Michigan Quarterly Review* 28, no. 1 (Winter 1989): 1–34.

Mullen, Harryette. " 'A Silence between Us Like a Language': The Untranslatability of Experience in Sandra Cisneros's *Woman Hollering Creek*." *MELUS* 21, no. 2 (Summer 1996): 3–20.

Muñoz, Carlos, Jr. *Youth, Identity, Power: The Chicano Movement*. New York: Verso, 1989.

NietoGomez, Anna. "La Feminista." In *Chicana Feminist Thought*, ed. Alma M. García, 86–92. New York: Routledge, 1997.

Olivares, Julián. "Sandra Cisneros' *The House on Mango Street* and the Poetics of Space." In *Chicana Creativity and Criticism: Charting New Frontiers in American Literature*, ed. María Herrera-Sobek and Helena María Viramontes. *Americas Review* 15, nos. 3–4 (1987): 160–69 (special issue).

Olsen, Tillie. *Yonnondio: From the Thirties*. New York: Delta Fiction, 1974.

Ong, Walter J. *Orality and Literacy: The Technologizing of the Word*. London: Methuen, 1982.

Ordóñez, Elizabeth J. "The Concept of Cultural Identity in Chicana Poetry." *Third Woman* 2 (1984): 75–82.

Ortega, Eliana. "Poetic Discourse of the Puerto Rican Woman in the United States: New Voices of Anacaonian Liberation." In *Breaking Boundaries: Latina Writings and Critical Readings*, ed. Asunción Horno-Delgado et al., 122–35. Amherst: University of Massachusetts Press, 1989.

Ortega, Eliana, and Nancy Saporta Sternbach. "At the Threshold of the Unnamed: Latina Literary Discourse in the Eighties." In *Breaking Boundaries: Latina Writings and Critical Readings*, ed. Asunción Horno-Delgado et al., 2–23. Amherst: University of Massachusetts Press, 1989.

Padilla, Genaro M. "The Recovery of Nineteenth-Century Chicano Autobiography." *American Quarterly* 40 (September 1988): 286–306.

Paredes, Américo. "Mexican Legendry and the Rise of the Mestizo: A Survey." In *American Folk Legend: A Symposium*, ed. Wayland D. Hand, 97–107. Berkeley: University of California Press, 1971.

————. "The Problem of Identity in a Changing Culture: Popular Expressions of Culture Conflict along the Lower Rio Grande Border." In *Views across the Border: The United States and Mexico*, ed. Stanley R. Ross, 68–94. Albuquerque: University of New Mexico Press, 1978.

————. *With His Pistol in His Hand: A Border Ballad and Its Hero*. Austin: University of Texas Press, 1958.

Partnoy, Alicia, ed. *You Can't Drown the Fire: Latin American Women Writing in Exile*. Pittsburgh: Cleis Press, 1988.

Pavletich, JoAnn, and Margot Gayle Backus. "With His Pistol in *Her* Hand: Rearticulating the Corrido Narrative in Helena María Viramontes' 'Neighbors.' " *Cultural Critique*, no. 27 (Spring 1994), 127–151.

Paz, Octavio. *The Labyrinth of Solitude*. Trans. Lysander Kemp. New York: Grove Press, 1961.

Peña, Manuel H. *The Texas-Mexican Conjunto: History of a Working-Class Music*. Mexican American Monographs no. 9. Austin: University of Texas Press, 1985.

Pérez, Laura Elisa. "Opposition and the Education of Chicana/os." In *Race, Identity and Representation in Education*, ed. Warren Crichlow and Cameron McCarthy, 268–79. New York: Routledge, 1992.

Ponce, Arcelia. "La Preferida." In *The Sexuality of Latinas,* ed. Norma Alarcón et al. *Third Woman* 4 (1989): 85–89 (special issue).

Ponce, Mary Helen. *The Wedding*. Houston: Arte Público Press, 1989.

Portillo Trambley, Estela. *Trini*. Binghamton, N.Y.: Bilingual Press/Editorial Bilingüe, 1986.

Posadas, Barbara M. "Mestiza Girlhood: Interracial Families in Chicago's Filipino Community since 1925." In *Making Waves: An Anthology of Writings by and about Asian American Women*, ed. Asian Women United of California, 273–82. Boston: Beacon Press, 1989.

Pratt, Mary Louise. "Yo Soy La Malinche: Chicana Writers and the Poetics of Ethnonationalism." *Callaloo* 16, no. 4 (1993): 859–73.

Quintana, Alvina E. *Home Girls: Chicana Literary Voices*. Philadelphia: Temple University Press, 1996.

Radway, Janice A. *Reading the Romance: Women, Patriarchy, and Popular Literature*. Chapel Hill: University of North Carolina Press, 1984.

Rebolledo, Tey Diana. "The Politics of Poetics; or, What Am I, a Critic, Doing in This Text Anyhow?" In *Chicana Creativity and Criticism: Charting New Frontiers in American Literature*, ed. María Herrera-Sobek and Helena María Viramontes. *Americas Review* 15, nos. 3–4 (1987) (special issue).

————. *Women Singing in the Snow: A Cultural Analysis of Chicana Literature*. Tucson: University of Arizona Press, 1995.

Rebolledo, Tey Diana, and Eliana S. Rivero, eds. *Infinite Divisions: An Anthology of Chicana Literature*. Tucson: University of Arizona Press, 1993.

Rendón, Armando B. *Chicano Manifesto*. New York: Macmillan, 1971.

Rios, Katherine. " 'And you know what I have to say isn't always pleasant': Translating the Unspoken Word in Cisneros's *Woman Hollering Creek*." In *Chicana (W)Rites on Word and Film*, ed. María Herrera-Sobek and Helena María Viramontes, 201–23. Berkeley: Third Woman Press, 1995.

Rivera, Tomás. . . . *Y no se lo tragó la tierra / And the Earth Did Not Part.* 1971. Berkeley: Justa Publications, 1976.

Rodríguez, Juan. Review of *The House on Mango Street,* by Sandra Cisneros. *Austin Chronicle,* Aug. 10, 1984.

Romano, Octavio Ignacio-V. "The Anthropology and Sociology of the Mexican-Americans: The Distortion of Mexican-American History." *El Grito* 2, no. 1 (Fall 1968): 13–26.

———. "Social Science, Objectivity, and the Chicanos." *El Grito* 4 (Fall 1970): 4–16.

Rosaldo, Michelle Zimbalist. "Woman, Culture, and Society: A Theoretical Overview." In *Woman, Culture, and Society,* ed. Michelle Zimbalist Rosaldo and Louise Lamphere, 17–42. Stanford: Stanford University Press, 1974.

Rowbotham, Sheila. "The Personal Is Political." *Zeta,* January 1989, 29–35.

Ruiz, Vicki. *Cannery Women, Cannery Lives: Mexican Women, Unionization, and the California Food Processing Industry, 1930–1950.* Albuquerque: University of New Mexico Press, 1987.

———. "Oral History and la Mujer: The Rosa Guerrero Story." In *Women on the U.S.–Mexico Border: Responses to Change,* ed. Vicki L. Ruiz and Susan Tiano, 219–31. Boston: Allen & Unwin, 1987.

Ruiz, Vicki, Lillian Schlissel, and Janice Monk, eds. *Western Women: Their Land, Their Lives.* Albuquerque: University of New Mexico Press, 1988.

Ruiz, Vicki, and Susan Tiano, eds. *Women on the U.S.–Mexico Border: Responses to Change.* Boston: Allen & Unwin, 1987.

Said, Edward. Foreword. In *Selected Subaltern Studies,* ed. Ranajit Guha and Gayatri Chakravorty Spivak, v–x. New York: Oxford University Press, 1988.

Saldívar, José David. "Calibán and Resistance: A Study of Chicano-Chicana Autobiography." Center for Chicano Research, Stanford University, April 1986.

———. *The Dialectics of Our America: Genealogy, Cultural Critique, and Literary History.* Durham: Duke University Press, 1991.

———. "The Limits of Cultural Studies." *American Literary History* 2 (Summer 1990): 251–66.

Saldívar, Ramón. *Chicano Narrative: The Dialectics of Difference.* Madison: University of Wisconsin Press, 1990.

Saldívar-Hull, Sonia. "Feminism on the Border: From Gender Politics to Geopolitics." Ph.D. dissertation, University of Texas at Austin, 1990.

Sánchez, George. "The American of Mexican Descent." *Chicago Jewish Forum* 20 (1961–62): 120–24.

Sánchez, George J. *Becoming Mexican American: Ethnicity, Culture, and Identity in Chicano Los Angeles, 1900–1945.* New York: Oxford University Press, 1993.

Sánchez, Marta Ester. *Contemporary Chicana Poetry: A Critical Approach to an Emerging Literature.* Berkeley: University of California Press, 1985.

Sánchez, Rosaura. "The Chicana Labor Force." In *Essays on la Mujer*, ed. Rosaura Sánchez and Rosa Martínez Cruz, 3–15. Los Angeles: Chicano Studies Research Center Publications, University of California, 1977.

———. "Ethnicity, Ideology, and Academia." *Americas Review* 15 (1987): 80–88.

Sandoval, Chela. "U.S. Third World Feminism: The Theory and Method of Oppositional Consciousness in the Postmodern World." *Genders* 10 (Spring 1991): 1–24.

Sangari, Kum Kum. "The Politics of the Possible." *Cultural Critique,* Fall 1987, 157–86.

Scott, Joan W. "Experience." In *Feminists Theorize the Political*, ed. Judith Butler and Joan W. Scott, 22–40. New York: Routledge, 1992.

Segura, Denise A. "Chicanas and Triple Oppression in the Labor Force." In *Chicana Voices: Intersections of Class, Race, and Gender*, ed. Teresa Córdova, Norma Cantú, Gilberto Cárdenas, Juan García, and Christine Sierra, 47–65. Austin: Center for Mexican American Studies, 1986.

Seiter, Ellen, Hans Borchers, Gabriele Kruetzner, and Eva-Maria Warth. " 'Don't Treat Us Like We're So Stupid': Towards an Ethnography of Soap Opera Viewers." In *Remote Control: Television, Audiences, and Cultural Power*, 223–47. New York: Routledge, 1989.

———, eds. *Remote Control: Television, Audiences, and Cultural Power*. New York: Routledge, 1989.

Showalter, Elaine. "The Feminist Critical Revolution." In *The New Feminist Criticism: Essays on Women, Literature, and Theory*, ed. Elaine Showalter, 3–17. New York: Pantheon Books, 1985.

———. *A Literature of Their Own: British Women Novelists from Brontë to Lessing*. Princeton: Princeton University Press, 1977.

Simo, Ana Maria. "What Do You See?" In *The Sexuality of Latinas*, ed. Norma Alarcón et al. *Third Woman* 4 (1989): 103–19 (special issue).

Sommer, Doris. " 'Not Just a Personal Story': Women's Testimonios and the Plural Self." In *Life/Lines: Theorizing Women's Autobiography,* ed. Bella Brodzki and Celeste Schenck, 107–30. Ithaca: Cornell University Press, 1988.

———. "Rigoberta's Secrets." *Latin American Perspectives* 18, no. 3 (1991): 32–50.

Sosa Riddell, Adaljiza. "Chicanas and El Movimiento." In *Chicana Feminist Thought,* ed. Alma M. García, 92–94. New York: Routledge, 1997.

Spillers, Hortense J. "Eva Peace, So Early in the Morning." Paper delivered to Division on Psychological Approaches to Literature, MLA convention, Washington, D.C., Dec. 28, 1989.

———. "Mama's Baby, Papa's Maybe: An American Grammar Book." *Diacritics* 17 (Summer 1987): 65–81.

Spivak, Gayatri Chakravorty. "Can the Subaltern Speak?" In *Marxism and the Interpretation of Culture*, ed. Cary Nelson and Lawrence Grossberg, 271–313. Urbana: University of Illinois Press, 1988.

———. "Marginality in the Teaching Machine." In *Outside in the Teaching Machine*, 53–76. New York: Routledge, 1993.

———. "The Problem of Self-Representation." Interview in *The Post-Colonial Critic: Interviews, Strategies, Dialogues*, ed. Sarah Harasym, 50–58. New York: Routledge, 1990.

———. "Woman in Difference." In *Outside in the Teaching Machine*, 77–95. New York: Routledge, 1993.

Stephen, Lynn. "Popular Feminism in Mexico." *Zeta*, December 1989, 102–6.

Stoll, David. *Rigoberta Menchú and the Story of All Poor Guatemalans*. Boulder, Colo.: Westview Press, 1999.

Suleri, Sara. "Woman Skin Deep: Feminism and the Postcolonial Condition." *Critical Inquiry* 18 (Summer 1992): 756–69.

Sweeney, Judith. "Chicana History: A Review of the Literature." In *Essays on la Mujer*, ed. Rosaura Sánchez and Rosa Martínez Cruz, 99–123. Los Angeles: Chicano Studies Research Center Publications, University of California, 1977.

Tabuenca Córdoba, María Socorro. "Teoría y creación en la prosa de Gloria Anzaldúa." In *Las Formas de Nuestras Voces: Chicana and Mexicana Writers in Mexico,* ed. Claire Joysmith, 153–65. Mexico City: Centro de Investigaciones sobre América del Norte México, Universidad Nacional Autónoma de México, 1995.

Tafolla, Carmen. "Federico y Elfiria." In *The Sexuality of Latinas*, ed. Norma Alarcón et al. *Third Woman* 4 (1989): 105–11 (special issue).

Trejo Delarbre, Raúl, ed. *Televisa: El quinto poder*. Mexico City: Claves Latinoamericanas, 1985.

Trujillo, Carla, ed. *Chicana Lesbians: The Girls Our Mothers Warned Us About*. Berkeley: Third Woman Press, 1991.

Valenzuela, Liliana. "Mexico's La Malinche: Mother or Whore, Creator or Traitor?" Master's report, University of Texas, Austin, 1988.

Valerio-Jiménez, Omar S. "Tejanos in Nineteenth-Century South Texas: Citizenship, Ethnicity, and Gender." Ph.D. dissertation, University of California, Los Angeles, 1999.

Vigil, Evangelina. *Thirty an' Seen a Lot*. Houston: Arte Público Press, 1982.

———, ed. *Woman of Her Word: Hispanic Women Write. Revista Chicano-Riqueña* 11, nos. 3–4 (1983) (special issue).

Villanueva, Tino. "Sobre el término 'chicano.' " In *Chicanos: Antología histórica y literaria*, ed. Tino Villanueva, 7–34. Mexico City: Fondo de Cultura Económica, 1980.

Villegas de Magnón, Leonor. *The Rebel*. Ed. Clara Lomas. Houston: Arte Público Press, 1994.

Viramontes, Helena María. "Miss Clairol." *Americas Review* 15 (Fall/Winter 1987): 101–5.

———. *The Moths and Other Stories*. Houston: Arte Público Press, 1985.

———. " 'Nopalitos': The Making of Fiction." In *Breaking Boundaries: Latina Writings and Critical Readings*, ed. Asunción Horno-Delgado et al., 33–38. Amherst: University of Massachusetts Press, 1989.

———. "Paris Rats in L.A. and Other Stories." Unpublished manuscript.

———. "Tears on My Pillow." In *New Chicana/Chicano Writing*, ed. Charles Tatum, 110–15. Tucson: University of Arizona Press, 1992.

———. *Under the Feet of Jesus*. New York: Dutton, 1995.

Viramontes, Helena María, and María Herrera-Sobek, eds. *Chicana Creativity and Criticism: Charting New Frontiers in American Literature. Americas Review* 15, nos. 3–4 (1987) (special issue).

Warmbold, Carolyn. "Women of the Mosquito Press: Louise Bryant, Agnes Smedley, and Margaret Randall as Narrative Guerrillas." Ph.D. dissertation, University of Texas, Austin, 1990.

Webb, Walter Prescott. *The Texas Rangers: A Century of Frontier Defense*. 2d ed. Austin: University of Texas Press, 1965.

Weber, Devra. "Sin Fronteras: Mexican Migration and Labor Struggles in the United States and Mexico." Paper presented at the American Studies conference, Toronto, Nov. 4, 1989.

Weigle, Marta. *Spiders and Spinsters: Women and Mythology*. Albuquerque: University of New Mexico Press, 1982.

Wells-Barnett, Ida B. *On Lynchings: Southern Horrors, a Red Record, Mob Rule in New Orleans*. New York: Arno Press, 1969.

Williams, Gareth. "Translation and Mourning: The Cultural Challenge of Latin American Testimonial Autobiography." *Latin American Literary Review* 21 (January–June 1993): 79–99.

Williams, Raymond. *Marxism and Literature*. Oxford: Oxford University Press, 1977.

Woolf, Virginia. *A Room of One's Own*. 1930. New York: Harcourt Brace Jovanovich, 1991.

Worsley, Peter. *The Three Worlds: Culture and World Development*. Chicago: University of Chicago Press, 1984.

Yamamoto, Hisaye. *Seventeen Syllables and Other Stories*. New York: Kitchen Table–Women of Color Press, 1988.

Yarbro-Bejarano, Yvonne. "Chicana Literature from a Chicana Feminist Perspective." In *Chicana Creativity and Criticism: Charting New Frontiers in American Literature,* ed. María Herrera-Sobek and Helena María Viramontes. *Americas Review* 15, nos. 3–4 (1987): 139–45 (special issue).

———. "Expanding the Categories of Race and Sexuality in Lesbian and Gay Studies." In *Professions of Desire: Lesbian and Gay Studies in Literature*, ed. George E. Haggerty and Bonnie Zimmerman, 124–35. New York: Modern Language Association of America, 1995.

———. "Gloria Anzaldúa's *Borderlands / La Frontera*: Cultural Studies, 'Difference,' and the Non-Unitary Subject." *Cultural Studies,* Fall 1994, 5–28.

———. "Primer encuentro de lesbianas feministas latinoamericanas y caribeñas." In *The Sexuality of Latinas*, ed. Norma Alarcón et al. *Third Woman* 4 (1989): 143–46 (special issue).

Yúdice, George. "Marginality and the Ethics of Survival." In *Universal Abandon? The Politics of Postmodernism*, ed. Andrew Ross, 214–36. Minneapolis: University of Minnesota Press, 1988.

Zambrano, Myrna M. *Mejor sola que mal acompañada: For the Latina in an Abusive Relationship*. Seattle: Seal Press, 1985.

Zavella, Patricia. "The Problematic Relationship of Feminism and Chicana Studies." In *Across Cultures: The Spectrum of Women's Lives*, ed. Emily K. Abel and Marjorie L. Pearson, 25–36. New York: Gordon & Breach, 1989.

———. *Women's Work and Chicano Families: Cannery Workers of the Santa Clara Valley*. Ithaca: Cornell University Press, 1987.

Index

Note: Page references in italics indicate figures.

academia: borderlands in, 67; Chicana struggle within, 52–54; Chicano Movement and, 29–34; legitimate fields in, 46, 54, 81–83; position and practice in, 181n6; as second to community activism, 163; White feminists in, 35–39

Acuña, Rodolfo: on Alamo, 173n4; on bracero program, 178n9; contributions of, 27; on farm laborers, 89; on Latinos in Midwest, 178n11; on terminology, 94

aesthetics, as practice, 125

African Americans: controlled through terror, 74–75; historical position of, 42–44; infanticide and, 118–19, 121, 179n22; literary context and, 36, 56–57; outdoors concept and, 89–90; specificities of, 90

African American women: Chicanas' links to, 45–46, 69–70; personal and political for, 40–44; spirituality of, 49–50. *See also* Black feminists

agency, discovery of, 121–22

Agosín, Marjorie, 183nn22–23

agriculture: Anglo agribusiness vs. sharecropper in, 76–77; workers for, 15, 24–25, 77, 89, 183n4. *See also* refugees

AIDS, fatalities from, 178n14

Alamo: counterhistory of, 173n4; use of term, 16, 17, 178n14

Alarcón, Norma: on *Borderlands,* 65, 66; contributions of, 27–28; on MacKinnon, 175n5; on *mujer,* 126; resistance of, 53–54; on speaking subject, 105; on subjectivity, 44–45; on symbolic contract, 181n8

¡Alarma! (magazine), 108, 109–10

Alegría, Claribel, 168

Allende, Isabel, 144

Althusser, Louis, 18, 53, 180n1

Alvarado, Elvia: identification with, 47–48, 51, 54–55; testimonio of, 161–62, 168–71

American: becoming, 2–4; gender and, 9–10; proof of being, 5

Americanos, los, use of term, 3

Americas Review, The (journal), 46

"Amor, ideología y enmascaramiento en Corín Tellado" (Erhart), 115

Anglo America. *See* United States; White supremacy

Anglo-American feminists. *See* White feminism

ansina/así, counterhistory of, 68–69

Anzaldúa, Gloria: contributions of, 25, 36; criticism on, 29, 65; on cultural traditions, 83; on heterosexism, 32–33;

Library of Congress Cataloging-in-Publication Data

Saldívar-Hull, Sonia.
    Feminism on the border : Chicana gender politics and literature / Sonia Saldívar-
Hull.
        p.   cm.
    Includes bibliographical references and index.
    ISBN 0-520-20732-7 (alk. paper) — ISBN 0-520-20733-5 (pbk. : alk. paper)
    1. American fiction—Mexican-American authors—History and criticism.   2. Amer-
ican fiction—Mexican-American Border Region—History and criticism.   3. Feminism
and literature—United States—History—20th century.   4. Women and literature—
United States—History—20th century.   5. American fiction—Women authors—History and criticism.   6. Mexican-American Border Region—In literature.   7. Mexican
American women—Intellectual life.   8. Sex role in literature.   I. Title.
PS374.M4837 S25   2000
813'.54099287'0896872—dc21   99-053297

                    Text: 10/13 Galliard
                 Display: Galliard
            Composition: Binghamton Valley Composition
   Printing and binding: Thomson-Shore
                   Index: Margie Towery